Neural Network-Based Deep Learning for Online Payment Fraud Detection

Yu Xie · Yue Tian · Jiamin Yao · Guanjun Liu

Neural Network-Based Deep Learning for Online Payment Fraud Detection

同濟大學出版社
TONGJI UNIVERSITY PRESS

Springer

Yu Xie
College of Information Engineering
Shanghai Maritime University
Shanghai, China

Jiamin Yao
College of Information Engineering
Shanghai Maritime University
Shanghai, China

Yue Tian
Department of Computer Science
and Technology
Shanghai Normal University
Shanghai, China

Guanjun Liu
Department of Computer Science
Tongji University
Shanghai, China

ISBN 978-981-95-8512-0 ISBN 978-981-95-8513-7 (eBook)
https://doi.org/10.1007/978-981-95-8513-7

Jointly published with Tongji University Press Co., Ltd.
The print edition is not for sale in Mainland China. Customers from Mainland China please order the print book from: Tongji University Press Co., Ltd.

This Springer imprint is published by the registered company Springer Nature Singapore Pte Ltd.
The registered company address is: 152 Beach Road, #21-01/04 Gateway East, Singapore 189721, Singapore

Competing Interests The authors have no competing interests to declare that are relevant to the content of this manuscript.

Contents

Notation

Nomenclature

z	A latent noise vector
$G(\cdot)$	The generator of a GAN-based model
$D(\cdot)$	The discriminator of a GAN-based model
x_f	A fraudulent sample
x_l	A legitimate sample
$\sigma(\cdot)$	The sigmoid activation function
$\odot$	The element-wise multiplication
$\tanh(\cdot)$	The hyperbolic tangent activation function
$\Delta T_{t-1,t}$	The temporal interval between the $t-1$-th and t-th transactions
X	The original online payment transaction dataset
X_f	The set of fraudulent samples
X_l	The set of legitimate samples
X_s	The set of synthetic samples
n_f	The number of fraudulent samples
n_l	The number of legitimate samples
u	A user
U	The set of users
x_i	A transaction record
R^x	A set of x_i
x_{i_j}	The j-th feature of x_i
x_i^u	The i-th transaction of user u
m	The number of features of x_i
n	The number of transactions
n^u	The number of u's transactions
R_u	u's transaction records
Φ	A feature mapping function
$\mathcal{F}$	The original feature set
s_i	The new transactional representation of x_i extracted by the feature-oriented extraction module

R^s	A set of s_i
v_i	The new transactional representation of x_i extracted by the transaction-oriented extraction module
R^v	A set of v_i
r_i	The new transactional representation of x_i extracted by the transactional representation interaction module
R^r	A set of r_i
g^u	The transaction group of u
d	The length of the transaction memory
T_r	The average time of training a model
I_r	The average time of detecting a transaction
A_v	The average value of a model's evaluation metrics
A_r	The average ranking of a model's evaluation metrics
T_P	The model correctly identifies a positive sample
T_N	The model correctly identifies a negative sample
F_P	The model incorrectly labels a negative sample as positive
F_N	The model incorrectly labels a positive sample as negative
P_r	The precision
R_e	The recall
F_1	The F_1-Score
G_m	The Geometric Mean
S_P	The pooled standard deviation
AUC	The area under the ROC curve
B_g	A batch generator
θ	Network parameters
n_b	The number of batches
b_{si}	The size of each batch
n_e	The number of epochs

Chapter 1
Introduction

In the digital economy, effective Online Payment Fraud Detection (OPFD) is essential for protecting financial security [33, 35]. However, fraudulent transactions are often well disguised and evolve over time, which causes many existing methods to fail in accurately detecting them [20]. These methods are also impacted by data imbalance, unclear or overlapping features, and concept drift [34]. As a result, these methods suffer from low detection accuracy, limited generalizability, and inadequate handling of new fraudulent patterns [29]. This chapter examines the evolution of the fraudulent ecosystem, highlights the weaknesses of traditional OPFD systems, and discusses potential solutions. The analysis presented here establishes a solid theoretical foundation for subsequent chapters and provides a clear framework for the study.

1.1 The Rise of Online Payments and the Fraud Landscape

Over the past decade, consumer behavior has undergone significant changes as internet technologies have advanced and external environments have evolved [26]. As commercial transactions have shifted from offline, cash-based payments to online platforms, online payments have become a dominant method of everyday transactions [52]. According to the Global Online Platform Market Size and Trend Study (2025), the global online transaction platform market reached USD 177 million by December 2024, reflecting a clear growth trend [11]. As shown in Fig. 1.1, the market is expected to grow at a compound annual growth rate of 4.8% and reach USD 269 million by 2033 [16].

With the rapid growth of online transactions, online payment fraud has also proliferated and now poses an increasingly serious threat to the economic security of individuals and businesses [3, 45]. Fraudsters exploit the convenience of online

Y. Xie et al., *Neural Network-Based Deep Learning for Online Payment Fraud Detection*,
https://doi.org/10.1007/978-981-95-8513-7_1

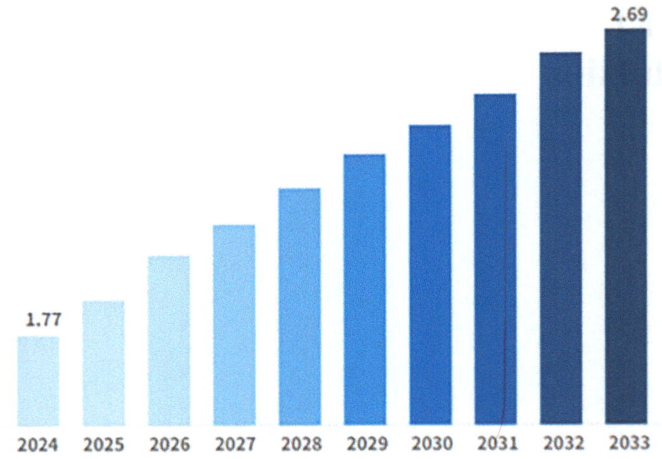

Fig. 1.1 Global online platform market size and trend analysis, 2024–2033

platforms and use techniques such as phishing and Trojan malware attacks to obtain users' account information [30]. The obtained access is then used to conduct unauthorized transactions and steal funds. According to projections by Juniper Research, losses from global online payment fraud will exceed USD 343 billion in the next 5 years [27]. To address this challenge, researchers have developed fraud detection models based on machine learning and behavioral analysis to identify abnormal transactions in real time and protect users [42].

As detection technologies advance, fraudulent behaviors have also become more sophisticated. New patterns have emerged across behavioral, temporal, and spatial dimensions. At the behavioral level, fraudsters often imitate the habits of legitimate users. Their transactions resemble legitimate ones in timing, amount, and frequency, allowing them to bypass traditional rule-based or threshold-based detection methods [40]. Fraudulent activity is no longer expressed as isolated outliers. Instead, fraudsters simulate a full transaction process, exhibiting continuity, operational coherence, and consistent intent [51]. These quasi-legitimate patterns blur the boundary between legitimate and fraudulent behavior and make detection more difficult.

At the temporal level, fraudsters adopt long-term, low-frequency behaviors combined with short bursts of high-frequency activity [1]. Unlike earlier one-time attacks, modern fraud exhibits clear temporal dependence. Fraudsters mimic the activity cycles of real users, follow realistic time intervals, and generate sequences with periodic fluctuations [4]. These strategies allow fraudulent transactions to blend into normal temporal patterns and evade detection methods that rely on fixed time windows or static thresholds [23].

At the spatial level, fraudsters move funds more swiftly across multiple accounts by shifting from random and isolated attacks to concentrated operations within a small geographic area or a specific network segment [31]. In practice, they rely on clusters of IP addresses, device groups, or geographically proximate accounts to create stable spatial activity patterns. These patterns appear legitimate within the local region and undermine detection methods that depend on anomalies in geographic distribution, movement continuity, or cross-region relationships [5]. This significantly improves the stealth and persistence of fraud.

In summary, the expansion of global online platforms and the widespread use of digital payments have led to fraud patterns that are more behaviorally similar to legitimate activity, more temporally dependent, and more spatially concentrated. These trends reduce the effectiveness of traditional rule-based or simple spatial-temporal anomaly detection methods and make fraud both harder to detect and easier to conceal [46]. Therefore, more fine-grained behavioral modeling and adaptive, intelligent detection methods are needed. Joint analysis across multiple dimensions and scales will be essential for the accurate identification and effective prevention of emerging online fraud [37, 41].

1.2 Limitations of Traditional Fraud Detection Systems

As online payment fraud becomes more complex, traditional fraud detection systems can no longer meet the requirements of modern OPFD tasks [8]. Fraudulent behaviors are highly concealed and evolve over time. As a result, existing methods struggle to accurately identify fraud and are easily affected by data imbalance, feature ambiguity, and concept drift. These issues lead to low detection accuracy, weak generalization, and poor adaptability to emerging fraud patterns [19]. Developing detection models with higher intelligence and adaptability has therefore become an essential direction for ensuring transaction security and maintaining the stability of financial systems. The key challenges in this field include the following:

(1) Model bias under imbalanced transaction data. In high-throughput transaction environments, fraudulent samples are extremely scarce compared with the large volume of legitimate samples. This imbalance distorts the decision boundary of detection models and makes it difficult for them to capture key fraud-related features [39]. As a result, models often develop cognitive bias and exhibit degraded generalization performance. Although data augmentation and few-shot learning methods have been used to alleviate this issue, several challenges remain: **(1) Limited diversity and representativeness of synthetic fraud samples**. Existing augmentation methods cannot fully capture the complexity and strategic nature of fraud. The generated samples often fail to reflect critical discriminative characteristics, reducing the model's ability to recognize complex fraud patterns in high-dimensional spaces [2]. **(2) Behavioral overlap between fraudulent and legitimate samples**. Due to the covert nature of fraud, the behavioral distributions of fraudulent and legitimate samples often overlap. Current approaches focus mainly on modeling fraudulent samples and ignore their similarity to legitimate samples [24]. As a result, synthetic samples are difficult to separate from legitimate ones near the decision boundary, which weakens the model's discriminative power. Therefore, balancing fraud-specific characteristics and inter-class similarity during optimization remains a key challenge for improving fraud identification accuracy.

(2) Feature separability under highly overlapping transactional behaviors. Fraudsters often imitate legitimate users, causing significant overlap between fraudulent and legitimate behaviors in the feature space. This overlap poses a significant challenge to existing detection methods [18]. Current methods rely heavily on expert-defined features and face several limitations: **(1) Insufficient temporal feature representation**. Many studies rely on static features from individual transactions [15]. Although these features support immediate risk assessment, they cannot capture long-term behavioral evolution. This limits the ability to distinguish fraud from legitimate behavior in the temporal dimension [32]. **(2) Restricted spatial-behavior representation**. Existing spatial modeling methods rely on predefined spatial-temporal grids and treat all historical records uniformly [6]. They ignore behavioral heterogeneity and dynamic evolution. As a result, high-frequency and cross-region coordinated fraud is fragmented into independent "within-grid" events, which makes these fraud patterns difficult to detect [49]. **(3) Single-view feature modeling**. Many methods extract features from only one perspective, such as time or space, without jointly considering temporal behavior patterns and transaction-space structures [14]. As a result, deep fraud-related features cannot be effectively captured. Thus, improving the separability of fraud-sensitive features under highly overlapping behavioral distributions is crucial for accurate OPFD.

(3) Model adaptability in dynamic and evolving fraud scenarios. Fraud strategies continuously evolve with technological advances and changes in users' living environments [47]. Existing models show several limitations: **(1) Insufficient ability to perceive evolving fraud patterns**. Most studies focus on individual temporal or spatial dynamics. However, real-world fraud often involves coordinated interactions among users, devices, and IP addresses [22]. Ignoring these interactions reduces model generalization and undermines detection performance for emerging fraud types. **(2) Slow model adaptation to rapid fraud outbreaks**. Many detection models rely on local static structural features or short-range dependencies within the transaction graph. These models perform well for stable long-term fraud but struggle to detect sudden outbreaks that involve long-range heterogeneous interactions and weak yet consistent structural signals [21]. This delay prevents timely identification of early-stage covert fraud. Therefore, developing OPFD models with rapid perception and adaptive capability in dynamic environments is essential for identifying transient and evolving fraud patterns.

1.3 The Promise of Deep Learning in Financial Security

As online payment fraud becomes increasingly sophisticated and adversarial, deep learning—owing to its strong representational capacity and adaptive modeling capabilities—offers a critical avenue for advancing OPFD beyond traditional paradigms. In contrast with conventional fraud detection systems that rely on static features and manually crafted rules, deep learning models can automatically uncover latent mechanisms of fraudulent behaviors within high-dimensional, nonlinear, and non-stationary transaction distributions. This enhances sensitivity and robustness to covert, sparse, and dynamically evolving fraud patterns [36]. With respect to the three core challenges in the current field, deep learning demonstrates the following targeted technical potentials:

(1) Adversarial data augmentation for imbalanced transactions. Under extreme class imbalance, detection models are prone to cognitive bias driven by the distribution dominated by legitimate samples. Generative adversarial networks (GANs), through the adversarial interplay between the generator and discriminator, can learn high-order distributional structures of fraudulent samples while maintaining inter-class discriminative boundaries, thereby providing more diverse and representative feature representations for fraud instances [48]. Unlike traditional augmentation techniques that rely on linear perturbations of local features, GANs characterize the compositionality and nonlinear evolution of fraud strategies in the latent space. They generate high-quality samples that closely resemble real fraudulent trajectories, thereby alleviating deficiencies in feature capture arising from data scarcity [9]. Moreover, conditional GANs [13] and boundary-aware GANs [25] explicitly constrain the structural similarity relationships between synthetic samples and legitimate distributions. This not only enhances the diversity of fraudulent behaviors but also prevents synthetic instances from collapsing into legitimate clusters, thereby achieving a balanced trade-off between fraud-specific modeling and inter-class similarity preservation [38]. Such capabilities ultimately improve detection accuracy and generalization in high-throughput scenarios involving covert fraud [44].

(2) Temporal dependence modeling for highly overlapping transactions. To address the substantial overlap between fraudulent and legitimate behaviors in the static feature space, long short-term memory networks (LSTMs) can capture long-range dependencies and stage-wise behavioral patterns across transaction sequences through their gated recurrent architecture [12]. This shifts the detection paradigm from "single-transaction static discrimination" to "sequence-level dynamic identification." The key advantage lies in LSTM's ability to model the non-stationarity inherent in user behavioral evolution over time: on one hand, LSTMs can learn implicit temporal cues—such as transaction rhythms, amount fluctuations, and operation intervals—to strengthen discrimination against camouflaged fraud [7]. On the other hand, by incorporating spatial-temporal joint embeddings or attention-enhanced LSTM variants, the model can adaptively select critical historical segments instead of treating entire histories uniformly, thereby capturing heterogeneous dynamic characteristics of high-frequency, cross-regional, and staged fraud more effectively [43]. Consequently, LSTMs provide an effective mechanism for decoupling fraud-sensitive patterns from highly overlapping behavioral trajectories, substantially mitigating the feature ambiguity caused by spatial-temporal entanglement.

(3) Relational structure learning for dynamically evolving fraud. In environments where fraud strategies evolve rapidly and collaborative behaviors intensify, graph neural networks (GNNs) can represent heterogeneous entities—such as users, devices, IPs, merchants, and transactions–as unified nodes within a heterogeneous transaction graph [28]. Through message-passing mechanisms, GNNs learn high-order interactions across entities and time, thereby enhancing the detection of emerging collaborative fraud. Unlike traditional methods that depend on local static structures, GNNs capture long-range heterogeneous dependencies and weak yet consistent structural signals, enabling earlier and more stable structural responses to short-term, bursty "flash fraud." By integrating dynamic graph modeling and incremental update strategies (e.g., temporal encoding, continuous subgraph sampling, and online contrastive learning), GNNs can rapidly adapt to structural drift in transaction graphs, assimilating newly formed interaction patterns while preserving historical knowledge [10]. This mitigates issues of model adaptation lag and insufficient generalization. Therefore, GNNs form the foundation for OPFD models with rapid perception, continual learning, and structural robustness.

In summary, GANs, LSTMs, and GNNs provide three complementary deep learning pathways that directly address the key bottlenecks in traditional fraud detection systems—namely "distribution reconstruction under data imbalance," "temporal disentanglement under behavioral overlap," and "structural adaptation under dynamic collaboration." These end-to-end representation learning paradigms not only promise substantial improvements in detection accuracy and recall for financial transaction security but also offer a systematic and research-significant direction for achieving robust intelligent defense in adversarial and evolving fraud environments.

1.4 Research Scope and Book Roadmap

Fraudulent behaviors in online transactions have become increasingly sophisticated, exhibiting pronounced sparsity, strong camouflage, and dynamic evolution, all of which pose substantial challenges to accurate OPFD. To address these issues, this book focuses on several key problems, including model bias under data imbalance, feature separability in highly overlapping transactional behaviors, and model adaptability under dynamically evolving fraud patterns. Guided by the core logic of "data-feature-model" collaborative optimization, this book conducts an in-depth investigation into transaction data augmentation and optimization, multi-dimensional feature extraction and behavioral representation, and graph-based model detection, culminating in several innovative solutions [50]. The research components are progressive and interdependent, forming a coherent framework. These developments not only facilitate the precise identification of complex online fraud but also provide critical support for safeguarding financial stability and promoting the healthy development of the digital economy. Figure 1.2 presents the overall research framework of this book. The specific contents are as follows:

This Chapter and Chap. 2 begin by elaborating on the security risks associated with the rapid growth of online payments and outlining the limitations of traditional rule-based OPFD systems and shallow models in highly dynamic and strongly camouflaged fraud environments. The chapters further clarify the concept of online payment

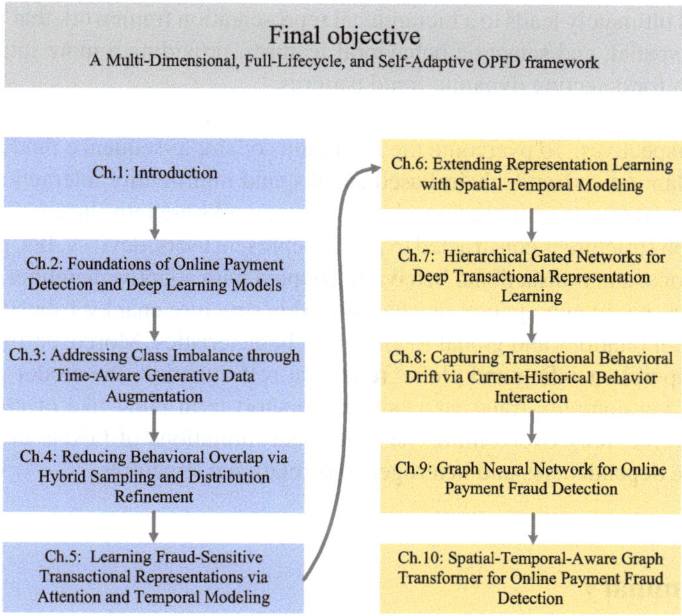

Fig. 1.2 The framework of neural network-based deep learning for online payment fraud detection

fraud, existing technical bottlenecks, and the central challenges in current practices. Building on this foundation, a deep neural network-based modeling perspective is introduced. Sequence modeling, structured data learning, and key evaluation metrics are systematically discussed to establish the theoretical groundwork for developing adaptive, robust, and interpretable fraud detection models in the subsequent chapters.

Chapters 3 and 4 address data-level challenges such as fraud sample scarcity and distributional shift. Under conditions of severe class imbalance, a time-aware generative augmentation model and density-penalized strategy are proposed to generate more representative minority-class fraud samples. A hybrid sampling framework is further constructed, combining generative data augmentation with neighborhood-adaptive denoising to jointly reshape the fraud distribution and refine overlapping regions. These steps create a clearer and more separable data space for subsequent deep learning models.

Building upon enhanced data quality, Chaps. 5–8 shift the focus to feature-level and behavioral modeling. A multi-dimensional transaction representation system is systematically developed. By introducing temporal gating mechanisms, attention networks, and long- and short-term behavioral modeling, the book proposes sequence representation methods capable of capturing fine-grained temporal patterns and behavioral shifts. The modeling scope is further extended to the geographical dimension to identify cross-regional behavioral anomalies. In addition, behavioral drift modeling enables dynamic comparison between a user's historical behavior and current transactions, effectively characterizing both gradual and abrupt fraud patterns. This ultimately leads to a hierarchical representation framework that integrates temporal, spatial, and semantic behavioral features, providing a more interpretable foundation for detecting dynamic fraud patterns.

Finally, Chaps. 9 and 10 advance the research toward structural and relational reasoning perspectives. To overcome the limitations of single-sequence models in capturing collaborative fraud, chain-based attacks, and multi-entity interactions, graph neural networks and spatial-temporal graph frameworks are introduced. A heterogeneous graph structure is constructed to jointly represent users, devices, IPs, geographical locations, and transactional behavior. Coupled with adaptive neighbor sampling and entropy-based aggregation mechanisms, this structure enables robust modeling of both local relations and global topological characteristics. Moreover, by incorporating temporal encoding and global relational self-attention, the model is capable of identifying complex fraud attacks that are short-term burst-like or cross-entity coordinated, thereby overcoming the traditional limitations of GNNs in modeling long-range dependencies and heterogeneous relational structures.

1.5 Summary

With the rapid proliferation of online payments and the continuous expansion of transactional volume, fraudulent activities have become increasingly camouflaged, temporally dependent, and structurally concentrated. Their behavioral patterns overlap extensively with those of legitimate transactions, substantially complicating accurate OPFD. Accordingly, this chapter provides a systematic analysis of the limitations inherent in traditional rule-based, threshold-driven, and shallow-model approaches, highlighting their issues of cognitive bias, insufficient feature separability, and delayed adaptability. Building on these observations, this chapter distills the fundamental contributions of deep learning to OPFD. GAN-based approaches address distributional imbalance by synthesizing high-fidelity, structure-preserving representations of fraudulent behaviors, thereby mitigating the discriminative bias inherent in skewed transaction distributions. Sequential models such as LSTMs, equipped with multi-scale dependency modeling, disentangle temporally entangled behavioral trajectories by capturing both long-range contextual evolution and short-range operational cues. GNNs further extend this capacity to the relational domain: through high-order message-passing and structure-aware aggregation, they model heterogeneous, multi-entity interaction patterns and transfer relational structure across evolving graph topologies. This enables early and stable detection of collaborative fraud phenomena and structural drift in dynamically shifting ecosystems [17]. Collectively, these insights form an integrated research framework for "data-feature-model" collaborative optimization, establishing the foundation for subsequent investigations spanning data distribution reconfiguration, spatial-temporal behavioral representation, and graph-structured relational reasoning.

References

1. Benchaji, I., Douzi, S., El Ouahidi, B., Jaafari, J.: Enhanced credit card fraud detection based on attention mechanism and LSTM deep model. Journal of Big Data **8**(1), 151 (2021)
2. Cao, R., Liu, G., Xie, Y., Jiang, C.: Two-level attention model of representation learning for fraud detection. IEEE Trans. on Computational Social Systems **8**(6), 1291–1301 (2021)
3. Chawla, N., Kumar, B.: E-commerce and consumer protection in india: the emerging trend. Journal of Business Ethics **180**(2), 581–604 (2022)
4. Cheng, D., Wang, X., Zhang, Y., Zhang, L.: Graph neural network for fraud detection via spatial-temporal attention. IEEE Trans. on Knowledge and Data Engineering **34**(8), 3800–3813 (2020)
5. Chu, G., Wang, J., Qi, Q., Sun, H., Tao, S., Yang, H., Liao, J., Han, Z.: Exploiting spatial-temporal behavior patterns for fraud detection in telecom networks. IEEE Trans. on Dependable and Secure Computing **20**(6), 4564–4577 (2022)
6. Cui, J., Yan, C., Wang, C.: ReMEMBeR: Ranking metric embedding-based multicontextual behavior profiling for online banking fraud detection. IEEE Trans. on Computational Social Systems **8**(3), 643–654 (2021)
7. Deng, Z., Xin, G., Liu, Y., Wang, W., Wang, B.: Contrastive graph neural network-based camouflaged fraud detector. Information Sciences **618**, 39–52 (2022)
8. Fanai, H., Abbasimehr, H.: A novel combined approach based on deep autoencoder and deep classifiers for credit card fraud detection. Expert Systems with Applications **217**, 119562 (2023)
9. Goodfellow, I.J., Pouget-Abadie, J., Mirza, M., Xu, B., Warde-Farley, D., Ozair, S., Courville, A., Bengio, Y.: Generative adversarial nets. Advances In Neural Information Processing Systems **27** (2014)
10. Guang, M., Li, Z., Yan, C., Xu, Y., Wang, J., Cheng, D., Jiang, C.: Multi-temporal partitioned graph attention networks for financial fraud detection. IEEE Trans. on Information Forensics and Security **20**, 9399–9412 (2025)
11. Guthrie, C., Fosso-Wamba, S., Arnaud, J.B.: Online consumer resilience during a pandemic: An exploratory study of e-commerce behavior before, during and after a COVID-19 lockdown. Journal of Retailing and Consumer Services **61**, 102570 (2021)
12. Hochreiter, S., Schmidhuber, J.: Long short-term memory. Neural Computation **9**(8), 1735–1780 (1997)
13. Kang, M., Zhang, R., Barnes, C., Paris, S., Kwak, S., Park, J., Shechtman, E., Zhu, J.Y., Park, T.: Distilling diffusion models into conditional gans. In: European Conference on Computer Vision. vol. 15086, pp. 428–447 (2024)
14. Kennedy, R.K., Villanustre, F., Khoshgoftaar, T.M., Salekshahrezaee, Z.: Synthesizing class labels for highly imbalanced credit card fraud detection data. Journal of Big Data **11**(1), 38 (2024)
15. Khodabandehlou, S., Golpayegani, A.H.: FiFrauD: unsupervised financial fraud detection in dynamic graph streams. ACM Trans. on Knowledge Discovery from Data **18**(5), 1–29 (2024)
16. Li, R., Liu, Z., Ma, Y., Yang, D., Sun, S.: Internet financial fraud detection based on graph learning. IEEE Trans. on Computational Social Systems **10**(3), 1394–1401 (2022)
17. Li, Y., Peng, X., Zhang, J., Li, Z., Wen, M.: DCT-GAN: Dilated convolutional transformer-based GAN for time series anomaly detection. IEEE Trans. on Knowledge and Data Engineering **35**(4), 3632–3644 (2023)
18. Li, Z., Huang, M., Liu, G., Jiang, C.: A hybrid method with dynamic weighted entropy for handling the problem of class imbalance with overlap in credit card fraud detection. Expert Systems with Applications **175**, 114750 (2021)
19. Lu, C., Wang, X., Yang, A., Liu, Y., Dong, Z.: A few-shot-based model-agnostic meta-learning for intrusion detection in security of internet of things. IEEE Internet of Things Journal **10**(24), 21309–21321 (2023)
20. Ma, J., Xiang, S., Li, Q., Yuan, L., Cheng, D., Jiang, C.: Parallel graph learning with temporal stamp encoding for fraudulent transactions detections. IEEE Trans. on Big Data **11**(4), 1945–1958 (2025)

21. Ma, W., Shi, J., Qiu, J., Wu, C., Chen, J., Jiang, L., Liu, S., Liu, Y., Yang, X.: Detecting defi fraud with a graph-transformer language model. IEEE Trans. on Information Forensics and Security **20**, 10051–10065 (2025)
22. Ma, X., Qu, J., Li, J., Lui, J.C., Li, Z., Liu, W., Guan, X.: Inferring hidden IoT devices and user interactions via spatial-temporal traffic fingerprinting. IEEE/ACM Trans. on Networking **30**(1), 394–408 (2021)
23. Ma, X., Wu, J., Xue, S., Yang, J., Zhou, C., Sheng, Q.Z., Xiong, H., Akoglu, L.: A comprehensive survey on graph anomaly detection with deep learning. IEEE Trans. on Knowledge and Data Engineering **35**(12), 12012–12038 (2021)
24. Ni, L., Li, J., Xu, H., Wang, X., Zhang, J.: Fraud feature boosting mechanism and spiral oversampling balancing technique for credit card fraud detection. IEEE Trans. on Computational Social Systems **11**(2), 1615–1630 (2023)
25. Pei, S., Zhang, X., Fan, B., Meng, G.: Out-of-distribution detection with boundary aware learning. In: European Conference on Computer Vision. vol. 13684, pp. 235–251 (2022)
26. Sağkaya Güngör, A., Ozansoy Çadırcı, T.: Understanding digital consumer: A review, synthesis, and future research agenda. International Journal of Consumer Studies **46**(5), 1829–1858 (2022)
27. Santos, M.S., Abreu, P.H., Japkowicz, N., Fernández, A., Santos, J.: A unifying view of class overlap and imbalance: Key concepts, multi-view panorama, and open avenues for research. Information Fusion **89**, 228–253 (2023)
28. Scarselli, F., Gori, M., Tsoi, A.C., Hagenbuchner, M., Monfardini, G.: The graph neural network model. IEEE Trans. on Neural Networks **20**(1), 61–80 (2008)
29. Sharief, F., Ijaz, H., Shojafar, M., Naeem, M.A.: Multi-class imbalanced data handling with concept drift in fog computing: A taxonomy, review, and future directions. ACM Computing Surveys **57**(1), 1–48 (2024)
30. Sharma, T., Rattan, D.: Characterization of android malwares and their families. ACM Computing Surveys **57**(5), 1–31 (2025)
31. Shehnepoor, S., Togneri, R., Liu, W., Bennamoun, M.: Spatio-temporal graph representation learning for fraudster group detection. IEEE Trans. on Neural Networks and Learning Systems **35**(5), 6628–6642 (2022)
32. Soltanzadeh, P., Feizi-Derakhshi, M.R., Hashemzadeh, M.: Addressing the class-imbalance and class-overlap problems by a metaheuristic-based under-sampling approach. Pattern Recognition **143**, 109721 (2023)
33. Tang, H., Wang, C., Zhu, H.: Enhancing online transaction fraud detection via heterogeneous source models. IEEE Trans. on Dependable and Secure Computing **22**(6), 7818–7834 (2025)
34. Van Belle, R., Baesens, B., De Weerdt, J.: CATCHM: A novel network-based credit card fraud detection method using node representation learning. Decision Support Systems **164**, 113866 (2023)
35. Vanini, P., Rossi, S., Zvizdic, E., Domenig, T.: Online payment fraud: from anomaly detection to risk management. Financial Innovation **9**(1), 66 (2023)
36. Wang, C., Chai, S., Zhu, H., Jiang, C.: Caesar:an online payment anti-fraud integration system with decision explainability. IEEE Trans. on Dependable and Secure Computing **20**(3), 2565–2577 (2022)
37. Wang, X., Yu, H., Guo, J., Li, P., Luo, X.: Towards fraud detection via fine-grained classification of user behavior. IEEE Trans. on Big Data **11**, 1994–2007 (2024)
38. Wei, J., Wang, S., Zhou, S.K., Cui, S., Li, Z.: Weakly supervised object localization through inter-class feature similarity and intra-class appearance consistency. In: European Conference on Computer Vision. vol. 13690, pp. 195–210 (2022)
39. Wu, Z., Yang, X., Wei, X., Yuan, P., Zhang, Y., Bai, J.: A self-supervised anomaly detection algorithm with interpretability. Expert Systems with Applications **237**, 121539 (2024)
40. Xie, Y., Hong, Y., Qiao, S., Yao, J., Liu, G., Pang, S.: A time-aware generative network for enhancing transaction security in consumer electronics. IEEE Trans. on Consumer Electronics **71**(2), 6818–6828 (2025)
41. Xie, Y., Liu, G., Yan, C., Jiang, C., Zhou, M.: Time-aware attention-based gated network for credit card fraud detection by extracting transactional behaviors. IEEE Trans. on Computational Social Systems **10**(3), 1004–1016 (2023)

42. Xie, Y., Liu, G., Yan, C., Jiang, C., Zhou, M., Li, M.: Learning transactional behavioral representations for credit card fraud detection. IEEE Trans. on Neural Networks and Learning Systems **35**(4), 5735–5748 (2024)
43. Xie, Y., Liu, G., Zhou, M., Wei, L., Zhu, H., Zhou, R., Cao, L.: A spatial–temporal gated network for credit card fraud detection by learning transactional representations. IEEE Trans. on Automation Science and Engineering **21**(4), 6978–6991 (2023)
44. Xie, Y., Shan, J., Wei, L., Yao, J., Zhou, M.: GAN-based hybrid sampling method for transaction fraud detection. IEEE Trans. on Knowledge and Data Engineering **37**(10), 5905–5918 (2025)
45. Xie, Y., Zhou, M., Liu, G., Wei, L., Zhu, H., De Meo, P.: A transactional-behavior-based hierarchical gated network for credit card fraud detection. IEEE/CAA Journal of Automatica Sinica **12**(7), 1489–1503 (2025)
46. Xu, R., Li, Y.: Interpretable spatial-temporal graph convolutional network for system log anomaly detection. Advanced Engineering Informatics **62**, 102803 (2024)
47. Yang, H., Gu, D., He, J.: A robust and efficient federated learning algorithm against adaptive model poisoning attacks. IEEE Internet of Things Journal **11**(9), 16289–16302 (2024)
48. Yousefimehr, B., Ghatee, M.: A distribution-preserving method for resampling combined with lightgbm-lstm for sequence-wise fraud detection in credit card transactions. Expert Systems with Applications **262**, 125661
49. Zeng, Q., Lin, L., Jiang, R., Huang, W., Lin, D.: NNEnsLeG: A novel approach for e-commerce payment fraud detection using ensemble learning and neural networks. Information Processing & Management **62**(1), 103916 (2025)
50. Zhang, W., Luo, C.: GE-GNN: Gated edge-augmented graph neural network for fraud detection. IEEE Trans. on Big Data **11**(4), 1664–1676 (2025)
51. Zhou, J., Qian, Y., Zou, Q., Liu, P., Xiang, J.: Deepsyslog: Deep anomaly detection on syslog using sentence embedding and metadata. IEEE Trans. on Information Forensics and Security **17**, 3051–3061 (2022)
52. Zhu, H., Wang, C., Chai, S.: Detecting evolving fraudulent behavior in online payment services: Open-category and concept-drift. IEEE Trans. on Services Computing **17**(5), 2180–2193 (2024)

Chapter 2
Foundations of Online Payment Fraud Detection and Deep Learning Models

In Chap. 1, we provide a high-level analysis of the evolution of online fraudulent transactions, the limitations of traditional OPFD systems, and the potential of deep learning in financial security. Building on this foundation, this chapter offers a systematic review of the foundational concepts and operational characteristics of online payment transactions, identifies the core challenges faced by OPFD, and introduces the deep learning model framework that will be used throughout the book. In addition, this chapter discusses commonly used evaluation metrics and assessment strategies in OPFD, establishing a unified methodological basis for model design, experimental comparison, and performance analysis in the subsequent chapters.

2.1 What Is Online Payment Fraud

With the rapid growth of the digital economy, online payment fraud has become increasingly prominent and poses a major threat to its healthy development [84]. Online payment fraud refers to illegal activities in which fraudsters gain unauthorized control of user accounts, forge transaction identities, manipulate payment processes, or exploit structural vulnerabilities in payment systems to induce victims to transfer funds involuntarily or under deceptive conditions [3]. Its core characteristic lies in the construction of highly deceptive pseudo-legitimate transaction processes across behavioral, temporal, and spatial dimensions, enabling fraudulent activities to exhibit statistical patterns and structural properties that closely resemble those of legitimate users.

At the behavioral level, fraudsters employ systematic disguise strategies to imitate the operational habits and behavioral patterns of legitimate users [90]. As a result, fraudulent transactions closely resemble legitimate ones across multiple feature dimensions, including temporal distribution, transaction amount, frequency, device

Y. Xie et al., *Neural Network-Based Deep Learning for Online Payment Fraud Detection*,
https://doi.org/10.1007/978-981-95-8513-7_2

and network environment, geographic location, and preferred transaction channels [11]. This leads to a strong "quasi-legitimate" behavioral pattern.

Instead of relying on extreme or abrupt actions, modern fraud operations pursue the goal of "using the account like a legitimate user." Fraudsters orchestrate transaction processes that are complete, continuous, and logically coherent [78]. These include initiating logins during the user's typical active periods, keeping transaction amounts within the user's historical mean and normal fluctuation range, maintaining familiar transaction rhythms and intervals, selecting merchants or transfer paths consistent with past preferences, and mimicking routine steps such as checking balances or browsing bills before initiating payments or transfers [14]. These actions increase the perceived legitimacy and realism of the entire behavior sequence.

Based on this pattern, fraudsters often further disguise their activities by conducting multiple small trial transactions or splitting fund transfers across several accounts [66]. Each individual transaction remains locally consistent with legitimate behavior, while the overall sequence appears smooth and continuous. For example, in mobile payment and online banking scenarios, a fraudster who has gained account access may first log in from a device and network environment similar to the account's historical usage [71]. The fraudster may then check account information or upcoming bills during the user's usual evening activity window, followed by several moderate transfers to recipients consistent with the user's past geographic or banking patterns. Finally, a larger transfer may be divided into multiple smaller transactions to obfuscate the outflow of funds.

Such behavior sequences intertwine with the user's historical patterns in terms of time, amount, frequency, and transaction pathways. Consequently, rule-based systems, static thresholds, and single-point anomaly detectors struggle to identify these risks in real time, significantly increasing the difficulty of precisely detecting and effectively blocking fraudulent activities [16].

At the temporal level, fraudsters often combine a "low-frequency long-period dormancy" strategy with a "high-frequency short-period burst" pattern [12]. This creates highly organized temporal characteristics across the entire account lifecycle [56]. Specifically, fraudsters deliberately control the frequency of operations over extended periods, embedding logins, queries, profile modifications, and small payments into normal-looking timelines. As a result, account activity exhibits daily, weekly, and monthly rhythms similar to those of legitimate users [57].

On top of this long-term disguise, fraudsters split large transfers into multiple consecutive, reasonably spaced transactions. They also perform short, intensive bursts of fund movement within critical time windows [87]. These crafted bursts exhibit both temporal continuity and inter-transaction intervals that match common user statistics [79]. Fraudsters not only mimic typical active hours but also draw on the empirical distribution of the user's historical transaction intervals. They generate access and transaction sequences with multiple periodic fluctuations, such as intraday cycles, weekday-weekend cycles, and billing cycles [62]. This makes each fraudulent transaction difficult to flag as an isolated anomaly.

For example, in online credit card payment scenarios, a fraudster who has obtained account information may first spend weeks performing only bill inquiries and small purchases during the user's usual evening activity window [31]. The attacker maintains operational intervals and timing patterns consistent with the user's historical records [35]. After the monitoring system forms a stable perception of this "new normal," the fraudster may switch to periods when the user occasionally made large purchases, such as Friday evenings or pre-holiday periods. Within 30–60 min, the fraudster then initiates several high-value transactions slightly below the suspicious threshold, keeping a few minutes between each transaction to mimic a common user pattern of "repeated comparison and split ordering." [81].

Throughout this process, the fraudulent sequence matches the legitimate user's long-term activity pattern at the macro level, while maintaining statistically plausible intervals and periodic patterns at the micro level [58]. These characteristics substantially reduce the effectiveness of traditional detection methods that rely on fixed time windows, static outlier thresholds, or simple temporal clustering, thereby increasing the concealment and persistence of fraudulent activities [52].

At the spatial level, modern online payment fraud often appears as clustered, high-frequency operations concentrated in specific geographic areas, network nodes, or device environments, rather than as isolated individual behaviors [15]. Fraudsters commonly rely on groups of IP address prefixes, mobile base stations, or network exit points within the same Autonomous System (AS), as well as clusters of devices with highly similar fingerprints and networks of geographically proximate accounts [80]. Within these constrained spatial regions, they repeatedly trigger key actions such as logins, bindings, payments, and transfers, forming stable and persistent false activity patterns.

During execution, fraudsters carefully manage the spatial attributes of devices and networks. They may operate for extended periods within a small set of IP prefixes or shared Wi-Fi hotspots and intentionally maintain location coordinates, base-station coverage, or city-level distributions similar to those of legitimate users [6]. As a result, both individual accounts and their related accounts exhibit spatial patterns that appear "locally dense yet globally reasonable." Attackers may further construct coordinated behaviors among multiple accounts in the same area [13]. By frequently activating, logging in, and transacting near the same residential community, office park, or commercial district, these accounts form high-similarity "behavior clusters" in the joint spatial-behavior feature space, while each account remains consistent with the typical pattern of local users when viewed individually.

By simulating seemingly legitimate transactional behavior within a localized region, fraudsters can effectively undermine traditional spatial detection rules based on abnormal geographic distribution, rapid cross-city or cross-country switching, discontinuous movement paths, or associations with high-risk cross-region nodes [3]. For example, in integrated online banking and third-party payment environments, fraud groups may recruit numerous"money-laundering accounts" within the same mid-tier city [76]. These accounts are configured to originate from a small number of shared IP address ranges and device fingerprint types, and they are collectively linked to commonly used local phone numbers and delivery addresses [95]. They then perform frequent fund-receiving and fund-transferring operations within the same city, following fund-flow paths such as "local merchant → local personal account → local relay account → cross-border exit account." At each step, the spatial distribution and merchant type remain similar to those of genuine local transactions.

As a result, the geographic location, IP address, and device origin of any single transaction appear highly consistent with normal local behavior. However, within the local spatial network, the accounts form a compact, densely connected fund-flow network. This structure undermines detection methods that rely on simple geographic-distance thresholds, cross-region switching rules, or limited high-risk region blacklists, significantly increasing the concealment, persistence, and adversarial nature of fraudulent activities in the spatial dimension.

2.2 Challenges in Online Payment Fraud Detection

With the rapid expansion of online transaction volume and the continuous emergence of new business models, fraudulent activities have become increasingly organized, intelligent, and covert. Traditional OPFD approaches largely rely on manually crafted rules or static supervised learning models. Although these methods were effective in earlier, relatively simple fraud scenarios, they struggle in today's high-frequency, high-dimensional, and adversarial environments.

Fraudulent behaviors exhibit strong camouflage and continuous evolution, making accurate identification by existing detection methods difficult. These methods are easily affected by data imbalance, feature confusion, and pattern drift, leading to low detection accuracy, limited generalization ability, and poor adaptability to emerging fraud patterns.

Model cognitive bias under Imbalanced Transaction Data. In online transaction scenarios, fraudulent samples are extremely rare, typically accounting for only 0.01%–0.1% of all transactions [92]. Traditional machine learning classifiers tend to label fraudulent transactions as legitimate to achieve a globally optimal objective under such imbalanced data distributions. This bias significantly undermines the ability of OPFD models to learn fraud-related patterns and prevents them from accurately distinguishing between legitimate and fraudulent transactions [66]. Therefore, effectively addressing class imbalance has become a critical step toward improving the performance of OPFD models.

Current mainstream data augmentation methods for addressing class imbalance include the Synthetic Minority Oversampling Technique (SMOTE) and GANs. Although these methods enhance the representation of minority-class samples and have shown promising improvements in many classification tasks, they still face clear limitations in OPFD [89]. Fraudulent transactions often involve coordinated activities across multiple accounts, devices, and regions, forming complex multi-entity behaviors. These behaviors exhibit complex characteristics, including strong temporal dependencies, structural heterogeneity, and long-range interactions within their high-dimensional feature space. However, existing augmentation strategies rely primarily on point-wise features or local distribution interpolation. Such approaches struggle to capture the cross-dimensional jumps, sparse distributions, and multicluster patterns characteristic of fraudulent transactions. As a result, the generated samples tend to cluster around locally dense regions and fail to cover global fraud patterns, thereby weakening the model's ability to detect weak signals, boundary cases, and structured fraud behaviors [23].

Fraudulent samples often overlap with legitimate samples in behavioral space, resulting in blurred class boundaries [83]. Because fraudsters intentionally mimic the behavioral patterns of legitimate users, the feature distribution of fraudulent transactions is frequently embedded within high-density regions or boundary areas of the legitimate class. This creates a pronounced overlapping structure in high-dimensional space. Under this setting, most existing methods focus on modeling the internal characteristics of minority samples but overlook the distributional similarity and boundary morphology between fraudulent and legitimate classes. Consequently, synthesized samples are overly embedded within the legitimate distribution and exhibit intertwined topological structures, causing the model to learn ambiguous decision boundaries and reducing detection performance [39].

Overall, in extremely imbalanced transaction environments with strong behavioral overlap, the key scientific problem in OPFD research is how to jointly model the essential characteristics of fraudulent behaviors, enhance the diversity and representativeness of synthetic samples, and explicitly account for the similarity and boundary structures between fraudulent and legitimate samples. Addressing these challenges is essential for improving the model's ability to identify highly camouflaged, weak-signal, and dynamically evolving fraud patterns.

Feature Separability Challenges in Highly Overlapping Transactional Behavior. In OPFD, fraudsters often disguise their behaviors to closely resemble those of legitimate users across multiple feature dimensions, resulting in a highly overlapping distribution in the feature space [83]. This overlap substantially increases the difficulty of identifying anomalous patterns. Under such conditions, feature construction approaches dominated by expert rules reveal clear limitations.

Insufficient temporal feature representation further reduces the separability of fraudulent behaviors. Most traditional methods rely on static attributes of individual transactions for classification [82]. Although these approaches enable immediate risk assessment, they overlook the temporal evolution of user behavior. Real-world fraudulent activity typically exhibits staged, gradual, or sudden dynamic patterns, such as subtle transitions from normal to abnormal behavior patterns that cannot be captured by single-point static features [80]. Without explicit temporal modeling, the model fails to learn gradual variations across behavioral trajectories, causing fraudulent samples to become even more entangled with legitimate ones in the high-dimensional space and ultimately weakening the model's discriminative capability.

Limited spatial representation further increases behavioral confusion [82]. Geographic and device-related spatial patterns in online transactions are highly dynamic and heterogeneous, yet existing spatial feature modeling typically relies on fixed regional partitions, static grids, or predefined spatial rules [60]. Such approaches cannot adapt to the cross-domain and cross-location jumps exhibited by fraudulent behaviors. Because all historical transactions are treated as homogeneous records, the model cannot capture the evolving trends of spatial usage patterns or identify concealed fraud chains formed across regions, nodes, or devices. This lack of spatial expressiveness fragments what should be continuous multi-region fraud activities into isolated local events, causing fraud patterns to appear as fragmented distributions in the feature space. As a result, the sensitivity of detection models to spatial anomalies is further reduced.

Relying on single-dimensional feature modeling makes it difficult to capture deep fraud patterns effectively. Many existing methods extract features from either temporal or spatial perspectives alone and fail to integrate the inherent relationships between temporal dynamics and spatial structures [84]. However, online transaction fraud often exhibits strong spatial-temporal dependencies, such as cross-region logins within short time windows, consecutive device switching, and rapid fund-transfer sequences. These behaviors form complex spatial-temporal interaction structures in the feature space [79]. Without a joint modeling mechanism, models are unable to capture these cross-dimensional, deeply coupled features, allowing fraudulent behaviors to remain hidden within the distribution of normal transactions. In summary, under highly overlapping behavioral spaces, a key research direction for improving OPFD accuracy is to disentangle fraud-sensitive features across multiple dimensions and to construct representations that reflect transaction dynamics and spatial-temporal correlations. Such advancements are essential for overcoming the feature entanglement caused by disguised behaviors.

Model Adaptation Challenges in Dynamically Evolving Environments. With continuous technological advancement and evolving social environments, online transaction fraud displays rapid evolution and strong dynamism, posing a significant challenge to the effectiveness of traditional fraud detection models in real-world settings. First, inadequate perception of fraud patterns is one of the core limitations of existing approaches [10]. Many studies focus primarily on constructing single-entity behavioral features in either temporal or spatial dimensions, emphasizing the local dynamics of individual transaction sequences or account activities [49].

However, real-world online fraud typically unfolds through multi-entity collaboration, involving complex interactions among user accounts, devices, IP addresses, payment channels, and proxy nodes. In the feature space, these collaborative behaviors often manifest as cross-node connections, cross-region switching, and nested multi-entity structures, which differ substantially from traditional single-entity patterns [19]. Due to the inability of current models to represent such multi-entity interaction structures, they struggle to capture the cooperative patterns and topological characteristics underlying correlated fraud. Consequently, their generalization capability deteriorates when facing emerging fraud strategies—such as device-sharing fraud, cluster-based attacks, and chained transfer fraud—leading to poor performance in detecting unseen patterns or weak-signal fraud behaviors.

Model adaptation lag further limits the performance of existing methods in rapidly evolving environments [37]. Online transaction networks are inherently dynamic, heterogeneous graph structures, yet most mainstream models rely on local static structural features or short-range dependencies [77]. While effective for long-standing, recurrent fraud patterns, such models struggle to adapt to sudden, short-term bursts of fraudulent activity.

In practice, fraud attacks often exhibit dense transactions, rapid path switching, and multi-entity participation within extremely short time windows. In the feature space, these behaviors appear as weak-signal but highly consistent structural patterns [81]. They frequently skip multiple intermediate nodes and display pronounced long-range dependencies and heterogeneous interactions. However, traditional models, which depend on local neighborhood information or short temporal windows, have difficulty capturing these rapidly propagating structural anomalies.

Moreover, when fraud strategies evolve quickly or behavior trajectories drift, models often fail to update their internal representations in time, resulting in performance degradation and detection delays [96]. In summary, in real-world environments where fraudulent behaviors continuously evolve, a central research challenge lies in developing OPFD models capable of rapidly perceiving complex structural changes, remaining sensitive to long-range interactions, and sustaining stable discriminative capability under dynamic conditions.

2.3 Neural Networks for Sequential and Structured Data

Generative Adversarial Networks. Proposed by Goodfellow et al. [23], GANs are a class of deep learning models based on a zero-sum game framework. A GAN consists of two adversarial neural networks: a generator and a discriminator. The generator learns the probability density distribution of real samples and produces synthetic samples that accurately capture the underlying patterns of the original data [98]. The discriminator, in turn, learns to distinguish between real and synthetic samples by modeling their feature differences and predicting the authenticity of the input [42]. During the adversarial training process, the generator continuously improves its ability to fool the discriminator, while the discriminator simultaneously enhances its capacity to detect forged samples [22]. Through this adversarial process, the two networks iteratively refine each other and eventually reach a Nash equilibrium [5]. Once training converges, the generator can produce synthetic samples that closely match the distribution of the real data and preserve its characteristic patterns while maintaining sufficient diversity [4].

The generator learns feature representations of real samples by modeling the data distribution in the latent space and produces synthetic samples that resemble the original ones. Its loss function is defined as follows:

$$L_G = -\mathbb{E}_{z \sim P_z(z)}\big[\log\big(D(G(z))\big)\big], \tag{2.1}$$

where z refer to the latent noise vector sampled from the prior noise distribution $P_z(z)$ and the synthetic sample $G(z)$ produced by the generator, respectively. The training objective of the generator is to learn the underlying patterns of real samples as accurately as possible and to confuse the discriminator such that it cannot distinguish between synthetic and real data. $D(G(z))$ denotes the probability predicted by the discriminator that the synthetic sample is real, where the value lies within the range [0, 1]. During the training process, the generator achieves its objective by maximizing $D(G(z))$.

The discriminator identifies whether an input sample is synthetic or real by analyzing and comparing the feature differences between generated samples and original samples. Its loss function is defined as follows:

$$L_D = \mathbb{E}_{x_f \sim P_f(x)}\big[\log D(x_f)\big] + \mathbb{E}_{z \sim P_Z(z)}\big[\log(1 - D(G(z)))\big], \tag{2.2}$$

where $x_f \sim P_f(x)$ represents a fraudulent sample from the distribution of fraudulent samples. The objective of the discriminator is to maximally distinguish a synthetic sample $G(z)$ from a fraudulent one x_f. $D(x_f)$ denotes the probability predicted by the discriminator that the fraudulent sample is genuine and the value lies within the range [0, 1]. During the training process, the discriminator increases $D(x_f)$ while decreasing $D(G(z))$ to maximize its objective. This optimization process drives the discriminator toward more effective separation between fraudulent and synthetic samples. Furthermore, to facilitate optimization, the loss function is commonly reformulated from a maximization problem into a minimization problem using standard optimization techniques.

Long Short-Term Memory Network. Long Short-Term Memory (LSTM), proposed by Hochreiter and Schmidhuber, is a gated recurrent neural network architecture designed to address the vanishing and exploding gradients in traditional recurrent neural networks [18]. The core structure of LSTM consists of four key components: the input gate, forget gate, output gate, candidate, and updated cell state. Through the coordinated operation of these components, LSTM can dynamically regulate how information is stored, forgotten, and output, enabling it to effectively capture both long-term and short-term patterns in sequential data.

The input gate regulates the extent to which the current input contributes to the update of the memory cell state [59]. Its primary role is to determine which new information should be written into long-term memory, ensuring that the network remains robust when processing redundant or noisy inputs [53].

$$i_t = \sigma(W_{ih}h_{t-1} + W_{ix}x_t + b_i), \tag{2.3}$$

where i_t is the input gate, $\sigma(\cdot)$ denotes the Sigmoid activation function, W_{ih} and W_{ix} denote the weight matrix, and b_i represent the bias term of the input gate. h_{t-1} and x_t denote the previous hidden state and the current input, respectively. Since the output of the input gate is constrained within the range [0, 1], values closer to 1 indicate that the model considers the corresponding information more important and assigns it a higher weight during subsequent memory updates.

The forget gate is a key component of LSTM designed to address the long-term dependency problem [36]. It determines how much historical information should be retained at the current time step and functions as a dynamic "memory filter" [44]. By selectively preserving relevant portions of past memory states, the model prevents irrelevant or outdated information from negatively affecting future predictions.

$$f_t = \sigma(W_{fh}h_{t-1} + W_{fx}x_t + b_f), \tag{2.4}$$

where f_t denotes the forget gate, W_{fh} and W_{fx} denote the weight matrix, and b_f represent the bias term of the forget gate. The output of the forget gate also lies within the range [0, 1]; a smaller value in a specific dimension indicates that the corresponding memory component will be partially or completely discarded at the current time step [67]. Through this mechanism, LSTM achieves flexible information selection along the temporal dimension, enabling the model to preserve essential long-term features while avoiding model degradation caused by redundant information [68].

The memory cell is the core component of LSTM and serves as an "information highway" that runs through the entire sequence, providing a state representation that can be continuously propagated along the temporal dimension [32]. Specifically, the candidate cell state $\tilde{c}_t$ is first generated based on the current input and the previous hidden state, encoding the new information to be integrated into the memory system. Then, by jointly leveraging the controls of the input gate and forget gate, LSTM selectively retains historical information from the previous cell state c_{t-1} and incorporates valid new information from $\tilde{c}_t$, thus yielding the updated cell state c_t. This mechanism enables a balanced integration of historical information and newly acquired information.

$$\widetilde{c_t} = tanh(W_{ch}h_{t-1} + W_{cx}x_t + b_c), \tag{2.5}$$

$$c_t = f_t \odot c_{t-1} + i_t \odot \widetilde{c}_t, \tag{2.6}$$

where $\odot$ denotes element-wise multiplication, $\tanh(\cdot)$ is the hyperbolic tangent activation function, W_{ch} and W_{cx} denote the weight matrix, and b_c represent the bias term of the memory cell. Through this update mechanism, the memory cell not only preserves stable long-term information but also integrates newly relevant features at the current time step. This effectively alleviates the rapid gradient decay that occurs during backpropagation and enables the network to maintain stable information flow across long temporal sequences [61].

The output gate determines which information from the memory cell at the current time step will be projected into the hidden state, allowing it to participate in subsequent computations or be passed to upper network layers [43]. The computation involves two steps: **(1)** the output gate produces a control signal, and **(2)** the signal is then combined with the current memory cell state to generate the final hidden state [63].

$$o_t = \sigma(W_{oh}h_{t-1} + W_{ox}x_t + b_o), \tag{2.7}$$

$$h_t = o_t \odot \tanh(C_t), \tag{2.8}$$

where o_t denotes the output gate, h_t represents the current hidden state, W_{oh} and W_{ox} denote the weight matrix, and b_o represent the bias term of the output gate. o_t enables the LSTM to selectively utilize the memory cell contents according to task requirements at each time step, thereby enhancing the model's representational capacity and generalization performance. In addition, during training, LSTM optimizes the parameters of all gates and memory cells through backpropagation, allowing the model to minimize the loss function while stably learning both short-term variations and long-term dependency patterns in sequential data [21].

Gated Recurrent Unit. The gated recurrent unit (GRU), proposed by Cho et al. [88], is a simplified variant of the LSTM. Its main objective is to achieve modeling capacity comparable to that of LSTM with fewer structural components, while further reducing the computational cost and the number of parameters during training. Unlike LSTM, GRU merges the memory cell and the hidden state, and employs two core gating structures, the update gate and the reset gate, to regulate the flow of information for input, forgetting, and output.

The update gate z_t is the key component of GRU. It determines to what extent the current hidden state should inherit the memory from the previous time step [88]. It functionally combines the roles of the LSTM's input and forget gates, jointly controlling the retention of past information and the incorporation of new input [2].

$$z_t = \sigma(W_z \cdot [h_{t-1}, x_t] + b_z) \, , \tag{2.9}$$

where $\sigma(\cdot)$ denotes the Sigmoid activation function, and W_z and b_z are the weight matrix and bias term of the update gate, respectively. The value of z_t lies in [0, 1]. When z_t is close to 1, the model tends to retain more information from the previous hidden state and to reduce the influence of new input information. Conversely, a small value of z_t indicates that the model prefers to incorporate more new input features. Through this dynamic control mechanism, the update gate effectively balances stability and flexibility, enabling the GRU to preserve long-term memory while avoiding excessive forgetting when modeling complex sequences [54].

The reset gate r_t controls how much historical information is used when computing the current candidate hidden state [30]. Its main role is to decide whether the past memory should be discarded and the current state recomputed [28].

$$r_t = \sigma(W_r \cdot [h_{t-1}, x_t] + b_r) \, . \tag{2.10}$$

A small value of r_t indicates that the model should rely less on the previous hidden state at the current time step and focus more on the current input features. When r_t is close to 1, the model treats the past context as still important and fully includes historical information in the computation of the candidate state. By introducing the reset gate, the GRU can flexibly handle abrupt or non-stationary sequence patterns while reducing the interference of irrelevant information on the learned representations [70].

Under the joint effect of the update and reset gates, the GRU captures the useful information at the current time step through the candidate hidden state $\tilde{h}_t$ [93].

$$\tilde{h}_t = \tanh(W_h \cdot [r_t \odot h_{t-1}, x_t] + b_h), \tag{2.11}$$

where $\odot$ represents the element-wise product, and $\tanh(\cdot)$ is the hyperbolic tangent activation function. By controlling the reset gate, the model can selectively ignore irrelevant historical information when computing the candidate state, which allows it to better adapt to sequence data with short-term shifts or local pattern changes [47]. This structure not only increases the model's sensitivity to feature variations but also improves the flexibility of sequence modeling. Moreover, compared with a traditional recurrent neural network (RNN), the final hidden state h_t of GRU is obtained by weighting the previous hidden state and the candidate state through the update gate [69].

$$h_t = (1 - z_t) \odot h_{t-1} + z_t \odot \tilde{h}_t. \tag{2.12}$$

This mechanism highlights the central role of the update gate in balancing the retention of historical information and the integration of new information [32]. When z_t is large, the model prefers to inherit the previous state; when z_t is small, the model adaptively incorporates more new information to update the current state. This linear interpolation scheme effectively mitigates the rapid decay of gradients over time in conventional RNNs, allowing GRUs to maintain stable gradient propagation when learning from long sequences [45].

Graph Neural Networks. GNNs are a class of deep learning models specifically designed for graph-structured data [24]. First formalized in their modern form by Scarselli et al., GNNs aim to provide effective representation learning mechanisms for nodes, edges, and entire graphs, thereby overcoming the limitation that conventional deep neural networks cannot directly handle non-Euclidean structured data [7]. A GNN model is typically composed of several key components, including a message-passing mechanism, a node update function, and a readout layer [1]. Through the joint effect of these modules, GNNs can efficiently model node features and structural semantics while preserving the integrity of the underlying graph topology [8].

The message-passing mechanism is the core component of a GNN. It propagates local neighborhood information between nodes, thereby establishing dependencies between each node and its neighbors [86]. Its primary function is to compute the information to be transmitted from each neighbor, forming the basis for generating discriminative node embeddings during subsequent aggregation [73]. A typical message-passing computation can be given by:

$$m_{u\to v}^{(t)} = \phi_m^{(t)}\left(h_u^{(t)}, h_v^{(t)}, e_{uv}\right), \tag{2.13}$$

where $m_{u\to v}^{(t)}$ denotes the message passed from node u to node v at the t-th iteration, $\phi_m^{(t)}(\cdot)$ is the message generation function, $h_u^{(t)}$ and $h_v^{(t)}$ are the current hidden representations of nodes u and v, respectively, and e_{uv} denotes the edge features between them. By introducing learnable parametric functions, the message-passing mechanism enables the model to extract rich structural dependencies and attribute semantics from multi-hop neighborhoods, thereby explicitly modeling the local graph structure [9].

The aggregation function compresses and combines information from neighboring nodes, and can be regarded as a summarizer of neighborhood information [55]. Since the number of neighbors of a node is usually not fixed, the aggregation function must be permutation-invariant. A typical aggregation operation is defined as follows:

$$a_v^{(t)} = \phi_{\text{agg}}^{(t)}\big(\{\, m_{u\to v}^{(t)} \mid u \in \mathcal{N}(v) \,\}\big), \tag{2.14}$$

where $a_v^{(t)}$ denotes the aggregated result for node v, and $\phi_{\text{agg}}^{(t)}(\cdot)$ can be implemented by summation, averaging, or max pooling. To enhance expressive power, advanced models like Graph SAmple and aggreGatE (GraphSAGE) [64] employ learnable aggregators (e.g., LSTM-based or attention-based aggregators), which allow the model to distinguish more precisely between different neighborhood structures and information patterns [75]. The aggregation mechanism is therefore a key step for GNNs to learn graph representations from local neighborhoods to global structures.

The node state update mechanism combines a node's own features with the aggregated neighborhood information to generate a new hidden representation $h_v^{(t+1)}$ [97]. Essentially, it is a recursive update process across iterations, analogous to the state update in recurrent neural networks.

$$h_v^{(t+1)} = \phi_u^{(t)}\big(h_v^{(t)}, a_v^{(t)}\big), \tag{2.15}$$

where $\phi_u^{(t)}(\cdot)$ denotes the node update function, which is usually implemented by a multilayer perceptron or a gated architecture. Through this process, each node iteratively integrates structural information from an expanding neighborhood with each layer, thereby enabling semantic propagation across multiple hops [27]. When multiple GNN layers are stacked, a node can eventually perceive the structural and feature information of its multi-hop neighbors, which forms the basis for learning global graph representations [38].

The readout layer maps node-level representations to graph-level or subgraph-level representations, enabling tasks such as graph classification, link prediction, and graph regression [41]. Its main role is to extract global semantic information from local node or edge representations [72]. A general form is given as follows:

$$h_G = \phi_{\text{readout}}\big(\{\, h_v^{(T)} \mid v \in G \,\}\big), \tag{2.16}$$

where h_G denotes the final embedding of the whole graph, and $\phi_{\text{readout}}(\cdot)$ can be implemented by sum pooling, mean pooling, or attention-based pooling. During training, the GNN optimizes the parameters in the message-passing, aggregation, and update functions through gradient descent and backpropagation, so that the model minimizes the loss for node classification, link prediction, or graph-level tasks [85]. Benefiting from a differentiable, end-to-end framework, GNNs can effectively learn structural dependencies in non-Euclidean spaces while maintaining high scalability [74]. These properties make them particularly well-suited for modeling the relational patterns inherent in online fraudulent transactions.

2.4 Key Metrics and Evaluation Strategies in OPFD

Confusion Matrix. The confusion matrix is a fundamental tool for evaluating the performance of classification models [50]. By cross-tabulating the true labels and the predicted labels, it reveals the discriminative behavior of the model in OPFD [48]. As shown in Table 2.1, the rows and columns of the matrix correspond to the true class of each transaction (fraudulent or legitimate) and the prediction, respectively. Specifically, T_P denotes the number of samples for which the model correctly identifies the fraudulent class, F_N denotes the number of fraudulent samples that the model fails to identify correctly, T_N denotes the number of samples for which the model correctly identifies the legitimate class, and F_P denotes the number of legitimate samples that the model fails to identify correctly [34].

Evaluation Metrics. In OPFD, the severe class imbalance between legitimate and fraudulent transactions renders traditional evaluation metrics inadequate for objectively assessing model performance [40]. To address this challenge, this chapter adopts F_1, G_m, and AUC as the core evaluation metrics and constructs a more scientific and reasonable performance evaluation framework. The components of F_1 and G_m, as well as their related descriptions, are detailed below.

Precision (P_r), also referred to as the positive predictive value, measures the proportion of correctly identified fraudulent transactions among all transactions predicted as fraudulent.

$$P_r = \frac{T_P}{T_P + F_P}. \tag{2.17}$$

Recall (R_e), also known as the true positive rate (TPR), measures the model's ability to recognize fraud patterns. It is defined as the proportion of detected fraudulent transactions among all actual fraudulent transactions.

$$R_e = \frac{T_P}{T_P + F_N}. \tag{2.18}$$

Table 2.1 Confusion matrix

Category	Actual fraudulent samples	Actual legitimate samples
Predicted fraudulent samples	T_P	F_P
Predicted legitimate samples	F_N	T_N

Specificity (S_p) measures the accuracy of recognizing legitimate patterns. It is defined as the proportion of correctly predicted legitimate transactions among all actual legitimate transactions.

$$S_P = \frac{T_N}{T_N + F_P}. \tag{2.19}$$

The F_1-score (F_1) is the harmonic mean of R_e and P_r. It attains a high value only when both P_r and R_e are high, indicating a model's robustness in identifying fraudulent patterns.

$$F_1 = \frac{2 * P_r * R_e}{P_r + R_e}. \tag{2.20}$$

The Geometric mean (G_m) combines recall and specificity. A high G_m score reflects a balance between identifying fraudulent transactions and correctly classifying legitimate transactions, indicating overall discriminative power.

$$G_m = \sqrt{R_e * S_P}. \tag{2.21}$$

The Area Under the Receiver Operating Characteristic Curve (AUC) measures the overall discriminative ability of a binary classification model across all possible classification thresholds. It quantifies the probability that the model will rank a randomly chosen positive instance higher than a randomly chosen negative instance.

$$AUC = P\left(\text{score}(x^+) > \text{score}(x^-)\right), \tag{2.22}$$

where $\text{score}(x^+)$ and $\text{score}(x^-)$ represent the prediction scores for a randomly selected positive sample and a randomly selected negative sample, respectively. AUC ranges from 0 to 1, where 0.5 indicates random guessing performance, and 1 represents perfect discrimination ability.

Evaluation Strategy. Evaluating models for OPFD requires not only general performance metrics but also experimental designs that reflect real-world business constraints and temporal dynamics [65]. In real-world settings, fraud strategies evolve over time, and the data distribution drifts continuously. Therefore, the evaluation protocol must reveal a model's stability and temporal generalization ability in such dynamic environments [26]. To mimic the real decision pattern of "using history to predict the future," experiments usually adopt a chronological split, where early transaction data are used for training and later data are used for testing [29]. This setup prevents data leakage from the future and specifically tests the model's ability to generalize to emerging fraud patterns [33]. At the same time, sliding-window evaluation strategies are widely used to further examine long-term performance under concept drift [46]. By moving the training and test windows forward over time, one can systematically observe the robustness of the model, the persistence of its performance, and its degradation trend under changing data distributions [91]. In addition, to verify whether the model effectively captures structural features that distinguish normal transactions from fraudulent ones, high-dimensional visualization tools such as t-Distributed Stochastic Neighbor Embedding (t-SNE) are often used to analyze the learned representation space [25]. These visual analyses help assess the feature expressiveness and class separability of different modules, such as attention mechanisms, temporal structures, and graph-structure encoders.

To thoroughly validate the effectiveness and relative advantages of a model design, the evaluation protocol usually also includes baseline comparison, ablation studies, and parameter sensitivity analysis [51]. Baseline comparison is conducted by systematically comparing the proposed model with multiple types of baselines—such as traditional machine learning models, deep temporal models, graph-based models, and resampling strategies—under the same data splits and metric definitions [20]. This setting allows us to objectively quantify the improvements in detection accuracy, stability, and generalization performance. Ablation studies remove or replace key components of the model step by step to examine the independent contribution of each module and to assess the necessity of the overall architecture [94]. Finally, parameter sensitivity analysis explores how the model's performance varies under different hyperparameter settings, thereby evaluating its dependence on hyperparameters and its stability in deployment [17]. Collectively, these evaluation strategies—emphasizing temporal consistency, structural analysis, and robustness—form a systematic experimental framework that enables credible and comprehensive validation of fraud detection models.

2.5 Summary

This chapter provides a systematic review of the theoretical foundations and methodological frameworks for OPFD. First, it defines fraudulent transactions and clarifies the essential properties of online payment fraud. These properties—namely low frequency, high camouflage, and strong adversariality—are manifested across behavioral, temporal, and spatial patterns. Second, it analyzes the core challenges faced by traditional OPFD models. Third, it summarizes the most representative deep learning approaches in this domain, including recurrent neural networks for modeling temporal dependencies, generative models for addressing extreme class imbalance and enriching fraud sample diversity, and graph neural networks for capturing multi-entity interactions and latent structural patterns. Finally, it constructs a systematic evaluation framework tailored to OPFD from the perspectives of metrics and experimental design, thereby establishing a rigorous basis for the experiments and analyses in subsequent chapters.

References

1. Abbahaddou, Y., Malliaros, F.D., Lutzeyer, J.F., Vazirgiannis, M.: ADMP-GNN: Adaptive depth message passing GNN. In: Proceedings of the 34th ACM International Conference on Information and Knowledge Management. pp. 4–13 (2025)
2. Addae, S., Kim, J., Kang, M.: Effective gas level prediction based on sensor array using deep learning in mixed gases: A comparative analysis of CNN-1D, LSTM, and GRU models. IEEE Trans. on Instrumentation and Measurement **74**, 1–9 (2025)
3. Awosika, T., Shukla, R.M., Pranggono, B.: Transparency and privacy: The role of explainable AI and federated learning in financial fraud detection. IEEE Access **12**, 64551–64560 (2024)
4. Bai, H., He, K., Li, Y., Chen, J., Li, H., Liu, Z., Yang, X., Du, R.: GetFed: Accurate, differentially private federated learning with GAN-Based data generation. IEEE Trans. on Dependable and Secure Computing **22**(6), 7463–7478 (2025)
5. Bianchi, L.A., Pregardier, R.C., Silva, L.A.L., dos Santos, C.R.P.: 2Pack-GAN: Exploring transfer learning to fine-tune generative adversarial networks for network packet generation. In: NOMS 2025-2025 IEEE Network Operations and Management Symposium. pp. 1–9 (2025)
6. de Castro Silva, G.M., Sichman, J.S.: Impersonation fraud detection on building access control systems: An approach based on anomalous social and spatio-temporal behaviors. Applied Soft Computing **118**, 108310 (2022)
7. Chang, J., Ren, H., Li, Z., Xu, Y., Lai, T.: A unified transductive and inductive learning framework for Few-Shot learning using graph neural networks. Applied Soft Computing **173**, 112928 (2025)
8. Chen, D., O'Bray, L., Borgwardt, K.: Structure-Aware transformer for graph representation learning. In: International Conference on Machine Learning. pp. 3469–3489. PMLR (2022)
9. Chen, J., Chen, S., Gao, J., Huang, Z., Zhang, J., Pu, J.: Exploiting neighbor effect: Conv-Agnostic GNN framework for graphs with heterophily. IEEE Trans. on Neural Networks and Learning Systems **35**(10), 13383–13396 (2024)
10. Cheng, D., Wang, X., Zhang, Y., Zhang, L.: Graph neural network for fraud detection via Spatial-Temporal attention. IEEE Trans. on Knowledge and Data Engineering **34**(8), 3800–3813 (2022)
11. Cheng, D., Xiang, S., Shang, C., Zhang, Y., Yang, F., Zhang, L.: Spatio-Temporal Attention-Based neural network for credit card fraud detection. In: Proceedings of the AAAI Conference on Artificial Intelligence. vol. 34, pp. 362–369 (2020)
12. Cheng, D., Zou, Y., Xiang, S., Jiang, C.: Graph neural networks for financial fraud detection: a review. Frontiers of Computer Science **19**(9), 199609 (2025)
13. Cheng, F., Yan, C., Liu, W., Lin, X.: Research on medical insurance anti-gang fraud model based on the knowledge graph. Engineering Applications of Artificial Intelligence **134**, 108627 (2024)
14. Cheng, L., Zhu, F., Shao, Q., Pu, J., Zeng, F.: Early detection of malicious crypto addresses with asset path tracing and selection. IEEE Trans. on Knowledge and Data Engineering **37**(3), 1154–1166 (2025)
15. Cherif, A., Ammar, H., Kalkatawi, M., Alshehri, S., Imine, A.: Encoder-decoder graph neural network for credit card fraud detection. Journal of King Saud University-Computer and Information Sciences **36**(3), 102003 (2024)
16. Chu, G., Wang, J., Qi, Q., Sun, H., Tao, S., Yang, H., Liao, J., Han, Z.: Exploiting Spatial-Temporal behavior patterns for fraud detection in telecom networks. IEEE Trans. on Dependable and Secure Computing **20**(6), 4564–4577 (2023)
17. Cong, Z., Shi, B., Li, S., Yang, J., He, Q., Pei, J.: FairSample: Training fair and accurate graph convolutional neural networks efficiently. IEEE Trans. on Knowledge and Data Engineering **36**(4), 1537–1551 (2024)
18. Creswell, A., White, T., Dumoulin, V., Arulkumaran, K., Sengupta, B., Bharath, A.A.: Generative adversarial networks: An overview. IEEE Signal Processing Magazine **35**(1), 53–65 (2018)

19. De Domenico, M.: More is different in real-world multilayer networks. Nature Physics **19**(9), 1247–1262 (2023)
20. Ding, H., Wei, Z., Ye, Y.: Scalable and effective graph neural networks via trainable random walk sampling. IEEE Trans. on Knowledge and Data Engineering **37**(2), 896–909 (2025)
21. Dong, J., Xu, M., Zhang, J., Li, J., Sun, Y., Han, S.: Short-Term power load forecasting under unstable data quality: A fuzzy deep neural network with LSTM and Self-Attention. IEEE Trans. on Industrial Informatics **21**(12), 9945–9956 (2025)
22. Dou, W., Kuang, H., Liu, X., Ma, X.: A multimodal emotion recognition framework based on generative adversarial networks. In: 2025 IEEE 6th International Seminar on Artificial Intelligence, Networking and Information Technology (AINIT). pp. 1670–1673 (2025)
23. Feng, Y., Meng, X., Zhou, F., Lin, W., Su, Z.: Real-World Non-Homogeneous haze removal by sliding Self-Attention wavelet network. IEEE Trans. on Circuits and Systems for Video Technology **33**(10), 5470–5485 (2023)
24. Feng, Z., Wang, R., Wang, T., Song, M., Wu, S., He, S.: A comprehensive survey of dynamic graph neural networks: Models, frameworks, benchmarks, experiments and challenges. IEEE Trans. on Knowledge and Data Engineering **38**(1), 26–46 (2026)
25. Fu, Y., Zhou, K., Zhu, G., Li, Z., Li, Y., Meng, P., Xu, Y., Lu, L.: A partial discharge signal separation method applicable for various sensors based on Time–Frequency feature extraction of t-SNE. IEEE Trans. on Instrumentation and Measurement **73**, 1–9 (2024)
26. Greco, S., Vacchetti, B., Apiletti, D., Cerquitelli, T.: Unsupervised concept drift detection from deep learning representations in Real-Time. IEEE Trans. on Knowledge and Data Engineering **37**(10), 6232–6245 (2025)
27. Guo, F., Yuan, Y., Wang, G., Chen, L., Lian, X., Wang, Z.: Cohesive group nearest neighbor queries on Road-Social networks under Multi-Criteria. IEEE Trans. on Knowledge and Data Engineering **33**(11), 3520–3536 (2021)
28. Guo, H., Lin, X., Zhu, K.: Pyramid LSTM network for tool condition monitoring. IEEE Trans. on Instrumentation and Measurement **71**, 1–11 (2022)
29. Guo, H., Zhang, Y., Wang, W.: Dynamical targeted ensemble learning for streaming data with concept drift. IEEE Trans. on Knowledge and Data Engineering **36**(12), 8023–8036 (2024)
30. Guo, K., Wang, N., Liu, D., Peng, X.: Uncertainty-Aware LSTM based dynamic flight fault detection for UAV actuator. IEEE Trans. on Instrumentation and Measurement **72**, 1–13 (2023)
31. Hajek, P., Abedin, M.Z., Sivarajah, U.: Fraud detection in mobile payment systems using an XGBoost-based framework. Information Systems Frontiers **25**(5), 1985–2003 (2023)
32. Han, H., Li, H., Wu, X., Yang, H., Qiao, J.: Generalized mapping fault diagnosis for industrial machine based on penalty gating LSTM. IEEE Trans. on Industrial Informatics **21**(11), 9159–9170 (2025)
33. He, G., Jin, D., Dai, L., Xin, X., Yu, Z., Chen, C.L.P.: Online learning of temporal association rule on dynamic multivariate time series data. IEEE Trans. on Knowledge and Data Engineering **36**(12), 8954–8966 (2024)
34. Heydarian, M., Doyle, T.E., Samavi, R.: MLCM: Multi-Label confusion matrix. IEEE Access **10**, 19083–19095 (2022)
35. Huang, H., Liu, B., Xue, X., Cao, J., Chen, X.: Imbalanced credit card fraud detection data: A solution based on hybrid neural network and clustering-based undersampling technique. Applied Soft Computing **154**, 111368 (2024)
36. Huang, R., Wei, C., Wang, B., Yang, J., Xu, X., Wu, S., Huang, S.: Well performance prediction based on long short-term memory (LSTM) neural network. Journal of Petroleum Science and Engineering **208**, 109686 (2022)
37. Jiang, J., Li, Y., He, B., Hooi, B., Chen, J., Kang, J.K.Z.: Spade: A Real-Time fraud detection framework on evolving GGraphs. Proceedings of the VLDB Endowment **16**(3), 461–469 (2022)
38. Jiao, Z., Zhang, H., Li, X.: Deep graph Multi-View representation learning with Self-Augmented view fusion. IEEE Trans. on Neural Networks and Learning Systems **36**(8), 14119–14130 (2025)
39. Jin, D., Yu, Z., Jiao, P., Pan, S., He, D., Wu, J., Yu, P.S., Zhang, W.: A survey of community detection approaches: From statistical modeling to deep learning. IEEE Trans. on Knowledge and Data Engineering **35**(2), 1149–1170 (2021)

40. Kennedy, R.K., Villanustre, F., Khoshgoftaar, T.M., Salekshahrezaee, Z.: Synthesizing class labels for highly imbalanced credit card fraud detection data. Journal of Big Data **11**(1), 38 (2024)
41. Koo, E., Lim, T.: Node classification in networks via simplicial interactions. IEEE Trans. on Neural Networks and Learning Systems **36**(8), 14428–14439 (2025)
42. Kumar, M., Sharma, A.K., Rathore, P.S.: Enhancing fashion design with conditional generative adversarial networks: A CGAN approach using the Fashion-MNIST dataset. In: 2024 12th International Conference on Internet of Everything, Microwave, Embedded, Communication and Networks (IEMECON). pp. 1–6 (2024)
43. Lahariya, M., Karami, F., Develder, C., Crevecoeur, G.: Physics-Informed LSTM network for flexibility identification in evaporative cooling system. IEEE Trans. on Industrial Informatics **19**(2), 1484–1494 (2023)
44. Landi, F., Baraldi, L., Cornia, M., Cucchiara, R.: Working memory connections for LSTM. Neural Networks **144**, 334–341 (2021)
45. Li, C., Lin, S., Zhang, H., Zhao, H., Liu, L., Jia, N.: A sequence and network embedding method for bus arrival time prediction using GPS trajectory data only. IEEE Trans. on Intelligent Transportation Systems **24**(5), 5024–5038 (2023)
46. Li, P., Yu, S., Li, J., Hu, X.: Semi-Supervised short text stream classification based on Drift-Aware incremental deep learning. IEEE Trans. on Knowledge and Data Engineering **37**(11), 6680–6693 (2025)
47. Lin, C., Wang, H., Fu, M., Yuan, J., Gu, J.: A gated recurrent Unit-Based particle filter for unmanned underwater vehicle state estimation. IEEE Trans. on Instrumentation and Measurement **70**, 1–12 (2021)
48. Liu, Y., Deng, A., Deng, M., Shi, Y., Zhou, Z., Hu, Q.: A fuzzy confusion Matrix-Based Self-Supervised learning method to mitigate class confusion for partial transfer fault diagnosis. IEEE Trans. on Instrumentation and Measurement **73**, 1–12 (2024)
49. Lou, C., Wang, Y., Li, J., Qian, Y., Li, X.: Graph neural network for fraud detection via context encoding and adaptive aggregation. Expert Systems with Applications **261**, 125473 (2025)
50. Lovell, D., Miller, D., Capra, J., Bradley, A.P.: Never mind the metrics—what about the uncertainty? visualising binary confusion matrix metric distributions to put performance in perspective. In: International Conference on Machine Learning. pp. 22702–22757. PMLR (2023)
51. Lu, X.S., Zhou, M., Qi, L., Liu, H.: Clustering-algorithm-based rare-event evolution analysis via social media data. IEEE Trans. on Computational Social Systems **6**(2), 301–310 (2019)
52. Lv, J., Wang, Y., Chen, S.: Adaptive multivariate Time-Series anomaly detection. Information Processing & Management **60**(4), 103383 (2023)
53. Ma, J., Liu, H., Peng, C., Qiu, T.: Unauthorized broadcasting identification: A deep LSTM recurrent learning approach. IEEE Trans. on Instrumentation and Measurement **69**(9), 5981–5983 (2020)
54. Ma, P., Li, G., Zhang, H., Wang, C., Li, X.: Prediction of remaining useful life of rolling bearings based on multiscale efficient channel attention CNN and bidirectional GRU. IEEE Trans. on Instrumentation and Measurement **73**, 1–13 (2024)
55. Mao, Y., Hao, Y., Cao, X., Gao, Y., Yao, C., Lin, X.: Boosting GNN-Based link prediction via PU-AUC optimization. IEEE Trans. on Knowledge and Data Engineering **37**(4), 1635–1649 (2025)
56. Motie, S., Raahemi, B.: Financial fraud detection using graph neural networks: A systematic review. Expert Systems with Applications **240**, 122156 (2024)
57. Mutemi, A., Bacao, F.: E-Commerce fraud detection based on machine learning techniques: Systematic literature review. Big Data Mining and Analytics **7**(2), 419–444 (2024)
58. Peng, F., Ma, R., Lu, X., Qian, Y., Xu, Y., Hu, Z., Wu, H.: MGRD: Multigranularity reconstruction deviation modeling for time series anomaly detection. IEEE Trans. on Instrumentation and Measurement **74**, 1–11 (2025)
59. Prakash, S., Mehta, U., Sharma, B.: Blending additive and multiplicative gates: New FlexGate-Long Short-Term memory architecture. Engineered Science **37**, 1785 (2025)

60. Shehnepoor, S., Togneri, R., Liu, W., Bennamoun, M.: Spatio-Temporal graph representation learning for fraudster group detection. IEEE trans. on neural networks and learning systems **35**(5), 6628–6642 (2022)
61. Sherstinsky, A.: Fundamentals of recurrent neural network (RNN) and long Short-Term memory (LSTM) network. Physica D: Nonlinear Phenomena **404**, 132306 (2020)
62. Stragapede, G., Vera-Rodriguez, R., Tolosana, R., Morales, A.: BehavePassDB: Public database for mobile behavioral biometrics and benchmark evaluation. Pattern Recognition **134**, 109089 (2023)
63. Tian, J., Zeng, G., Zhao, J., Zhu, X., Zhang, Z.: A Data-Driven modeling method of virtual synchronous generator based on LSTM neural network. IEEE Trans. on Industrial Informatics **20**(4), 5428–5439 (2024)
64. Van Belle, R., De Weerdt, J.: SHINE: A scalable heterogeneous inductive graph neural network for large imbalanced datasets. IEEE Trans. on Knowledge and Data Engineering **36**(9), 4904–4915 (2024)
65. Wang, C., Wang, C., Zhu, H., Cui, J.: LAW: Learning automatic windows for online payment fraud detection. IEEE Trans. on Dependable and Secure Computing **18**(5), 2122–2135 (2021)
66. Wang, C., Zhu, H.: Representing Fine-Grained Co-Occurrences for Behavior-Based fraud detection in online payment services. IEEE Trans. on Dependable and Secure Computing **19**(1), 301–315 (2022)
67. Wang, J., Deng, Z., Shen, K.: Virtual gyros construction and evaluation method based on BILSTM. IEEE Trans. on Instrumentation and Measurement **71**, 1–10 (2022)
68. Wang, P.F., Zhu, Q.X., He, Y.L.: Novel multiscale trend decomposition LSTM based on feature selection for industrial soft sensing. IEEE Trans. on Industrial Informatics (2024)
69. Wang, Q., Mao, Y., Zhu, K.: Melt pool size prediction of laser powder bed fusion by process and image feature fusion. IEEE Trans. on Instrumentation and Measurement **73**, 1–12 (2024)
70. Wang, X., Guo, J., Luo, X., Yu, H.: DyHDGE: Dynamic heterogeneous transaction graph embedding for safety-centric fraud detection in financial scenarios. Journal of Safety Science and Resilience **5**(4), 486–497 (2024)
71. Wang, X., Yu, H., Guo, J., Li, P., Luo, X.: Towards fraud detection via Fine-Grained classification of user behavior. IEEE Trans. on Big Data **11**(4), 1994–2007 (2025)
72. Wang, Y., Wu, M., Jin, R., Li, X., Xie, L., Chen, Z.: Local–Global correlation Fusion-Based graph neural network for remaining useful life prediction. IEEE Trans. on Neural Networks and Learning Systems **36**(1), 753–766 (2025)
73. Wang, Y., Hu, X., Gan, Q., Huang, X., Qiu, X., Wipf, D.: Efficient link prediction via GNN layers induced by negative sampling. IEEE Trans. on Knowledge and Data Engineering **37**(1), 253–264 (2025)
74. Wu, Y., Wang, Y., Hu, L., Hu, J.: DCGNN: Adaptive deep graph convolution for heterophily graphs. Information Sciences **666**, 120427 (2024)
75. Xia, J., Lin, H., Xu, Y., Tan, C., Wu, L., Li, S., Li, S.Z.: GNN cleaner: Label cleaner for graph structured data. IEEE Trans. on Knowledge and Data Engineering **36**(2), 640–651 (2024)
76. Xia, M., Wang, Z., Lan, X., Liu, W., Wu, J.: Confidence-driven under-sampling decision forest for imbalanced credit scoring. Engineering Applications of Artificial Intelligence **147**, 110278 (2025)
77. Xia, W., Zhang, Y., Yang, Y., Xue, J.H., Zhou, B., Yang, M.H.: GAN inversion: A survey. IEEE Trans. on Pattern Analysis and Machine Intelligence **45**(3), 3121–3138 (2022)
78. Xiang, S., Zhang, G., Cheng, D., Zhang, Y.: Enhancing Attribute-Driven fraud detection with risk-aware graph representation. IEEE Trans. on Knowledge and Data Engineering **37**(5), 2501–2512 (2025)
79. Xie, Y., Hong, Y., Qiao, S., Yao, J., Liu, G., Pang, S.: A time-aware generative network for enhancing transaction security in consumer electronics. IEEE Trans. on Consumer Electronics **71**(2), 6818–6828 (2025)
80. Xie, Y., Liu, G., Yan, C., Jiang, C., Zhou, M.: Time-aware attention-based gated network for credit card fraud detection by extracting transactional behaviors. IEEE Trans. on Computational Social Systems **10**(3), 1004–1016 (2023)

81. Xie, Y., Liu, G., Yan, C., Jiang, C., Zhou, M., Li, M.: Learning transactional behavioral representations for credit card fraud detection. IEEE Trans. on Neural Networks and Learning Systems **35**(4), 5735–5748 (2024)
82. Xie, Y., Liu, G., Zhou, M., Wei, L., Zhu, H., Zhou, R., Cao, L.: A spatial–temporal gated network for credit card fraud detection by learning transactional representations. IEEE Trans. on Automation Science and Engineering **21**(4), 6978–6991 (2024)
83. Xie, Y., Shan, J., Wei, L., Yao, J., Zhou, M.: GAN-based hybrid sampling method for transaction fraud detection. IEEE Trans. on Knowledge and Data Engineering **37**(10), 5905–5918 (2025)
84. Xie, Y., Zhou, M., Liu, G., Wei, L., Zhu, H., De Meo, P.: A transactional-behavior-based hierarchical gated network for credit card fraud detection. IEEE/CAA Journal of Automatica Sinica **12**(7), 1489–1503 (2025)
85. Xu, K., Zhang, M., Jegelka, S., Kawaguchi, K.: Optimization of graph neural networks: Implicit acceleration by skip connections and more depth. In: International Conference on Machine Learning. pp. 11592–11602. PMLR (2021)
86. Xu, L., He, Z.Y., Wang, K., Wang, C.D., Huang, S.Q.: Explicit Message-Passing heterogeneous graph neural network. IEEE Trans. on Knowledge and Data Engineering **35**(7), 6916–6929 (2023)
87. Yu, J., Wang, H., Wang, X., Li, Z., Qin, L., Zhang, W., Liao, J., Zhang, Y., Yang, B.: Temporal insights for Group-Based fraud detection on e-Commerce platforms. IEEE Trans. on Knowledge and Data Engineering **37**(2), 951–965 (2025)
88. Yuan, J., Jin, R., Wang, L., Wang, T.: A nonintrusive load identification method based on Dual-Branch attention GRU fusion network. IEEE Trans. on Instrumentation and Measurement **73**, 1–10 (2024)
89. Zeng, Q., Gong, Z., Wu, S., Zhuang, C., Li, S.: Measuring cyclists' subjective perceptions of the street riding environment using K-means SMOTE-RF model and street view imagery. International Journal of Applied Earth Observation and Geoinformation **128**, 103739 (2024)
90. Zhang, G., Wu, J., Yang, J., Beheshti, A., Xue, S., Zhou, C., Sheng, Q.Z.: FRAUDRE: Fraud detection dual-resistant to graph inconsistency and imbalance. In: 2021 IEEE International Conference on Data Mining (ICDM). pp. 867–876 (2021)
91. Zhang, R., Tang, J., Xia, H., Yu, W., Qiao, J.: CO emission prediction for MSWI process based on Dual-Space nested Dual-Window drift detection. IEEE Trans. on Instrumentation and Measurement **74**, 1–15 (2025)
92. Zhao, J., Lau, R.Y., Zhang, W., Zhang, K., Chen, X., Tang, D.: Extracting and reasoning about implicit behavioral evidences for detecting fraudulent online transactions in e-Commerce. Decision Support Systems **86**, 109–121 (2016)
93. Zhao, Y., Li, Y., Cao, Y., Jiang, L., Wan, J., Rehtanz, C.: An RNN with small sequence trained by Multi-Level optimization for SOC estimation in Li-Ion battery applications. IEEE Trans. on Vehicular Technology **72**(9), 11469–11481 (2023)
94. Zhong, Z., Li, C.T., Pang, J.: Multi-Grained Semantics-Aware graph neural networks. IEEE Trans. on Knowledge and Data Engineering **35**(7), 7251–7262 (2023)
95. Zhou, J., Wang, X., Wang, J., Ye, H., Wang, H., Zhou, Z., Han, D., Ying, H., Wu, J., Chen, W.: FraudAuditor: A visual analytics approach for collusive fraud in health insurance. IEEE Trans. on Visualization and Computer Graphics **29**(6), 2849–2861 (2023)
96. Zhou, M., Lu, J.: Continuous graph Learning-Based Self-Adaptation for Multi-Stream concept drift. IEEE Trans. on Cybernetics **55**(8), 3760–3773 (2025)
97. Zhu, Y., Tong, L., Li, G., Luo, X., Zhou, K.: FocusedCleaner: Sanitizing poisoned graphs for robust GNN-Based node classification. IEEE Trans. on Knowledge and Data Engineering **36**(6), 2476–2489 (2024)
98. Zuo, Y., Wang, Y., Chen, D., Zomaya, A.Y., Wang, F., Gao, T., Chen, J.: High-fidelity EEG generation: Generative adversarial network highlighting time-frequency-spatial features regulated by global dynamics supervision. IEEE Trans. on Neural Systems and Rehabilitation Engineering **33**, 4432–4443 (2025)

Chapter 3
Addressing Class Imbalance Through Time-Aware Generative Data Augmentation

Deep neural network-based models excel at capturing intricate patterns of fraudulent behavior. However, in OPFD, their performance is fundamentally constrained by severe class imbalance, which substantially compromising their ability to detect the minority fraud class. To address this issue, this chapter proposes a GAN-based data augmentation framework that integrates distributional learning with temporal dependency modeling. Supported by theoretical analysis and empirical validation, the proposed approach yields significant improvements over traditional methods on key metrics such as F_1 and G_m, thereby providing a robust and effective direction for advancing generative solutions in OPFD.

3.1 Impact of Class Imbalance in Online Payment Fraud

The Essence and Impact of Class Imbalance. Over the past decade, driven by the continuous evolution of internet technologies and the dynamic shifts in the external environment, consumer behavior has undergone profound transformations, with online transactions progressively supplanting traditional offline commerce as the dominant mode of consumption [2, 39]. Concurrently, the rapid expansion of online transaction volume has exacerbated the risks of transactional fraud, posing significant systemic threats to individual financial security, corporate operational stability, and the resilience of national financial infrastructures [7, 14]. In this context, machine learning-based OPFD models have been widely employed [23, 36]. However, their effectiveness is severely constrained by the pervasive challenge of class imbalance [5, 27]. The root cause of this issue lies in the markedly skewed distribution of training data: legitimate transactions dominate both in quantity and in feature-space representation, steering the model's optimization process toward majority-class patterns [8, 12]. In contrast, fraudulent transactions are extremely scarce and often employ feature-obfuscation and behavioral-camouflage techniques to embed

Y. Xie et al., *Neural Network-Based Deep Learning for Online Payment Fraud Detection*,
https://doi.org/10.1007/978-981-95-8513-7_3

themselves within the distributional domain of legitimate samples, making it difficult for models to learn sufficiently discriminative representations of fraudulent behavior [20, 21].

Class imbalance affects OPFD models across four critical dimensions [18, 38]. During training, gradient updates are dominated by legitimate transactions, leading to a skewed decision boundary that prioritizes overall accuracy at the cost of higher false-negative rates [9, 42]. Concurrently, the evasive tactics employed by fraudsters—such as transaction dispersion, high-concurrency requests, and behavioral trajectory spoofing—obfuscate discriminative features, thereby impeding the effectiveness of pattern recognition [30, 44]. Furthermore, the extreme scarcity of fraudulent samples leads to overfitting to spurious local patterns associated with specific merchants or channels, compromising generalization capability and adaptability to evolving fraud strategies [33]. Ultimately, the small number of fraudulent samples causes significant volatility in key metrics like recall and precision, where even minor misclassifications lead to substantial performance fluctuations, thus undermining both experimental reproducibility and deployment reliability [19].

Class Imbalance Methods. Class imbalance, a pervasive challenge in machine learning, is particularly acute in OPFD. Given the much smaller number of fraudulent samples compared to legitimate ones, OPFD models tend to establish decision boundaries $p_z(z)$ biased toward legitimate samples, thereby impairing their ability to detect fraud [26]. Current solutions to this issue primarily fall into three categories: cost-sensitive methods, data sampling methods, and ensemble learning methods [13, 35]. Although cost-sensitive and ensemble learning approaches hold theoretical promise for enhancing performance, their practical application is constrained by challenges such as model complexity, tuning difficulty, and high computational costs [28, 32]. In contrast, data sampling methods have garnered considerable attention owing to their operational simplicity and robust scalability.

As an important branch of data sampling methods, data augmentation enhances the representation of minority-class samples through feature-space transformations or local linear interpolation mechanisms [43]. Comparative experiments conducted by Japkowicz and other scholars on various public datasets have demonstrated that data augmentation methods significantly outperform data cleaning methods in key evaluation metrics such as F_1 and G_m [6]. This provides strong empirical support for the use of data augmentation in addressing imbalanced classification problems [3]. In the specific context of OPFD, traditional data augmentation methods face fundamental technical challenges. The highly concealed, dynamic, and context-dependent nature of fraudulent behaviors, combined with significant nonlinear and temporal correlations in their features, makes it difficult for conventional linear interpolation and feature transformation methods to accurately reconstruct their intrinsic distributions [40]. As a result, synthetic samples fail to accurately replicate the key distinguishing features between fraudulent and legitimate samples, thereby impairing the model's ability to generalize and reducing its robustness in real-world scenarios. Consequently, developing novel data augmentation methods that can accurately preserve the essential characteristics of fraudulent samples has become a key breakthrough for improving OPFD model performance [1, 34].

3.2 Boundary-Constrained Wasserstein GAN for Minority Oversampling

Method Overview. This chapter addresses the issue of synthetic samples in OPFD failing to capture the key discriminative features of fraudulent samples by proposing a Boundary-constrained Wasserstein GAN (BWGAN). The method optimizes the generation process of fraudulent samples through two core mechanisms. First, a sample selection mechanism guides the generator to focus on fraudulent samples with discriminative information, enhancing the representativeness of synthetic samples. Second, a distribution constraint mechanism identifies and strengthens the discriminative features between synthetic samples and legitimate samples by focusing on key features, thereby effectively improving the separability in the feature space and reducing confusion. The proposed method ensures the authenticity of synthetic samples while significantly enhancing their discriminative capability. It effectively alleviates issues of sample scarcity and distribution skew under extreme class imbalance, thus improving the overall performance of fraud detection models.

Sample selection mechanism. In OPFD, training data often suffers from severe class imbalance, with fraudulent samples being both scarce in quantity and sparsely distributed within the classification boundary regions [37]. Boundary samples play a crucial role in defining the decision boundary of classification tasks [41]. Therefore, GANs should emphasize the focused learning of fraudulent samples within boundary regions when fitting the data distribution. This approach enhances their ability to model key discriminative features. To achieve this, this chapter introduces a sample selection mechanism based on a discriminative evaluation of sample features. This mechanism assigns differentiated selection probabilities to legitimate samples, encouraging the discriminator to prioritize learning the distinguishing features between fraudulent and legitimate samples near the decision boundary. This targeted learning approach enhances the generator's ability to capture the key discriminative features of fraudulent samples.

As illustrated in Fig. 3.1, sample selection is performed based on inter-sample distances. The core idea is defined as follows: let the set of fraudulent samples be $X_f = \{x_i \mid i = 1, 2, \ldots, n_f\}$ and the set of legitimate samples be $X_l = \{y_i \mid i = 1, 2, \ldots, n_l\}$. For any legitimate sample $x_i \in X_l$, the average Euclidean distance D_i between x_i and the fraudulent sample set X_f is calculated. Subsequently, a selection probability $p(x_i)$ is assigned to each legitimate sample based on D_i. Finally, in accordance with the aforementioned probability distribution, a fitness-proportional selection strategy is adopted to extract n_{sel} legitimate samples from X_l that are prone to being confused with fraudulent samples. The specific formulas are as follows:

$$D_i = \frac{1}{n_{pos}} \sum_{j=1}^{n_{pos}} \|x_i - y_j\|_2, \quad i = 1, 2, \ldots, n_{neg}, \tag{3.1}$$

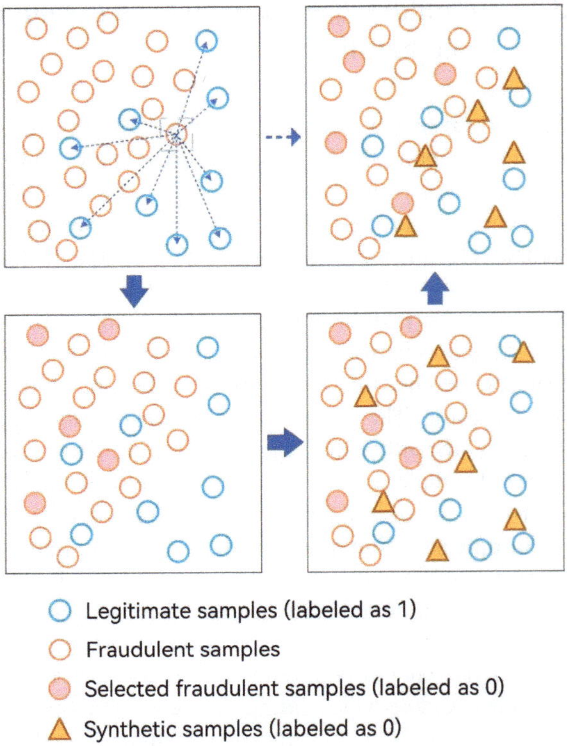

Fig. 3.1 Schematic diagram of sample selection strategy

$$p(x_i) = \frac{D_i}{\sum_{j=1}^{n_{neg}} D_j}, \quad i = 1, 2, \ldots, n_{neg}, \tag{3.2}$$

$$n_{\text{sel}} = r \times n_{\text{pos}}. \tag{3.3}$$

Among them, the selection ratio r is set to a default value of 0.1. During the training process of BWGAN, the selected sample set N_{sel} and synthetic samples are uniformly labeled as 0, while real fraudulent samples are labeled as 1, so as to construct the training data for the discriminator. Guided by this mechanism, the discriminator can more intensively perceive legitimate samples highly correlated with the fraudulent distribution, thereby prompting the generator to generate fraudulent samples with stronger discriminative power near the decision boundary.

Distribution Constraint Mechanism. The quality of the decision boundary has a decisive impact on model performance. To enhance the discriminability of synthetic samples, this chapter introduces a Kernel Density Estimation (KDE)-based distribution constraint loss function into the generator, explicitly constraining the distribution of synthetic samples in the feature space to improve their separability from legitimate samples. Specifically, BWGAN incorporates information from legitimate samples to strengthen the discriminative differences between synthetic and legitimate data.

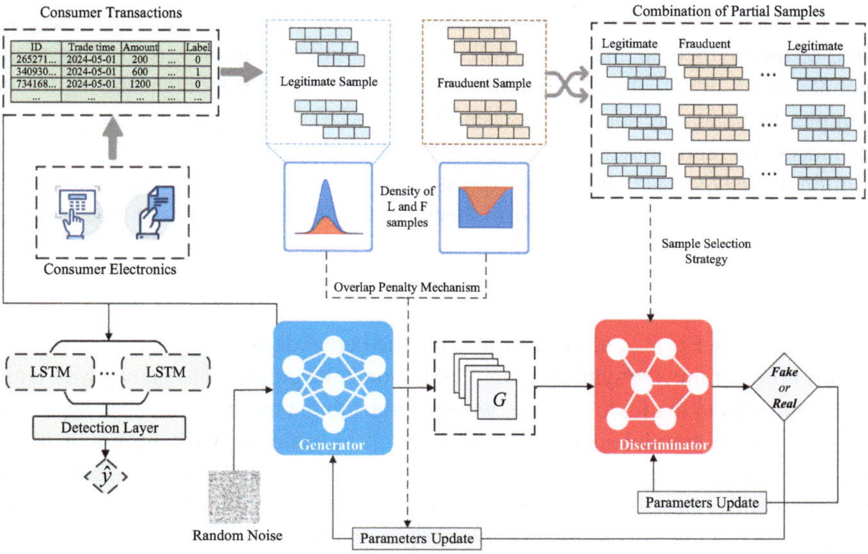

Fig. 3.2 Framework of BWGAN for OPFD

As illustrated in Fig. 3.2, by computing the kernel densities $\hat{f}_p(x)$ and $\hat{f}_n(x)$ for fraudulent and legitimate samples in the training set, respectively, and applying the distribution constraint loss $L_{S_0}(G)$ to synthetic samples falling within the overlapping region S_0 of the two distributions, the generator is guided to produce data with pronounced fraudulent characteristics. This approach not only enhances the fraud attributes of synthetic samples but also improves the classifier's ability to discriminate between fraudulent and legitimate transactions. The specific formulation is as follows:

$$\hat{f}(x) = \frac{1}{nh}\sum_{i=1}^{n} K\left(\frac{x - x_i}{h}\right), \tag{3.4}$$

$$K(u) = \frac{1}{\sqrt{2\pi}} e^{-\frac{u^2}{2}}, \tag{3.5}$$

$$h = \left(\frac{4\hat{\sigma}^5}{3n}\right)^{\frac{1}{5}} \approx 1.06\hat{\sigma} n^{-\frac{1}{5}}, \tag{3.6}$$

$$x_i \in S_o \Leftrightarrow \begin{cases} 1, & \text{if } \min(\hat{f}_p(x), \hat{f}_n(x)) > 0 \\ 0, & \text{otherwise} \end{cases} \tag{3.7}$$

$$L_{S_o}(G) = \mathbb{E}_{z \sim P_z}\left[-\log(\hat{f}_p(G(z))) + \log(\hat{f}_n(G(z)))\right], \tag{3.8}$$

where K denotes the Gaussian kernel function, h is the bandwidth estimated using the rule-of-thumb method, and $G(z)$ represents the synthetic samples. According to the defined loss function, the distributional differences between fraudulent and legitimate samples in the feature space are measured using KDE. During training, the generator enhances the representation of core fraud features by maximizing $\hat{f}_p(G(z))$, while simultaneously strengthening the expression of key discriminative features by minimizing $\hat{f}_n(G(z))$. In alignment with this objective, the final generator loss function is defined as follows:

$$L_G = L(D, G) + L_{S_o}(G). \tag{3.9}$$

As shown in Fig. 3.3, after incorporating the kernel density estimation-based distribution constraint, the synthetic samples demonstrate greater consistency with legitimate samples in the feature space, while establishing a more pronounced separable boundary from fraudulent samples. This result indicates that the proposed distribution constraint mechanism effectively enhances both intra-class consistency and inter-class discriminability of the synthetic samples. On the one hand, the synthetic samples better preserve the intrinsic distribution characteristics of legitimate samples, improving their authenticity and representativeness. On the other hand, the strengthened separability enables classifiers to distinguish more clearly between legitimate and fraudulent samples, thereby significantly increasing the effectiveness of the synthetic samples in OPFD.

Collectively, this mechanism not only alleviates common issues such as mode collapse and distributional shift that arise in traditional generative models trained

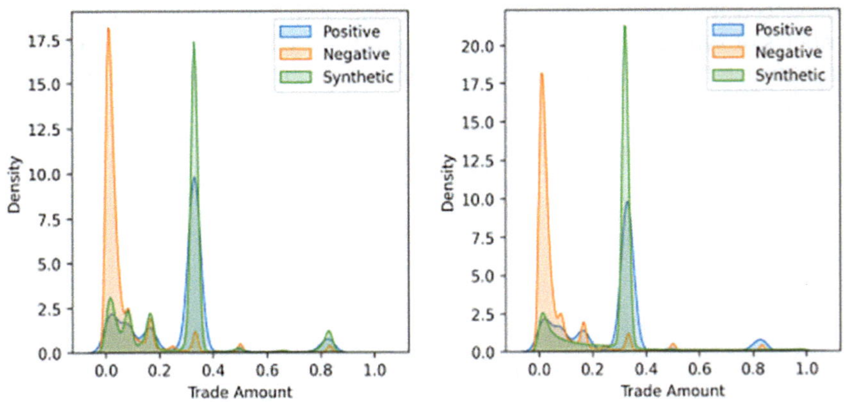

(a) Before applying the overlap penalty mechanism (b) After applying the overlap penalty mechanism

Fig. 3.3 The distribution of trade amount for positive, negative, and synthetic samples

on highly imbalanced datasets, but also supplies downstream detection models with higher-quality and more discriminative augmented data, thereby improving the overall system's generalization ability and robustness in fraud detection.

3.3 Time-Aware Encoding for Transaction Context

Method Overview. BWGAN effectively alleviates class imbalance and reduces distribution overlap at the data level. However, it solely relying on sample-level augmentation proves insufficient for fully capturing the temporal dynamics inherent in user behavior. Specifically, fraudulent transactions often exhibit highly concentrated, short-term, and intensive behavioral patterns. Conversely, legitimate users' transactions are typically spaced further apart and follow more regular rhythms [29]. Therefore, effectively modeling the temporal relationships among transactions is crucial for further improving fraud detection performance.

To address this, this chapter introduces a Time-aware Gated Recurrent Network (TaGRN), which explicitly incorporates time-interval information into the recurrent neural network structure. This integration enhances the model's ability to represent temporal patterns of fraud during the feature encoding stage, strengthening its capacity to capture sequential behavioral nuances critical for OPFD.

Design Motivation and Model Structure. Traditional recurrent network architectures (e.g., LSTM and GRU) primarily rely on the sequential order of inputs to capture dependencies [17]. However, they typically assign equal weights to all historical inputs, thereby overlooking the impact of varying time intervals between transactions on user behavior [16]. For instance, a short interval between two transactions often implies potential abnormal risk, whereas a long interval indicates relatively stable behavior.

To overcome this limitation, this chapter introduces the TaGRN, which explicitly incorporates a time-aware gating mechanism. This design enables the network to dynamically regulate the degree of memory retention and decay based on transaction intervals, thereby enhancing its ability to distinguish fraudulent patterns from legitimate ones. Specifically, when updating the hidden state, TaGRN relies not only on the previous hidden state and the current input but also incorporates the time-interval $\Delta T_{t-1,t}$, which represents the elapsed time between the t-th and $(t-1)$-th transactions. By embedding time-interval information into the gating mechanism, the model dynamically modulates the balance between information retention and forgetting according to the elapsed time, thereby enhancing its sensitivity to short-term, high-frequency transaction patterns while reducing dependence on temporally distant transactions. This design allows the model to capture fraud-related behavioral signals with greater precision. The specific formulation is as follows:

$$d_t = \tanh(W_s \cdot [h_{t-1}, x_t, D_t] + b_s), \tag{3.10}$$

$$f_t = \sigma(W_{fh} \cdot [h_{t-1}, x_t] + W_{fd} \cdot d_t + b_f), \ s.t. \ W_{fd} < 0, \tag{3.11}$$

$$i_t = \sigma(W_i \cdot [h_{t-1}, x_t, d_t] + b_i), \tag{3.12}$$

$$\tilde{C}_t = \tanh(W_c \cdot [h_{t-1}, x_t] + b_c), \tag{3.13}$$

$$C_t = f_t * C_{t-1} + i_t * \tilde{C}_t, \tag{3.14}$$

$$o_t = \sigma(W_o \cdot [h_{t-1}, x_t, d_t] + b_o), \tag{3.15}$$

$$\hat{h}_t = o_t * \tanh(C_t), \tag{3.16}$$

where h_{t-1} denotes the hidden state at the previous time step $t-1$, x_t is the input at the current time step t, f_t is the forget gate, i_t is the input gate, $\tilde{C}_t$ is the candidate cell state, σ represents the Sigmoid activation function, o_t is the output gate, and $\hat{h}_t$ is the updated hidden state. $\Delta T_{t-1,t}$ represents the raw time interval between the t-th and $(t-1)$-th transactions, while d_t denotes the time-sensitive cell state derived from $\Delta T_{t-1,t}$ and other inputs. By incorporating these time intervals, d_t integrates current transactional behavior with historical patterns and temporal dynamics, enabling the forget gate to more effectively evaluate the relevance of past behaviors in the presence of concept drift arising from evolving user activity.

For example, if the previous transaction occurred a long time ago, this may signal a substantial shift in the consumer's behavioral patterns. In such cases, the forget gate assigns lower weights to historical behaviors, reflecting the diminished relevance of outdated patterns amid evolving transactional dynamics. This adjustment shifts the model's emphasis toward present transactional signals, thereby improving its adaptability to emerging fraud strategies and shifts in legitimate behavior. Conversely, if the preceding transaction occurred recently, suggesting temporal stability in behavioral patterns, the forget gate assigns higher weights to past behaviors, reinforcing continuity with historical patterns.

By dynamically adjusting the degree of historical information decay in response to concept drift, this module ensures that the model captures the most relevant and up-to-date information, thereby enhancing its fraud detection capability even when user behavior changes. The cell state C_t is updated by combining the forget gate, input gate, and candidate cell state. W_s, W_{fh}, W_{fd}, W_i, W_c, and W_o are the weight matrices for different gates and states, while b_s, b_f, b_i, b_c, and b_o are the corresponding bias vectors.

Specifically, when transaction intervals are short, TaGRN reinforces memory and attention toward recent transactional behavior, effectively capturing high-frequency fraud patterns. Conversely, when intervals are long, the influence of distant information is substantially attenuated, suppressing noise and enhancing the model's response to meaningful discriminative signals. This explicit time-aware mechanism not only enhances the model's ability to dynamically process variable-length transaction sequences but also improves its discriminative capability against sophisticated fraud strategies, all without introducing significant additional parameter overhead.

3.4 Experimental Validation and Interpretability Analysis

To validate the effectiveness of the proposed methods, this chapter conducts a series of systematic experiments encompassing data-partitioning strategies, feature-space visualization analyses, and ablation studies, supplemented by a preliminary interpretability analysis of the model's decision mechanisms. Since TaGRN is specifically designed to leverage the temporal intervals between uses' consecutive transactions to differentiate behavior patterns in overlapping regions, it is evaluated using a real transaction dataset containing time-interval features. In contrast, experiments on publicly available imbalanced datasets aim to examine whether BWGAN can generate more discriminative synthetic samples that closely match the distribution of real fraudulent transactions in highly imbalanced online transaction settings, thereby effectively enhancing the generalization and robustness of downstream OPFD models.

Baseline Model. To comprehensively evaluate the performance of the proposed TaGRN and BWGAN in OPFD, this section employs eight widely recognized methods in the field of imbalanced classification as benchmark comparisons. A concise overview of the underlying principles and key advantages of each method is presented below.

(1) Random Oversampling (ROS) [22]: It balances the dataset by randomly duplicating minority-class samples. Its primary advantages are simplicity and computational efficiency. However, it may increase the risk of overfitting.
(2) Synthetic Minority Oversampling Technique (SMOTE) [4]: It generates synthetic samples by interpolating between a minority sample and its nearest neighbors in feature space. This helps augment the dataset and can improve the classifier's discrimination capability by better delineating the decision boundary.
(3) Adaptive Synthetic Sampling (ADASYN) [15]: It calculates the required number of synthetic samples for each minority sample based on its local density and generates them through linear interpolation. Its key advantage is focusing on hard-to-learn regions by generating more samples where the class imbalance is most severe.
(4) Wasserstein GAN (WGAN) [10]: It incorporates the Wasserstein distance into the GAN framework, stabilizing training and mitigating mode collapse. This enables the generator to learn the minority-class distribution more reliably, producing diverse synthetic samples that can enhance model generalization in imbalanced settings.
(5) Borderline-SMOTE (BSMOTE) [25]: It extends SMOTE by specifically oversampling minority samples near the decision boundary. By identifying and augmenting these "hard-to-classify" boundary samples, it enhances classifier discrimination in critical regions and reduces misclassification due to class overlap.
(6) Edited Nearest Neighbor (ENN) [31]: It cleans the dataset by removing samples whose class label differs from that of the majority of their nearest neighbors. This effectively reduces noise and outliers, smoothing the decision boundary and improving classifier robustness.

(7) Random Undersampling (RUS) [24]: It balances the dataset by randomly removing majority-class samples. It is simple and reduces computational cost but may discard potentially useful information. It is therefore often combined with oversampling methods in hybrid approaches.
(8) Generative Adversarial Network (GAN) [11]: It employs an adversarial training framework where a generator learns to produce synthetic samples that a discriminator cannot distinguish from real data. For class imbalance, it can generate realistic minority-class samples, thereby augmenting the class and enhancing the model's ability to recognize it.

Imbalanced dataset experiment. This chapter employs a real-world transaction dataset provided by a major Chinese financial institution. The dataset comprises 5.12 million business-to-consumer transactions from 107,192 customers, exhibiting severe class imbalance with fraudulent transactions constituting only a small minority. Each record contains 11 variables: the target variable Sign (1 for fraudulent, 0 for legitimate), the temporal feature Time_intervals (elapsed seconds from the observation start), and the monetary feature Trade_amount (in Chinese Yuan, RMB). To preserve privacy, the remaining eight numerical variables are transformed via Principal Component Analysis (PCA) into eight derived features, denoted as $V_1 \sim V_8$. Due to data confidentiality agreements, the original business semantics of these principal components are unavailable, and some components may capture noise or fraud-irrelevant variations. The detailed structure of the dataset is summarized in Table 3.1.

To ensure a realistic evaluation of the model's predictive accuracy, the datasets are partitioned into training and testing sets based on the chronological order of transactional dates. In the initial phase of this division, transactions from January are assigned to the training set, while those from February are used as the testing set. As shown in Table 3.2, this sequential allocation pattern continues consistently over the subsequent months.

As shown in Table 3.3, TaGRN achieves the highest P_r and R_e across the three test sets of the real-world online transaction dataset, while also exhibiting the best average performance. This indicates that the model can detect fraudulent transactions while maintaining a relatively low false-positive rate. In terms of F_1, TaGRN outperforms its peers across all test sets and on average. Although its G_m is slightly lower than that of certain competing approaches, the overall performance remains stable and reliable. Overall, TaGRN effectively mitigates behavioral overlap in the feature space arising

Table 3.1 Transaction dataset information

Variable	Attribute
Sign	1 denotes fraudulent transaction, 0 denotes legitimate transaction
Time_intervals	Transaction to dataset start time offset, in seconds
Trade_amount	Transaction scale, in RMB
$V_1 \sim V_8$	Other characteristic variable

Table 3.2 Data partitioning

Dataset	#Legitimate	#Fraudulent	#Total	#Ratio
Jan.	656416	28175	666591	0.043
Feb.	657899	33762	691661	0.051
Mar.	226206	10601	264807	0.047
Apr.	1229764	23271	1243035	0.019
May.	1189117	27122	1216299	0.023
Jun.	1017816	24898	1042714	0.024
Total	4977218	165829	5125047	0.033

Table 3.3 OPFD performance of nine methods

Train	Test	Criteria	ROS	GAN	WGAN	SMOTE	BSMOTE	ENN	RUS	ADASYN	TaGRN
Jan.	Feb.	P_r	0.7443	0.7506	0.7594	0.6508	0.7486	0.7904	0.3790	0.6552	**0.8214**
		R_e	0.6456	0.6700	0.6684	0.8223	0.7419	0.7811	**0.9460**	0.8065	0.8143
		F_1	0.6915	0.7080	0.7110	0.7265	0.7452	0.7857	0.5412	0.7230	**0.8178**
		G_m	0.7989	0.8139	0.8131	0.8965	0.8558	0.8791	**0.9331**	0.8882	0.8946
Feb.	Mar.	P_r	0.8491	**0.8601**	0.8562	0.8241	0.8453	0.8380	0.7406	0.8123	0.8524
		R_e	0.7806	0.7699	0.7748	0.8800	0.8151	0.8739	0.9284	0.8724	**0.9328**
		F_1	0.8135	0.8125	0.8135	0.8511	0.8299	0.8556	0.8239	0.8413	**0.8908**
		G_m	0.8730	0.8680	0.8704	0.9229	0.8913	0.9212	**0.9364**	0.9178	0.9151
Mar.	Apr.	P_r	0.3060	0.3704	0.3636	0.2667	0.4147	0.3292	0.1216	0.2990	**0.5156**
		R_e	0.5741	0.5787	0.5804	0.6938	0.6866	0.6801	0.7843	0.6798	**0.9654**
		F_1	0.3992	0.4517	0.4471	0.3853	0.5171	0.4436	0.2105	0.4154	**0.6721**
		G_m	0.7524	0.7567	0.7576	0.8243	0.8243	0.8185	**0.8581**	0.8174	0.7156
Apr.	May.	P_r	0.7315	**0.7429**	0.7309	0.5855	0.6927	0.7348	0.3129	0.5755	0.6943
		R_e	0.7339	0.7463	0.6959	0.8194	0.8091	0.8234	0.9647	0.8051	0.8917
		F_1	0.7327	0.7456	0.7130	0.6830	0.7464	0.7766	0.4726	0.6712	**0.7807**
		G_m	0.8542	0.8613	0.8318	0.8992	0.8958	**0.9043**	0.9582	0.8912	0.8280
May.	Jun.	P_r	0.6764	0.6640	0.6692	0.5730	0.6437	0.6704	0.3993	0.5575	**0.6807**
		R_e	0.7849	0.7247	0.7528	0.8531	0.8126	0.8667	0.9511	0.8245	0.9757
		F_1	0.7275	0.6930	0.7086	0.6855	0.7184	0.7561	0.5639	0.6652	**0.8019**
		G_m	0.8829	0.8475	0.8637	0.9164	0.8965	0.9261	**0.9619**	0.9007	0.8239
A_v		P_r	0.6615	0.6776	0.6759	0.5800	0.6690	0.6726	0.3907	0.5799	**0.7129**
		R_e	0.7038	0.6979	0.6945	0.8137	0.7731	0.8051	0.9149	0.7977	**0.9160**
		F_1	0.6729	0.6822	0.6786	0.6663	0.7114	0.7235	0.5224	0.6632	**0.7927**
		G_m	0.8323	0.8295	0.8273	0.8919	0.8727	0.8899	**0.9296**	0.8831	0.8354
A_r		P_r	4.2	2.8	3.4	7.4	4.8	3.6	9	7.6	**2.2**
		R_e	8	8	8	3.2	5.4	4	1.6	5.2	**1.6**
		F_1	6	5.8	5.6	5.8	3.4	2.6	8.4	6.2	**1**
		G_m	7.4	7.4	7.4	2.4	4.8	3.2	**1**	4.4	7

Table 3.4 Public datasets

Dataset	#S	#A	#IR
cmc_data	1473	9	3.42
adult_data	30963	14	3.12
heart_data	270	13	1.25
german_data	1000	20	2.33
housing_data	506	13	3.77

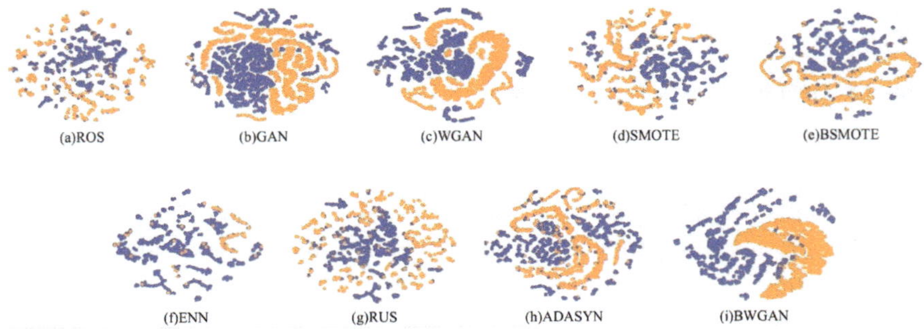

Fig. 3.4 Visualization of varied transactional representations

from fraudsters' covert strategies, thereby significantly enhancing fraud detection capability in imbalanced transaction data.

Furthermore, this study selects five imbalanced datasets from the UCI[1] repository for experimentation, originating from diverse domains, with feature counts ranging from 9 to 20 and sample sizes from 162 to 30,963. Detailed information on these public imbalanced datasets is provided in Table 3.4, where Column 1 lists the dataset ID, and Columns 2–5 indicate the dataset name, number of minority-class samples, number of majority-class samples where the imbalance ratio, respectively.

As shown in Table 3.5, when RF is employed as the classifier, BWGAN exhibits significant advantages. It achieves the highest scores across multiple evaluation metrics, with particularly notable performance on heart_data. On average, it attains the highest P_r, F_1, and G_m. This demonstrates that BWGAN can accurately recognize minority-class samples while maintaining overall robustness, thereby providing strong augmentation support for OPFD tasks.

As shown in Table 3.6, when SVM is employed as the classifier, BWGAN also delivers impressive performance. On average, it achieves the highest values and rankings for both P_r and F_1, while demonstrating strong performance across multiple datasets. This indicates that BWGAN can accurately identify minority-class samples while substantially lowering the false-positive rate. It equips classifiers with enhanced

[1] https://archive.ics.uci.edu/ml/index.php.

Table 3.5 Experiments on public datasets when RF is used a classifier

Dataset	Criteria	ROS	GAN	WGAN	SMOTE	BSMOTE	ENN	RUS	ADASYN	BWGAN
cmc_data	P_r	0.4396	0.4531	0.4776	0.4545	0.4624	0.4036	0.3543	0.4787	**0.5000**
	R_e	0.3810	0.2762	0.3048	0.4286	0.4095	**0.6381**	0.5905	0.4286	0.3048
	F_1	0.4082	0.3432	0.3721	0.4412	0.4343	**0.4945**	0.4429	0.4523	0.3787
	G_m	0.5686	0.4975	0.5226	0.5999	0.5906	**0.6713**	0.6265	0.6052	0.5252
adult_ data	P_r	0.6811	0.7331	0.7375	0.6588	0.6511	0.5877	0.5806	0.6446	**0.7440**
	R_e	0.7056	0.6445	0.6413	0.7142	0.7254	0.8407	**0.8582**	0.7263	0.6536
	F_1	0.6932	0.6860	0.6861	0.6854	0.6862	0.6918	0.6926	0.6830	**0.6959**
	G_m	0.7951	0.7726	0.7715	0.7943	0.7979	0.8254	**0.8313**	0.7967	0.7794
heart_ data	P_r	0.8462	0.6667	0.7857	0.8095	0.8333	0.6786	0.8571	0.8750	**0.8846**
	R_e	0.7097	0.7200	0.8462	0.6800	0.6452	0.7600	0.6923	0.6774	**0.8846**
	F_1	0.7719	0.6923	0.8148	0.7391	0.7273	0.7170	0.7660	0.7636	**0.8846**
	G_m	0.7956	0.7313	0.8154	0.7761	0.7586	0.7514	0.7862	0.7890	**0.8887**
german_ data	P_r	0.5526	0.6034	0.5714	0.5733	0.5432	0.4599	0.4880	0.5238	**0.6479**
	R_e	0.5060	0.4217	0.3855	0.5181	0.5301	**0.7241**	0.7011	0.5301	0.5287
	F_1	0.5283	0.4965	0.4604	0.5443	0.5366	0.5625	0.5755	0.5269	**0.5823**
	G_m	0.6533	0.6140	0.5856	0.6646	0.6631	**0.6874**	0.7003	0.6576	0.6831
housing_ data	P_r	0.5833	**0.6667**	0.6250	0.5600	0.5172	0.4808	0.4259	0.6296	0.6452
	R_e	0.3784	0.3243	0.2703	0.3784	0.4054	0.6410	0.5897	0.4595	**0.8696**
	F_1	0.4590	0.4364	0.3774	0.4516	0.4545	0.5495	0.4946	0.5313	**0.7407**
	G_m	0.5878	0.5544	0.5061	0.5850	0.5967	0.6985	0.6542	0.6477	**0.8919**
A_v	P_r	0.6206	0.6246	0.6394	0.6112	0.6014	0.5221	0.5412	0.6304	**0.6843**
	R_e	0.5361	0.4773	0.4896	0.5438	0.5431	**0.7208**	0.6864	0.5644	0.6483
	F_1	0.5721	0.5309	0.5422	0.5723	0.5678	0.6030	0.5943	0.5914	**0.6564**
	G_m	0.6801	0.6340	0.6402	0.6840	0.6814	0.7268	0.7197	0.6992	**0.7537**
A_r	P_r	5.0	4.2	4.0	5.0	5.6	8.2	7.6	4.2	**1.2**
	R_e	6.0	7.4	7.2	5.4	5.2	**1.8**	2.8	4.2	4.2
	F_1	4.4	8.2	6.8	5.8	5.6	3.6	3.2	5.2	**2.2**
	G_m	5.4	8.4	7.4	5.4	5.0	3.0	**2.4**	4.2	3.8

discriminatory capability for minority-class recognition, highlighting its advantages in both precise identification and effective mitigation of misclassification errors.

As shown in Table 3.7, BWGAN continues to demonstrate robust performance when paired with the MLP classifier. It achieves the highest P_r across all five datasets, while both P_r and F_1 record the highest A_v. In terms of G_m, the model's performance falls short of the optimal by no more than 1.05%. These results indicate that BWGAN can effectively enhance the discriminative accuracy of minority-class samples in class imbalance scenarios, thereby providing a reliable technical foundation for OPFD.

Visualization Analysis. To systematically evaluate the impact of various sampling methods on the distribution of online transaction samples, this chapter employs t-SNE to project high-dimensional features in a two-dimensional embedding space. The corresponding visualization results are illustrated in Fig. 3.4. ROS (Fig. 3.4a) generates synthetic samples via random selection, producing an approximately uniform distribution in the feature space; however, these samples often overlap with legitimate data, thereby degrading classifier performance. GAN (Fig. 3.4b) produces dispersed samples through adversarial training, yet the outputs may exhibit artifacts

Table 3.6 Experiments on public datasets when SVM is used a classifier

Dataset	Criteria	ROS	GAN	WGAN	SMOTE	BSMOTE	ENN	RUS	ADASYN	BWGAN
cmc_data	P_r	0.3676	0.3158	0.3333	0.3673	0.3482	0.3765	0.3667	0.3493	**0.4037**
	R_e	0.7143	0.1714	0.3714	0.6857	0.7429	0.6095	0.7333	**0.7619**	0.4190
	F_1	0.4854	0.2222	0.3514	0.4784	0.4742	0.4655	**0.4889**	0.4790	0.4112
	G_m	0.6640	0.3893	0.5343	0.6583	0.6489	0.6464	**0.6663**	0.6520	0.5816
adult_data	P_r	0.5329	0.6500	0.7158	0.5411	0.4945	0.5220	0.5185	0.4949	**0.6815**
	R_e	0.8733	0.6252	0.5942	0.8737	0.9110	0.8731	0.8899	**0.9155**	0.6604
	F_1	0.6619	0.6373	0.6493	0.6683	0.6410	0.6534	0.6552	0.6425	**0.6708**
	G_m	0.8141	0.7476	0.7416	**0.8184**	0.8024	0.8085	0.8116	0.8038	0.7722
heart_data	P_r	0.7188	0.7500	0.7857	0.8148	0.8333	0.6875	0.7692	0.7778	**0.9211**
	R_e	**0.8846**	0.8077	0.7097	0.6286	0.5714	0.8462	0.7692	0.8400	0.7778
	F_1	0.7931	0.7778	0.7458	0.7097	0.6780	0.7586	0.7692	0.8077	**0.8434**
	G_m	0.7748	0.7783	0.7711	0.7485	0.7223	0.7375	0.7774	0.8162	**0.8444**
german_data	P_r	0.5743	0.5294	0.5733	0.5521	0.4597	0.5154	0.5115	0.4741	**0.6625**
	R_e	0.6042	0.5422	0.5181	0.5521	0.6867	**0.7204**	**0.7204**	0.6627	0.5521
	F_1	0.5888	0.5357	0.5443	0.5521	0.5507	0.6009	0.5982	0.5528	**0.6023**
	G_m	0.6905	0.6650	0.6646	0.6601	0.6890	**0.7079**	0.7055	0.6902	0.6921
housing_data	P_r	0.4154	0.4857	0.4750	0.4510	0.4259	0.4889	0.3659	0.4259	**0.5227**
	R_e	0.7105	0.4595	0.5135	0.6216	0.6216	0.5641	**0.7692**	0.6216	0.6053
	F_1	0.5243	0.4722	0.4935	0.5227	0.5055	0.5238	0.4959	0.5055	**0.5610**
	G_m	0.6882	0.6225	0.6479	0.6858	0.6738	0.6703	0.6444	0.6738	**0.7027**
A_v	P_r	0.5218	0.5462	0.5766	0.5453	0.5123	0.5180	0.5063	0.5044	**0.6383**
	R_e	0.7574	0.5212	0.5414	0.6723	0.7067	0.7227	**0.7764**	0.7603	0.6029
	F_1	0.6107	0.5291	0.5568	0.5862	0.5699	0.6004	0.6015	0.5975	**0.6177**
	G_m	0.7263	0.6406	0.6719	0.7142	0.7073	0.7141	0.7210	**0.7272**	0.7186
A_r	P_r	5.2	5.4	4.0	4.0	6.6	5.0	6.8	6.6	**1.2**
	R_e	3.4	7.6	8.2	5.2	3.8	4.4	2.8	**2.4**	6.2
	F_1	2.8	8.0	7.4	4.8	6.8	4.4	4.0	4.4	**2.2**
	G_m	**3.0**	7.2	7.6	4.6	6.0	5.0	3.6	4.0	3.8

or implausible instances. WGAN (Fig. 3.4c) stabilizes training its Wasserstein-based loss, yielding samples that more closely align with the true data distribution, although small-scale outliers and residual overlap remain. SMOTE and ADASYN (Fig. 3.4d, h) generate new samples by linearly interpolating neighboring points, resulting in localized sample clusters around the original data and consequently limited distributional generalization. BSMOTE (Fig. 3.4e) emphasizes boundary regions, which inadvertently increases inter-class overlap and diminishes the model's ability to distinguish fraudulent from legitimate transactions in OPFD. ENN (Fig. 3.4f) removes noisy instances, yielding a sparser distribution concentrated near class boundaries. In contrast, RUS (Fig. 3.4g) achieves class balance by randomly discarding majority-class samples, but this approach often results in substantial information loss.

Table 3.7 Experiments on public datasets when MLP is used as a classifier

Dataset	Criteria	ROS	GAN	WGAN	SMOTE	BSMOTE	ENN	RUS	ADASYN	BWGAN
cmc_data	P_r	0.4375	0.4396	0.3623	0.4275	0.4775	0.3632	0.3604	0.4338	**0.4615**
	R_e	0.4118	0.3810	0.2381	0.5333	0.5048	**0.6952**	0.6762	0.5619	0.4000
	F_1	0.4242	0.4082	0.2874	0.4746	0.4907	**0.4771**	0.4702	0.4896	0.4286
	G_m	0.5885	0.5686	0.4550	0.6439	0.6464	0.6566	0.6507	**0.6584**	0.5847
adult_ data	P_r	0.5568	0.6514	0.6849	0.6129	0.5398	0.5220	0.5468	0.5312	**0.6673**
	R_e	0.8018	0.6038	0.6085	0.7263	0.8166	**0.8731**	0.8319	0.8301	0.6637
	F_1	0.6572	0.6267	0.6445	0.6648	0.6500	0.6534	0.6599	0.6478	**0.6655**
	G_m	0.8004	0.7356	0.7449	0.7888	0.7985	**0.8085**	0.8072	0.7991	0.7712
heart_ data	P_r	0.7742	0.7500	0.7333	0.7857	0.7500	0.7368	0.7742	0.7143	**0.8148**
	R_e	0.7742	0.8077	0.8462	0.6286	0.6774	0.8000	0.6857	0.7692	0.8462
	F_1	0.7742	0.7778	0.7857	0.6984	0.7119	0.7671	0.7273	0.7407	**0.8302**
	G_m	0.8032	0.7783	0.7774	0.7393	0.7513	0.7913	0.7625	0.7412	**0.8337**
german_ data	P_r	0.4945	0.5106	0.4941	0.5195	0.4842	0.4641	0.4478	0.4607	**0.6207**
	R_e	0.5422	0.5783	0.5060	0.4819	0.5542	**0.7634**	0.6452	0.4940	0.6207
	F_1	0.5172	0.5424	0.5000	0.5000	0.5169	0.5772	0.5286	0.4767	**0.6207**
	G_m	0.6536	0.6751	0.6370	0.6323	0.6550	0.6790	0.6438	0.6202	**0.7242**
housing_ data	P_r	0.5313	0.5882	0.5714	0.5588	0.7143	0.4483	0.4490	0.5833	**0.7200**
	R_e	0.4595	0.5405	0.5882	0.5135	0.5405	**0.6667**	0.5641	0.5676	0.4865
	F_1	0.4928	0.5634	0.5797	0.5352	**0.6154**	0.5361	0.5000	0.5753	0.5806
	G_m	0.6321	0.6890	**0.7166**	0.6682	0.7092	0.6913	0.6552	0.7025	0.6759
A_v	P_r	0.5589	0.5880	0.5692	0.5809	0.5932	0.5069	0.5156	0.5447	**0.6569**
	R_e	0.5979	0.5823	0.5574	0.5767	0.6187	**0.7597**	0.6806	0.6446	0.6034
	F_1	0.5731	0.5837	0.5594	0.5746	0.5970	0.6022	0.5772	0.5861	**0.6251**
	G_m	0.6956	0.6893	0.6662	0.6945	0.7121	**0.7253**	0.7039	0.7043	0.7179
A_r	P_r	4.6	3.4	5.4	4.0	4.2	7.8	7.0	6.8	**1.4**
	R_e	6.2	5.8	5.4	7.0	5.4	**1.6**	3.4	4.6	5.2
	F_1	5.8	5.6	6.0	5.8	4.4	4.2	5.4	5.6	**2.2**
	G_m	5.0	5.8	6.0	7.0	4.4	**2.4**	5.0	5.0	4.4

Overall, although existing resampling methods offer modest improvements in classification performance, they remain constrained by two fundamental limitations: excessive sample overlap and significant information loss. By contrast, BWGAN-generated samples (Fig. 3.4i) demonstrate strong generalization with minimal noise and boundary overlap, thus effectively enhancing fraudulent transaction detection performance.

Ablation Study. To evaluate the contribution of each module to the overall model performance, this chapter conducts a systematic ablation study. As shown in Table 3.8, the experiments conduct a sequential comparison of performance—measured by P_r, R_e, F_1, and G_m—across model configurations ranging from the baseline A_0 to the full model incorporating $A_1 + A_2 + A_3$.

The baseline model A_0 exhibited notably low recall in identifying fraudulent samples, indicating its limited ability to capture discriminative characteristics of such instances. With the incremental incorporation of the sample selection module A_1, the distribution constraint module A_2, and the temporal-aware module A_3, all per-

Table 3.8 Ablation study

Test	Criteria	A_0	A_1	A_2	$A_1 + A_2$	$A_1 + A_2 + A_3$
Feb.	P_r	0.6032	0.7432	0.7568	0.8013	**0.8127**
	R_e	0.6396	0.5996	0.6422	0.6883	**0.8325**
	F_1	0.6208	0.6672	0.6941	0.7405	**0.8225**
	G_m	0.7911	0.77307	0.7978	0.8260	**0.8910**
Mar.	P_r	0.8382	0.8493	0.8890	**0.8966**	0.8445
	R_e	0.7608	0.7499	0.8280	0.7979	**0.9352**
	F_1	0.7976	0.7965	0.8574	0.8444	**0.8876**
	G_m	0.8612	0.8561	0.9019	0.8862	**0.9111**
Apr.	P_r	0.3048	0.3794	0.4381	0.4426	**0.5194**
	R_e	0.5803	0.5498	0.6053	0.6303	**0.9653**
	F_1	0.3997	0.4490	0.5083	0.5201	**0.6754**
	G_m	0.7563	0.7379	0.7747	**0.7905**	0.7192
May.	P_r	0.6012	0.7178	**0.7831**	0.7592	0.6952
	R_e	0.7285	0.7442	0.7781	0.7815	**0.8911**
	F_1	0.6588	0.7308	0.7806	0.7702	**0.7811**
	G_m	0.8488	0.8598	0.8799	**0.8815**	0.8285
Jun.	P_r	0.5793	0.6346	0.6817	0.6829	**0.6971**
	R_e	0.7181	0.7151	0.7702	0.7597	**0.9783**
	F_1	0.6413	0.6725	0.7232	0.7193	**0.8141**
	G_m	0.8420	0.8414	**0.8737**	0.8678	0.8340

formance metrics demonstrate consistent improvement. The full model achieves the best performance across most evaluation periods, demonstrating a clear synergistic effect among the modules. Taking the February data for illustrative purposes, the F_1 increases substantially from 0.6208 to 0.8225, and the G_m improves from 0.7911 to 0.8910, indicating that the incorporated modules effectively strengthen the discriminative power of the synthetic samples. Specifically, A_1 improves attention to critical discriminative features, A_2 reinforces the representation of key characteristics, and A_3 captures temporal dependencies within transaction sequences. Collectively, these enhancements significantly boost the OPFD model's capability to identify fraudulent samples.

3.5 Summary

Targeting the class imbalance issue in OPFD, this chapter introduces a generative adversarial framework integrating distribution constraints and time awareness. First, it systematically analyzes the constraints imposed by class imbalance on the performance of OPFD models, pointing out the degradation of model discriminative capability and the deviation of decision boundaries caused by the scarcity of fraudulent samples. Based on this analysis, a data augmentation method based on BWGAN is proposed. By introducing a sample selection strategy and a distribution constraint mechanism, the method enhances the discriminability of synthetic fraudulent samples while ensuring their quality. Subsequently, a time-aware gated recurrent network is further designed to explicitly embed transaction interval information into feature representations, thereby improving the model's ability to model the dynamic patterns of user behavior. Finally, experiments conducted on real transaction scenarios and public datasets demonstrate that the proposed framework significantly outperforms baseline methods in terms of precision, robustness, and interpretability. However, in real-world online transaction environments, there exists distribution overlap between fraudulent and legitimate samples, which severely impairs the model's discriminative performance and generalization ability. To address this challenge, the next chapter will propose a GAN-based hybrid sampling framework. By avoiding the generation of samples in overlapping regions and proactively cleaning legitimate samples with high ambiguity, the framework aims to further enhance the stability and generalization performance of OPFD models in complex online transaction scenarios.

References

1. Aftabi, S.Z., Ahmadi, A., Farzi, S.: Expert systems with applicationsexpert systems with applications. Expert Systems with Applications **227**, 120144 (2023)
2. Agarwal, S., Qian, W., Ren, Y., Tsai, H.T., Yeung, B.: The real impact of FinTech: Evidence from mobile payment technology. Management Science (2025)
3. Belhaouari, S.B., Islam, A., Kassoul, K., Al-Fuqaha, A., Bouzerdoum, A.: Oversampling techniques for imbalanced data in regression. Expert systems with applications **252**, 124118 (2024)
4. Blagus, R., Lusa, L.: SMOTE for high-dimensional class-imbalanced data. BMC Bioinformatics **14**(1), 106 (2013)
5. Breskuvienė, D., Dzemyda, G.: Enhancing credit card fraud detection: Highly imbalanced data case. Journal of Big Data **11**(1), 182 (2024)
6. Cao, J., Luo, M., Yu, J., Yang, M.H., He, R.: ScoreMix: A scalable augmentation strategy for training GANs with limited data. IEEE Trans. on Pattern Analysis and Machine Intelligence **45**(7), 8920–8935 (2023)
7. Chatterjee, P., Das, D., Rawat, D.B.: Digital twin for credit cardfraud detection: opportunities, challenges, and fraud detection advancements. Future Generation Computer Systems **158**, 410–426 (2024)
8. Chen, J., Chen, Q., Jiang, F., Guo, X., Sha, K., Wang, Y.: SCN_GNN: A GNN-based fraud detection algorithm combining strong node and graph topology information. Expert Systems with Applications **237**, 121643 (2024)
9. Chen, Z.M., Cui, Q., Zhang, X., Deng, R., Xia, C., Lu, S.: Towards gradient equalization and feature diversification for Long-Tailed Multi-Label image recognition. IEEE Trans. on Multimedia **27**, 3489–3500 (2025)
10. Courville, A., Bengio, Y.: Generative adversarial nets. Advanc in Neural **27**, 3 (2014)
11. Creswell, A., White, T., Dumoulin, V., Arulkumaran, K., Sengupta, B., Bharath, A.A.: Generative adversarial networks: An overview. IEEE Signal Processing Magazine **35**(1), 53–65 (2018)
12. Deng, J., Wang, D., Gu, J., Chen, C.: SGO: An innovative oversampling approach for imbalanced datasets using SVM and genetic algorithms. Information Sciences **690**, 121584 (2025)

13. Gnip, P., Kanasz, R., Zoričak, M., Drotar, P.: An experimental survey of imbalanced learning algorithms for bankruptcy prediction. Artificial Intelligence Review **58**(4), 104 (2025)
14. Hafez, I.Y., Hafez, A.Y., Saleh, A., Abd El-Mageed, A.A., Abohany, A.A.: A systematic review of AI-enhanced techniques in credit card fraud detection. Journal of Big Data **12**(1), 6 (2025)
15. He, H., Bai, Y., Garcia, E.A., Li, S.: ADASYN: Adaptive synthetic sampling approach for imbalanced learning. In: 2008 IEEE International Joint Conference on Neural Networks (IEEE World Congress on Computational Intelligence). pp. 1322–1328. IEEE (2008)
16. Jiang, Y., Liu, G., Wu, J., Lin, H.: Telecom fraud detection via Hawkes-Enhanced sequence model. IEEE Trans. on Knowledge and Data Engineering **35**(5), 5311–5324 (2023)
17. Li, L., Zhu, Y., Zhu, Z.: Automatic modulation classification using ResNeXt-GRU with deep feature fusion. IEEE Trans. on Instrumentation and Measurement **72**, 1–10 (2023)
18. Liu, C.L., Hsieh, P.Y.: Model-Based synthetic sampling for imbalanced data. IEEE Trans. on Knowledge and Data Engineering **32**(8), 1543–1556 (2020)
19. Liu, Y., Du, G., Yin, C., Zhang, H., Wang, J.: Clustering-based incremental learning for imbalanced data classification. Knowledge-Based Systems **292**, 111612 (2024)
20. Lou, C., Wang, Y., Li, J., Qian, Y., Li, X.: Graph neural network for fraud detection via context encoding and adaptive aggregation. Expert Systems with Applications **261**, 125473 (2025)
21. Mengzhe, Z., Jindong, C., Wen, Z., Zhihua, Y.: Fraud detection based on GNNs with local augmentation and adaptive relation aggregation. Expert Systems with Applications **299**, 130110 (2025)
22. Mohammed, R., Rawashdeh, J., Abdullah, M.: Machine learning with oversampling and undersampling techniques: Overview study and experimental results. In: 2020 11th International Conference on Information and Communication Systems (ICICS). pp. 243–248. IEEE (2020)
23. Motie, S., Raahemi, B.: Financial fraud detection using graph neural networks: A systematic review. Expert Systems with Applications **240**, 122156 (2024)
24. Prusa, J., Khoshgoftaar, T.M., Dittman, D.J., Napolitano, A.: Using random undersampling to alleviate class imbalance on tweet sentiment data. In: 2015 IEEE International Conference on Information Reuse and Integration. pp. 197–202. IEEE (2015)
25. Smiti, S., Soui, M.: Bankruptcy prediction using deep learning approach based on borderline SMOTE. Information Systems Frontiers **22**(5), 1067–1083 (2020)
26. Sun, H., Li, J., Zhu, X.: A novel expandable borderline smote Over-Sampling method for class imbalance problem. IEEE Trans. on Knowledge and Data Engineering **37**(5), 2183–2199 (2025)
27. Tong, G., Shen, J.: Financial transaction fraud detector based on imbalance learning and graph neural network. Applied Soft Computing **149**, 110984 (2023)
28. Wang, C., Yang, J., Jie, H., Tao, Z., Zhao, Z.: A lightweight progressive joint transfer ensemble network inspired by the markov process for imbalanced mechanical fault diagnosis. Mechanical Systems and Signal Processing **224**, 111994 (2025)
29. Wang, C.: The behavioral sign of account theft: Realizing online payment fraud alert cheng wang. In: Proceedings of the Twenty-Ninth International Conference on International Joint Conferences on Artificial Intelligence. pp. 4511–4618 (2021)
30. Wang, Y., Zheng, Q., Li, X., Wang, L., Lin, L.: CoSemiGNN: Blockchain fraud detection with dynamic graph neural networks based on co-association of semi-supervised. Expert Systems with Applications **298**, 129853 (2025)
31. Wilson, D.L.: Asymptotic properties of nearest neighbor rules using edited data. IEEE Trans. on Systems, Man, and Cybernetics (3), 408–421 (2007)
32. Xia, M., Wang, Z., Lan, X., Liu, W., Wu, J.: Confidence-driven under-sampling decision forest for imbalanced credit scoring. Engineering Applications of Artificial Intelligence **147**, 110278 (2025)
33. Xie, Y., Hong, Y., Qiao, S., Yao, J., Liu, G., Pang, S.: A time-aware generative network for enhancing transaction security in consumer electronics. IEEE Trans. on Consumer Electronics **71**(2), 6818–6828 (2025)
34. Xie, Y., Liu, G., Yan, C., Jiang, C., Zhou, M.: Time-aware attention-based gated network for credit card fraud detection by extracting transactional behaviors. IEEE Trans. on Computational Social Systems **10**(3), 1004–1016 (2023)

35. Xie, Y., Liu, G., Yan, C., Jiang, C., Zhou, M., Li, M.: Learning transactional behavioral representations for credit card fraud detection. IEEE Trans. on Neural Networks and Learning Systems **35**(4), 5735–5748 (2024)
36. Xie, Y., Liu, G., Zhou, M., Wei, L., Zhu, H., Zhou, R., Cao, L.: A spatial–temporal gated network for credit card fraud detection by learning transactional representations. IEEE Trans. on Automation Science and Engineering **21**(4), 6978–6991 (2024)
37. Xie, Y., Shan, J., Wei, L., Yao, J., Zhou, M.: GAN-based hybrid sampling method for transaction fraud detection. IEEE Trans. on Knowledge and Data Engineering **37**(10), 5905–5918 (2025)
38. Xie, Y., Zhou, M., Liu, G., Wei, L., Zhu, H., De Meo, P.: A transactional-behavior-based hierarchical gated network for credit card fraud detection. IEEE/CAA Journal of Automatica Sinica **12**(7), 1489–1503 (2025)
39. Xiong, Y., Cui, X., Yu, L.: Impact of COVID-19 pandemic on online consumption share: Evidence from china's mobile payment data. Journal of Retailing and Consumer Services **81**, 103976 (2024)
40. Xu, Y., Yu, Z., Chen, C.L.P., Liu, Z.: Adaptive subspace optimization ensemble method for High-Dimensional imbalanced data classification. IEEE Trans. on Neural Networks and Learning Systems **34**(5), 2284–2297 (2023)
41. Yang, L., Peng, X., Guo, K., Liu, D.: MSFE-AD: Multiscale Feature-Enhanced early satellite sensor data anomaly detection based on rare boundary samples. IEEE Trans. on Instrumentation and Measurement **74**, 1–12 (2025)
42. Yu, S., Lin, L., Yu, Y.: Balanced contrast Class-Incremental learning. CAAI Trans. on Intelligence Technology (2025)
43. Zhang, W., Zhang, Y., Zhang, L.: Multiplanar data augmentation and lightweight skip connection design for Deep-Learning-Based abdominal CT image segmentation. IEEE Trans. on Instrumentation and Measurement **72**, 1–11 (2023)
44. Zhu, H., Wang, C., Chai, S.: Detecting evolving fraudulent behavior in online payment services: Open-Category and Concept-Drift. IEEE Trans. on Services Computing **17**(5), 2180–2193 (2024)

Chapter 4
A Hybrid Sampling and Distribution Refinement Method for Reducing Behavioral Overlap

Extending the generative data augmentation method proposed in Chap. 3, this chapter addresses the challenge posed by the substantial overlap between fraudulent and legitimate samples. This chapter proposes a GAN-based Hybrid Sampling (GANHS) framework [33], which integrates a Behavior-Boundary Aware Generative Adversarial Network (BBAGAN) for data augmentation with an Adaptive Neighborhood Cleaning Strategy (ANCS). This approach simultaneously generates high-quality fraudulent samples while eliminating ambiguous legitimate samples. It is particularly effective in detecting fraudulent activities characterized by weak discriminatory signals and strong concealment, such as micro-payment abuse and behavioral-camouflage transactions [14].

4.1 When Fraud Mimics Legitimate Behavior: The Challenge of Behavioral Concealment

Behavioral Overlap. In imbalanced classification, model performance is typically not severely compromised by numerical imbalance alone, provided that the feature space is well-separated [8]. Theoretical work shows that when classes are linearly separable, i.e., when a clear hyperplane can perfectly separate them, models such as Support Vector Machines (SVM) can maintain strong performance even under severe class imbalance [22]. The reason is that separability ensures the existence of a discriminative hyperplane; class imbalance may shift its position but does not fundamentally weaken the classifier's discriminative capability.

However, the challenge becomes far more severe when class imbalance coincides with substantial feature-space overlap [23]. In OPFD, fraudsters intentionally mimic the behavioral patterns of legitimate users. They achieve this through high-fidelity imitation across multiple dimensions such as transactional amount, temporal

Y. Xie et al., *Neural Network-Based Deep Learning for Online Payment Fraud Detection*,
https://doi.org/10.1007/978-981-95-8513-7_4

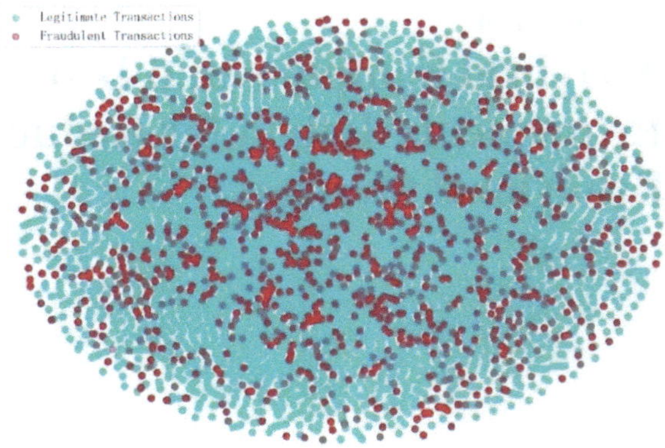

Fig. 4.1 Visualization of real-world transactions

patterns, geographic location, and device fingerprints [13]. This strategic camouflage creates substantial feature similarity, embedding many fraudulent samples into the distribution of legitimate ones and leading to significant behavioral overlap [1, 34].

To further illustrate the high similarity between fraudulent and legitimate samples, we employ *t*-SNE to visualize real transaction data. Figure 4.1 shows that fraudulent samples do not form distinct clusters but are densely embedded within the legitimate sample distribution, exhibiting an intertwined and highly overlapping topology. This reflects strong structural similarity and low inter-class separability, which fundamentally complicates the classification task. Specifically, this overlap: (1) exacerbates classification bias, making the classifier prone to labeling overlapping samples as legitimate, and (2) undermines feature-space separability, hindering both linear and nonlinear models from establishing confident decision boundaries in these regions.

Imbalanced Classification under Behavioral Overlap. Current mainstream methods for addressing class imbalance in data augmentation primarily involve SMOTE [24] and GAN-based methods [40]. Although these methods enhance the representativeness of minority-class samples and show improved performance in various tasks [10, 32], they exhibit significant limitations when applied to OPFD. First, they struggle to capture the discriminative patterns that arise within overlapping regions. This leads to synthetic samples with insufficient fidelity, which fail to reinforce genuinely discriminative features [5, 30]. Second, the augmentation process is adversely affected by overlapping samples, causing many synthetic samples to be embedded within the legitimate feature space and, in turn, blurring the decision boundary [31]. Consequently, synthetic samples often exhibit high similarity to legitimate ones, inadvertently intensifying the pre-existing behavioral overlap [27]. Thus, behavioral overlap emerges as a key bottleneck that fundamentally constrains the effectiveness of data augmentation in OPFD.

4.2 GAN-Based Hybrid Sampling Architecture

Method Framework. To address the significant behavioral overlap in OPFD, this chapter proposes a GANHS framework. As illustrated in Fig. 4.2, GANHS integrates two key components: a BBAGAN-based data augmentation module and an ANCS-driven data cleaning mechanism. This integrated design aims to mitigate the performance degradation caused by behavioral overlap [9, 26].

The data augmentation phase employs a BBAGAN with a dual-discriminator architecture to collaboratively optimize synthetic sample generation [6, 25]. The generator produces candidate fraudulent samples by sampling from a latent space distribution. The behavior-recognition discriminator assesses the authenticity of synthetic samples, thereby guiding the generator to mimic real fraud. Concurrently, the overlap-penalty discriminator explicitly models the decision boundary between legitimate and synthetic samples, constraining the generation process through an overlap-penalty mechanism. This dual-feedback ensures that synthetic samples enhance fraud-class representation while maintaining separability, thereby alleviating the boundary blurring prevalent in traditional data augmentation methods. In the subsequent data cleaning phase, an ANCS method is applied. It quantifies the behavioral overlap risk of each legitimate sample from three perspectives [15, 21]:

(1) Density Perspective: The Density-Based Spatial Clustering of Applications with Noise (DBSCAN) algorithm identifies high-overlap risk regions via density-based clustering.
(2) Hierarchical Perspective: Agglomerative Clustering (AC) constructs a hierarchical tree to reveal inter-class mixing at different granularities.

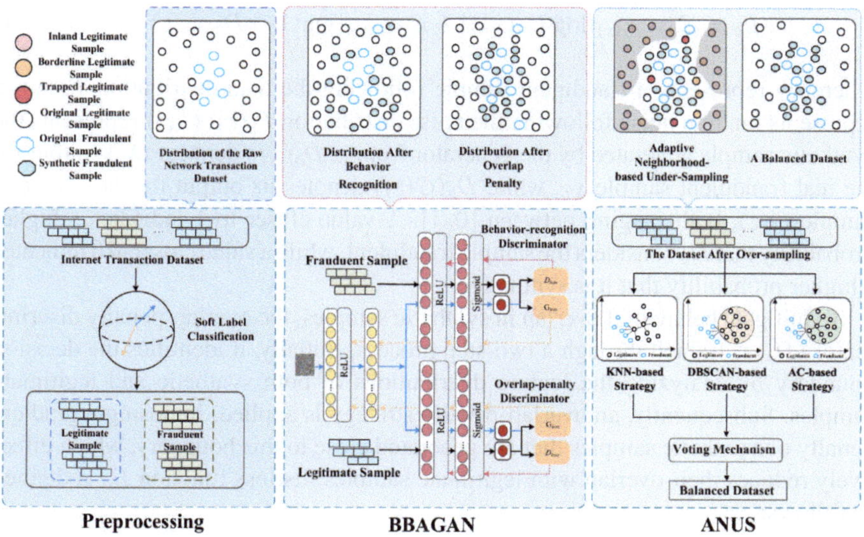

Fig. 4.2 Illustration of the structure of GANHS

(3) Distance Perspective: The K-Nearest Neighbors (KNN) algorithm calculates the proportion of fraudulent samples within the neighborhood of each legitimate sample, thereby characterizing local class confusion [12]. Finally, a weighted voting mechanism integrates these multi-dimensional scores to remove high-risk legitimate samples, further sharpening the decision boundary.

4.3 Enhanced Minority-Class Pattern Distillation

Model Overview. To address the behavioral overlap limitations of existing data augmentation methods in OPFD, this chapter proposes a BBAGAN-based augmentation framework. BBAGAN achieves dual optimization through a collaborative adversarial mechanism: (1) The generator and the behavior-recognition discriminator form a feature-level adversarial path that enhances the generator's capacity to capture discriminative fraud-related patterns. (2) The generator and the overlap-penalty discriminator form a boundary-aware adversarial path that employs an overlap penalty to prevent behavioral overlap between synthetic and legitimate samples. This decoupled strong-weak adversarial mechanism ensures that the generator produces synthetic samples possessing both fidelity to fraud patterns and inter-class discriminability, thereby improving the detection capability and robustness of OPFD models.

Behavior-recognition and Overlap-penalty Discriminators. The BBAGAN-based data augmentation method employs a dual-discriminator collaborative mechanism to improve the authenticity and inter-class separability of synthetic samples. The behavior-recognition discriminator (D_b) enhances synthetic sample quality through feature-level adversarial training. Its loss function L_b is defined as follows:

$$L_b = \mathbb{E}_{x_f \sim P_f(x)}[\log D_b(x_f)] + \mathbb{E}_{z \sim P_z(z)}[\log(1 - D_b(G(z)))], \tag{4.1}$$

where x_f represents a fraudulent sample following the data distribution $P_f(x)$; z represents random noise following the noise distribution $P_z(z)$; $G(z)$ represents the synthetic sample generated by the generator from z. $D_b(x_f)$ denotes D_b's output for the real fraudulent sample x_f, while $D_b(G(z))$ denotes its output for the synthetic sample $G(z)$, both ranging between [0, 1]. A value closer to 1 indicates a higher probability that D_b considers the sample fraudulent, while a value closer to 0 indicates a higher probability that it is synthetic.

To mitigate behavioral overlap in synthetic samples, the overlap-penalty discriminator (D_o) is trained through a two-step process. Initially, it identifies the decision boundary by analyzing the feature distributions of both synthetic and legitimate samples. Subsequently, an overlap-penalty strategy is applied, imposing a gradient penalty on synthetic samples that are generated close to this boundary, which effectively reduces their overlap with legitimate samples. Its loss function L_o is defined as follows:

$$L_o = \mathbb{E}_{x_l \sim P_l(x)}[\log D_o(x_l)] + \mathbb{E}_{z \sim P_z(z)}[\log(1 - D_o(G(z)))], \tag{4.2}$$

where x_l represents a legitimate sample following the data distribution $P_l(x)$. $D_o(x_l)$ denotes D_o's discrimination result for x_l, and $D_o(G(z))$ denotes its result for $G(z)$, also ranging between [0, 1]. To facilitate the use of standard optimization algorithms, this chapter converts the maximization problem into a minimization problem by negating the loss functions L_b and L_o, and then optimizes the model parameters using standard minimization techniques like Root Mean Square Propagation (RMSprop) [2].

Generator. In BBAGAN, the generator enhances its capacity to model fraudulent behavioral patterns through adversarial collaboration with a pair of discriminators. As shown in Fig. 4.3, the generator produces candidate synthetic samples based on the latent space distribution. The behavior-recognition discriminator evaluates the authenticity of these synthetic samples. Through the adversarial training process, the generator continuously optimizes the synthetic samples to increase their similarity to fraudulent samples. Concurrently, in the second adversarial path, the overlap-penalty discriminator mines boundary information between legitimate and synthetic samples in the feature space and feeds it back to the generator as an overlap-penalty signal. The generator adjusts its generation strategy accordingly to avoid behavioral overlap between synthetic and legitimate samples in the feature space. The three components, the generator and the two discriminators, collaboratively and adversarially optimize their joint objective until convergence to a Nash equilibrium state. At this point, the generator produces synthetic samples that align with the distribution of fraudulent samples in the feature space, while their joint distinctly separable from legitimate samples. The generator's loss function is defined as follows:

$$L_g = -\mathbb{E}_{z \sim P_z(z)}[\log(D_b(G(z))) + L_f], \tag{4.3}$$

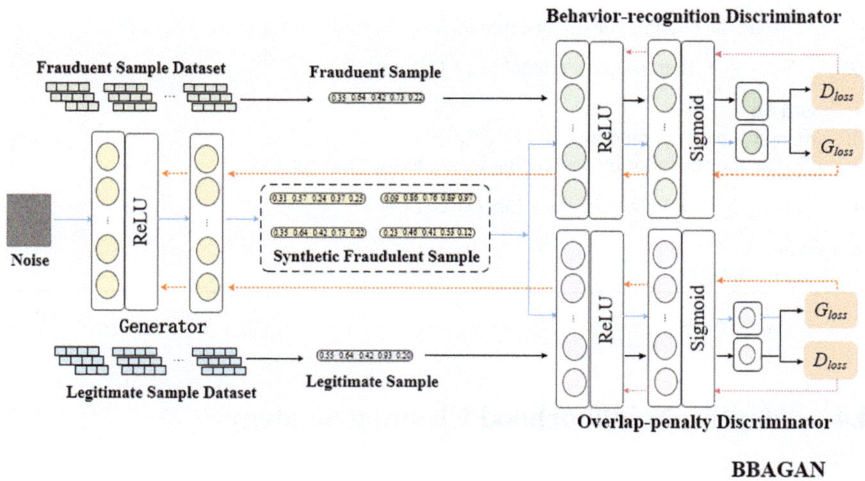

Fig. 4.3 Illustration of the structure of BBAGAN

where z is random noise following distribution $P_z(z)$; $G(z)$ is the synthetic sample generated from z; L_f is a penalty factor defined as follows:

$$L_f = -log D_o(G(z)). \tag{4.4}$$

The introduction of the penalty factor L_f into L_g creates a dual optimization guidance mechanism for the generator. Specifically, on the one hand, the generator aims to increase the value of $D_b(G(z))$, i.e., to enhance the probability that the behavior-recognition discriminator classifies the synthetic sample as fraudulent, thereby ensuring that fraudulent pattern features are correctly expressed. On the other hand, the penalty factor L_f drives the generator to decrease the output value of $D_o(G(z))$, i.e., to reduce the probability that the overlap-penalty discriminator considers the synthetic sample legitimate, thereby increasing inter-class separation. The detailed training algorithm for BBAGAN is outlined as follows:

Algorithm 1 Training algorithm for BBAGAN.

Input: The set of fraudulent sample: X_f; The set of legitimate samples: X_l; Synthetic sample: X_s; Epoch number: n_e.

Output: BBAGAN.

for *epoch* $\in \{1, ..., n_e\}$ **do**
  for k steps **do**
    Sample $\{x^i\}_{i=1}^m \sim X_f$;
    Sample $\{z^i\}_{i=1}^m \sim X_s$;
    Update the behavior-recognition discriminator by ascending its stochastic gradient:
    $\nabla_{\theta(D)} \frac{1}{m} \sum_{i=1}^{m} [\log(D_b(x_i)) + log(1 - D_b(G(z)))]$
    Sample $\{x^i\}_{i=1}^m \sim X_l$;
    Sample $\{z^i\}_{i=1}^m \sim X_s$;
    Update the overlap-penalty discriminator by ascending its stochastic gradient:
    $\nabla_{\theta(D)} \frac{1}{m} \sum_{i=1}^{m} [\log(D_o(x_i)) + \log(1 - D_o(G(z)))]$
  end for
  Sample a batch of random noise $\{z^i\}_{i=1}^m \sim X_s$;
  Update the generator by descending its stochastic gradient:
  $\nabla_{\theta(G)} \frac{1}{m} \sum_{i=1}^{m} [-\log(D_b(G(z))) + \log(D_o(G(z)))]$
end for
Return BBAGAN

4.4 Adaptive Neighborhood Cleaning Strategy

Method Framework. As illustrated in Fig. 4.4, the ANCS framework employs a multi-strategy collaborative assessment mechanism. It employs three complementary algorithms—DBSCAN, AC, and KNN—to evaluate the risk of behavioral overlap

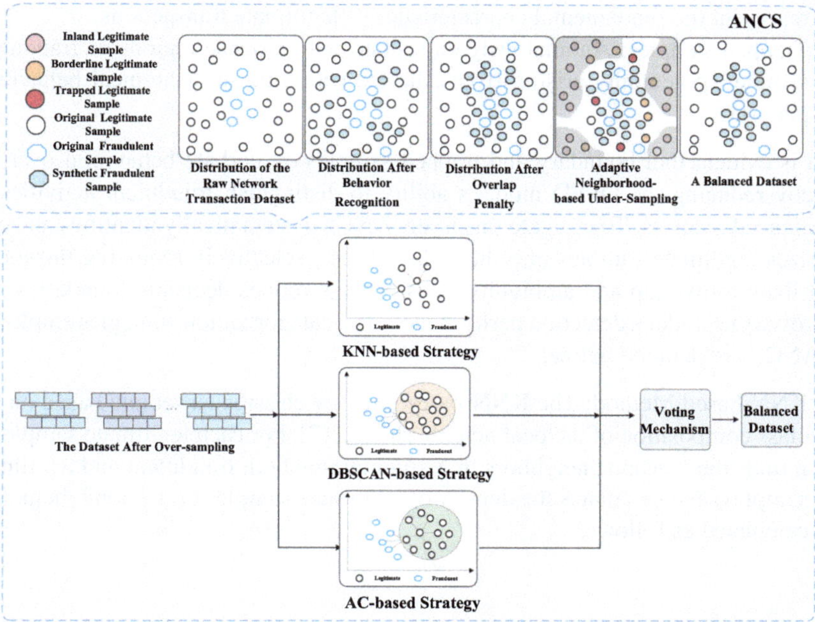

Fig. 4.4 Illustration of the structure of ANCS

for each legitimate sample from the perspectives of density, hierarchy, and distance. These algorithms are selected for their complementary strengths in assessing spatial relationships: (1) DBSCAN accurately identifies sample clusters in high-density areas through local density clustering, thereby effectively detecting local behavioral overlap [29]. (2) AC constructs a hierarchical clustering tree that reveals distributional structures across multiple scales, thereby identifying multi-level behavioral overlap patterns [19]. (3) KNN performs nearest-neighbor analysis to quantify the degree of class intermixing within a sample's local neighborhood [16]. To effectively integrate the multi-dimensional evaluation results, ANCS adopts a weighted voting mechanism for final decision-making: a sample is retained if it is classified as an "inland sample" by at least two of the three algorithms; otherwise, it is deleted. This consensus-based decision mechanism ensures both the reliability of the assessment and the clarity of the final decision boundary.

Partitioning Strategy. ANCS categorizes each legitimate sample into one of three groups according to its location in the feature space:

(1) Border samples: Located near the decision boundary, these samples exhibit features highly similar to fraudulent instances and constitute the primary source of behavioral overlap.

(2) Inland samples: Positioned within the dense core of legitimate instances, they represent the fundamental characteristics of legitimate transactions.
(3) Trapped samples: Anomalously embedded within dense regions of fraudulent samples, potentially arising from data collection noise or atypical behavioral patterns.

It is evident that boundary and trapped samples exacerbate behavioral overlap, thereby reducing the OPFD model's ability to distinguish fraudulent activities in imbalanced datasets. To mitigate this issue, ANCS systematically identifies and categorizes legitimate samples into these three types, selectively removing those that contribute to overlap and ambiguity. This process refines decision boundaries and improves the model's detection performance. The categorization strategies employed by ANCS are detailed below:

(1) KNN-based Method: The KNN-based strategy classifies a sample based on the class composition of its local neighborhood [17]. For each legitimate sample x_l, it finds the k nearest neighbors in X_t (containing both fraudulent and legitimate samples) and calculates the density of legitimate samples (T_l) among them. It is calculated as follows:

$$T_l = \frac{n_l}{k}, \tag{4.5}$$

where n_l is the number of legitimate samples among the k nearest neighbors. Classification is then based on T_l and a density threshold α: if $T_l \geq \alpha$, the sample is classified as an inland sample. If $T_l < \alpha$ and all k neighbors are fraudulent samples, it is classified as a trapped sample. If $T_l < \alpha$ and the k neighbors include at least one legitimate sample, it is classified as a border sample. To align with the binary classification nature of OPFD [28], the threshold α is set to $\frac{1}{2}$. This method effectively captures distance variations and identifies legitimate samples near the decision boundary that contribute to behavioral overlap.
(2) DBSCAN-based Method: This method classifies samples using local neighborhood density and inter-sample distances [37]. First, the dataset X_t is partitioned into clusters ($L_i \in \{L_1, ..., L_{\tilde{n}}\}$, where $L_i \cap L_j = \emptyset$ for any $i \neq j$). Then, for each legitimate sample within a cluster L_i, KNN is used to find its nearest neighbors. The density $\rho(x_l)$ of samples sharing the same cluster membership or the same label among these neighbors is calculated as follows:

$$\rho(x_l) = \frac{|N_{L_i(x_l)}| + |N^*_{L_i(x_l)}|}{k}, \tag{4.6}$$

where $N_{L_i(x_l)}$ is the number of nearest neighbors belonging to cluster L_i, and $N^*_{L_i(x_l)}$ is the number of nearest neighbors within L_i that also share the same class label. Classification is based on $\rho(x_l)$ and a threshold β: if $\rho(x_l) \geq \beta$, the sample is classified as an inland one; if $\rho(x_l) < \beta$ and at least one of the k nearest neighbors is a fraudulent sample, it is classified as a boundary one. If $\rho(x_l) < \beta$ and all k nearest neighbors are fraudulent samples, it is classified as a trapped one. The threshold β is set adaptively according to the following:

$$\beta = \frac{x_l}{x_l + x_f}, \tag{4.7}$$

where x_l and x_f are the number of legitimate and fraudulent samples in the original dataset, respectively. This adaptive setting ensures β reflects the inherent class imbalance, enabling flexible classification consistent with the data distribution.

(3) AC-based Method: This method uses hierarchical relationships and distances between samples for classification. It first applies AC to the dataset. Then, for legitimate samples within each resulting cluster, the same classification procedure as described in the DBSCAN-based method is applied. This hierarchical perspective helps capture multi-scale structural relationships, potentially improving the identification of overlap patterns.

A voting mechanism integrates the results from these three methods. A sample is retained only if it is classified as an Inland sample by at least two of the three methods; otherwise, it is deleted. This approach assesses legitimate samples from distance, density, and hierarchy perspectives, effectively reducing the degree of behavioral overlap between legitimate and fraudulent samples. The detailed procedure is outlined as follows:

Algorithm 2 An adaptive neighborhood-based cleaning method.

Input: Original fraudulent transactions: $X_f = \{x_1, ..., x_f\}$; Original legitimate transactions: $X_l = \{x_1, ..., x_l\}$; The set of synthetic samples: $X_s = \{x_1, ..., x_s\}$.

Output: A balanced dataset for OPFD.

Merging synthetic samples, fraudulent samples, and legitimate samples to form a transaction set: $X_t \longleftarrow X_f \cup X_S \cup X_l$;

Employ the KNN-based strategy to process X_t and divide X_l into inland samples I_1, borderline samples B_1, trapped samples T_1;

Employ the DBSCAN-based strategy to process X_t and divide X_l into inland samples I_2, borderline samples B_2, trapped samples T_2;

Employ the AC-based strategy to process X_t and divide X_l into inland samples I_3, borderline samples B_3, trapped samples T_3;

for x_i in P_l **do**

    Calculate the number of times x_i is identified as inland sample n;

    if $n \geq 2$ **then**

        Save x_i;

    else

        Delete x_i;

    end if

end for

Return A balanced dataset for OPFD

4.5 Experimental Validation and Interpretability Analysis

Baseline Models. In this chapter, nine common and representative imbalanced classification methods are selected as baseline comparisons. These methods have been extensively validated for handling extreme class imbalance and provide a solid reference for comparative experiments with GANHS. The specific methods include:

(1) ROS [38]: It balances the dataset by randomly duplicating minority-class samples. Its core advantages lie in simple implementation, high computational efficiency, and the complete preservation of the original minority-class distribution.
(2) SMOTE [3]: It generates synthetic samples by interpolating between a minority instance and its nearest neighbors in feature space. Its primary strength is effectively increasing the sample density near the decision boundary, thereby enhancing the classifier's discriminative ability in boundary regions.
(3) ADASYN [11]: It generates synthetic samples adaptively, assigning more samples to minority instances in denser majority neighborhoods via linear interpolation. A key advantage is its focus on "hard-to-learn" regions (i.e., minority samples surrounded by many majority samples). By generating more samples in these areas, it effectively improves the quality of the classification boundary.
(4) SMOTE-ENN (SMEN) [41]: It combines SMOTE-based oversampling with ENN-based cleaning to address both class imbalance and noisy majority samples near the boundary. This dual mechanism addresses class imbalance while also reducing behavioral overlap through data cleaning, ultimately improving classifier performance.
(5) ADASYN-ENN (ADEN) [33]: It integrates ADASYN's density-aware oversampling with ENN cleaning to achieve balance and purify local neighborhoods. This process ensures a balanced data distribution and stable local structures.
(6) SMOTE-TOMEK LINKS (SMTL) [20]: It applies SMOTE for oversampling, then uses Tomek Links to remove cross-class pairs of mutually nearest neighbors, clarifying the decision boundary.
(7) WGAN [18]: It uses the Wasserstein distance to stabilize GAN training and mitigate mode collapse, enabling more reliable generation of minority-class samples.
(8) Roulette wheel selection-based GAN (RGAN) [7]: It incorporates a roulette-wheel selection mechanism that prioritizes samples near the decision boundary, guiding the generator to produce more discriminative synthetic samples. Consequently, RGAN guides the generator to produce synthetic samples that are both representative of the minority-class and distant from the decision boundary, improving classification accuracy.
(9) Noisy-sample-removed Undersampling (NUS) [39]: It uses a neural model to learn the minority distribution, then removes majority samples whose predicted membership contradicts their geometric proximity. It then filters and removes the majority-class samples that contribute to behavioral overlap by evaluating the discrepancy between predicted values and Euclidean distances.

Experiments on OPFD. To evaluate the effectiveness of GANHS in addressing behavioral overlap within OPFD, a systematic comparative experiment is conducted.

Nine representative imbalanced learning methods are selected as baselines. These methods are evaluated using three widely adopted baseline classifiers: SVC, RF, and MLP. These classifiers are chosen for their distinct and representative characteristics: (1) SVC is renowned for its robust boundary delineation, making it suitable for high-dimensional imbalanced data [36]. (2) RF, as an ensemble learning method, excels at capturing complex nonlinear feature relationships [35]. (3) MLP, a typical neural network model, demonstrates strong adaptability and performance in modeling large-scale financial transaction data [4]. To ensure a fair comparison, all GAN-based methods (including WGAN, RGAN, and GANHS) utilize identical generator and discriminator network architectures. Furthermore, the results for each experimental group are averaged over ten independent runs to guarantee the robustness and reliability of the conclusions.

The experimental results with SVC as the base classifier are presented in Table 4.1. The results indicate that GANHS demonstrates a clear advantage in F_1, achieving the best performance in four out of the six monthly test cycles. Overall, its average F_1 improves by 1.0% compared to the second-best method and by 8.7% compared to the worst-performing method. In terms of G_m, GANHS maintains the best performance in all months except March, yielding average improvements of 0.4% over the second-best method and 2.9% over the worst-performing method. Notably, GANHS achieves the best A_r in both F_1 and G_m among all its peers, further confirming its stability when used with this boundary-sensitive classifier.

When RF is used as the base classifier, the performance of GANHS is reported in Table 4.2. The results show that GANHS improves the average F_1 by 0.8% over the second-best method and by 2.8% over the worst-performing method. In terms of G_m, GANHS achieves the best results in four months, with average improvements of 1.0% and 3.9%, over the second-best and worst-performing methods, respectively. Furthermore, GANHS ranks first in the overall evaluation for both key metrics, validating its robustness and superiority within the ensemble learning framework for modeling nonlinear features.

The results using MLP as the base classifier are shown in Table 4.3. GANHS achieves the best F_1 in three of the six months, with average improvements of 0.5% and 8.3% over the second-best and worst-performing methods, respectively. Regarding the G_m metric, although SMTL slightly outperforms GANHS in average performance and ranking, GANHS still performs notably well among most GAN-based oversampling methods, demonstrating its effectiveness in mitigating class overlap. It is noteworthy that traditional oversampling methods often underperform in adversarial data distributions, whereas GANHS, by incorporating dynamic generation and selective filtering mechanisms, significantly mitigates these negative effects, thereby enhancing the model's generalization capability in complex scenarios.

Visualization of Varied Representations for OPFD. To comprehensively validate the effectiveness of GANHS in addressing the class overlap problem caused by the concealment of fraudulent activities in OPFD, t-SNE is employed for visualization analysis. Figure 4.5 illustrates the data distributions generated by various baseline methods, where red, blue, and yellow points represent legitimate transactions, fraudulent transactions, and synthetic samples, respectively. As shown in Fig. 4.5a, ROS

Table 4.1 OPFD performance of ten methods when SVC Is used as a base classifier

Train	Test	Criteria	ROS	SMOTE	ADASYN	SMEN	ADEN	SMTL	NUS	RGAN	WGAN	GANHS
Jan.	Feb.	F_1	0.7359	0.7414	0.6849	0.7518	0.6567	0.7445	0.6976	0.6830	0.7249	**0.7555**
		G_m	0.9188	0.9209	0.8978	0.9246	0.8846	0.9219	0.9033	0.8892	0.9179	**0.9258**
Feb.	Mar.	F_1	0.7372	0.7363	0.6949	0.7468	0.6915	0.7383	0.6890	0.7454	0.7447	**0.7605**
		G_m	0.9248	0.9241	0.9070	0.9281	0.9054	0.9249	0.9043	0.9276	0.9273	**0.9331**
Mar.	Apr.	F_1	0.7871	0.7883	0.6172	0.7906	0.6196	0.7901	0.7682	0.7000	0.7891	**0.7907**
		G_m	0.9228	0.9231	0.8568	0.9234	0.8584	0.9235	0.9145	0.9177	0.9229	**0.9237**
Apr.	May.	F_1	0.7363	0.7368	0.7355	0.7375	0.7356	0.7364	0.7371	**0.8165**	0.7458	0.7696
		G_m	0.9209	0.9211	0.9208	0.9213	0.9206	0.9210	0.9212	0.9130	0.9197	**0.9308**
May.	Jun.	F_1	0.7353	0.7374	0.7360	0.7403	0.7381	0.7407	0.7361	**0.8017**	0.7990	0.7983
		G_m	0.9204	0.9182	0.9224	0.9190	0.9225	0.9191	0.9183	0.9048	0.9037	**0.9318**
A_v		F_1	0.7464	0.7480	0.6937	0.7534	0.6883	0.7500	0.7256	0.7653	0.7627	**0.7749**
		G_m	0.9215	0.9215	0.9010	0.9233	0.8983	0.9221	0.9123	0.9116	0.9183	**0.9268**
A_r		F_1	7.0000	5.8000	9.0000	3.0000	8.6000	4.4000	7.6000	4.2000	3.8000	**1.6000**
		G_m	5.6000	5.6000	7.2000	3.0000	7.6000	4.0000	7.0000	7.0000	7.0000	**1.0000**

Table 4.2 OPFD performance of ten methods when RF is used as a base classifier

Train	Test	Criteria	ROS	SMOTE	ADASYN	SMEN	ADEN	SMTL	NUS	RGAN	WGAN	GANHS
Jan.	Feb.	F_1	0.8428	0.8214	0.7763	**0.8431**	0.7941	0.8198	0.7612	0.8183	0.8111	0.8384
		G_m	0.9296	0.9492	0.9453	0.9371	0.9449	0.9494	0.9409	0.9521	**0.9622**	0.9576
Feb.	Mar.	F_1	0.8167	0.8108	0.8090	0.8107	0.8028	0.8200	0.8198	0.8124	0.8057	**0.8211**
		G_m	0.9201	0.9211	0.9284	0.9086	0.9174	0.9282	0.9609	0.9592	0.9573	**0.9694**
Mar.	Apr.	F_1	0.7561	0.7658	0.7745	0.7765	0.8011	0.8006	**0.8541**	0.7601	0.7476	0.7821
		G_m	0.7945	0.8608	0.8226	0.8294	0.8837	0.8349	0.9085	0.8941	0.8841	**0.9097**
Apr.	May.	F_1	0.8986	0.8654	0.8870	0.8962	0.8483	0.8709	0.8814	0.9109	0.8792	**0.9191**
		G_m	0.9777	0.9753	0.9686	0.9701	0.9694	0.9771	0.9666	0.9678	0.9542	**0.9785**
May.	Jun.	F_1	0.9081	0.9112	0.9043	0.9061	0.8843	**0.9161**	0.8853	0.9002	0.8955	0.9096
		G_m	0.9806	0.9750	0.9764	0.9554	0.9791	0.9774	0.9696	0.9752	0.9701	**0.9813**
A_v		F_1	0.8445	0.8349	0.8302	0.8465	0.8261	0.8455	0.8404	0.8404	0.8278	**0.8541**
		G_m	0.9205	0.9363	0.9283	0.9201	0.9389	0.9334	0.9493	0.9497	0.9456	**0.9593**
A_r		F_1	4.4000	5.6000	6.8000	4.4000	8.0000	3.8000	5.8000	5.6000	8.2000	**2.4000**
		G_m	6.4000	5.8000	6.4000	8.4000	6.0000	4.8000	6.0000	4.6000	5.4000	**1.2000**

Table 4.3 OPFD performance of ten methods when MLP is used as a base classifier

Train	Test	Criteria	ROS	SMOTE	ADASYN	SMEN	ADEN	SMTL	NUS	RGAN	WGAN	GANHS
Jan.	Feb.	F_1	0.8434	0.8552	0.7644	0.8445	0.8018	0.8522	0.8053	0.8601	0.8421	**0.8673**
		G_m	0.9510	0.9517	0.9301	0.9501	0.9409	0.9520	0.9411	**0.9586**	0.9221	0.9528
Feb.	Mar.	F_1	0.6897	0.8657	0.8185	0.8638	0.8310	**0.8663**	0.8211	0.8436	0.8225	0.8425
		G_m	**0.9649**	0.9647	0.9508	0.9642	0.9544	0.9648	0.9526	0.9425	0.9093	0.9314
Mar.	Apr.	F_1	0.8444	0.8429	0.8436	0.8428	0.8453	0.8440	0.8106	0.8558	0.8402	**0.8757**
		G_m	0.9167	0.9168	0.9190	0.9186	0.9192	0.9169	0.9183	0.9417	0.9095	**0.9485**
Apr.	May.	F_1	0.8362	0.8355	0.7849	0.8239	0.7734	0.8307	0.7608	**0.8797**	0.8490	0.8793
		G_m	0.9517	0.9515	0.9387	0.9488	0.9353	0.9512	0.9298	0.9323	0.9343	**0.9524**
May.	Jun.	F_1	0.8841	0.8943	0.7914	0.8831	0.7562	0.8954	0.7467	0.8958	0.8562	**0.8969**
		G_m	0.9615	0.9620	0.9412	0.9603	0.9292	**0.9624**	0.9246	0.9478	0.9413	0.9501
A_v		F_1	0.8196	0.8587	0.8005	0.8516	0.8016	0.8577	0.7889	0.8670	0.8420	**0.8723**
		G_m	0.9491	0.9494	0.9360	0.9484	0.9358	**0.9495**	0.9333	0.9446	0.9223	0.9470
A_r		F_1	5.8000	4.2000	8.2000	5.8000	7.2000	3.8000	9.2000	2.2000	6.6000	**2.0000**
		G_m	4.0000	4.0000	6.8000	4.8000	6.4000	**3.4000**	7.8000	5.2000	9.0000	3.6000

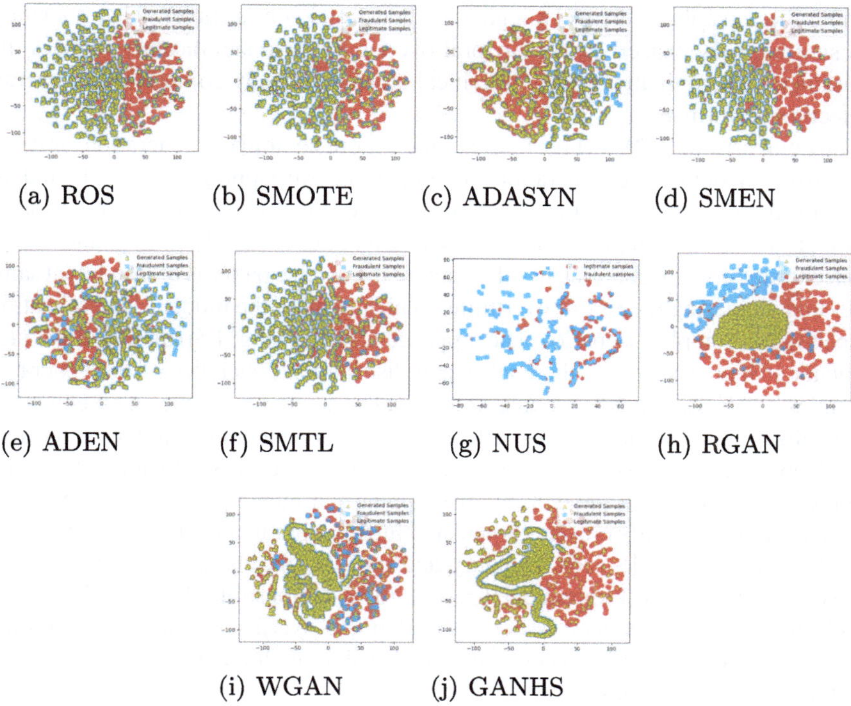

Fig. 4.5 Explorative visualization of diverse OPFD representations. It illustrates the spatial distribution of synthetic samples (yellow dots), legitimate samples (red dots), and fraudulent samples (blue dots). Each subplot corresponds to a specific generation method

balances the dataset by replicating minority-class samples. While this enhances the representation of fraudulent transactions, the simple replication mechanism tends to cause model overfitting, disproportionately amplifies the importance of minority features, and weakens the model's generalization capability. In contrast, SMOTE and ADASYN (Fig. 4.5b and c) generate synthetic samples through interpolation, causing yellow points to cluster closely around original minority-class samples. Although this increases the sample size, the limited diversity of synthetic samples restricts generalization ability and raises the risk of overfitting.

Regarding NUS (Fig. 4.5g), the majority-class samples are downsampled to balance the distribution. However, the scattered red points indicate that NUS discards critical feature information as a consequence of majority downsampling, thereby weakening the classifier's ability to distinguish between legitimate and fraudulent transactions. Hybrid data balancing methods, such as SMEN, ADEN, and SMTL (Fig. 4.5d, e, and f), as well as some GAN-based methods like WGAN (Fig. 4.5i), more closely approximate the original distribution by generating synthetic samples. Nevertheless, these methods still exhibit significant limitations: the synthetic samples tend to drift toward overlapping regions near the decision boundary, thereby diminishing the separability between legitimate and fraudulent samples. This boundary erosion not only exacerbates behavioral overlap but also significantly reduces the classifier's discriminative ability in critical areas, ultimately compromising overall detection performance.

In comparison, RGAN (Fig. 4.5h) adopts a more centralized generation strategy, effectively avoiding the generation of samples in overlapping decision boundary regions, thereby enhancing the separability between legitimate and fraudulent samples. However, the samples generated by RGAN have relatively limited and overly concentrated coverage, failing to fully capture the diverse patterns of fraudulent samples and increasing the risk of overfitting, which reduces the model's generalization capability in complex scenarios. The proposed GANHS (Fig. 4.5j) demonstrates significant advantages in both the quality and distribution coherence of the generated samples. GANHS not only produces high-quality synthetic samples with enhanced generalization capability but also effectively avoids generating samples in critical overlapping areas between legitimate and fraudulent samples. Notably, almost no yellow points appear in the densely overlapping red-blue regions. This generation mechanism successfully prevents boundary blurring, significantly reduces behavioral overlap, sharpens the decision boundary, and enhances the classifier's discriminative power in key regions. Experimental results fully demonstrate that GANHS effectively mitigates the common issues of overlap and overfitting found in traditional methods while maintaining a coherent data distribution, thereby achieving superior performance in OPFD tasks.

Parameter Sensitivity. To further validate the robustness and generalization ability of the proposed method, a sensitivity analysis is conducted on two key hyperparameters: the number of hidden layers n_l in BBAGAN, and the neighborhood size k in ANCS. The former directly influences the expressive capacity of the generator and discriminator, determining the model's ability to fit complex fraud patterns. The latter controls the granularity of local structure characterization during cleaning, playing a critical role in balancing the sample distribution while preserving feature diversity.

The results are summarized in Tables 4.4 and 4.5. Overall, the performance of the GANHS model remains relatively stable when the number of hidden layers n_l is within the reasonable range of 2 to 5. Similarly, the model demonstrates robust performance for k values of 4, 5, 6, or 7. Specifically, as shown in Table 4.4, a four-layer network architecture achieves the optimal trade-off between model performance and complexity, yielding an F_1 of 0.8211 and a G_m of 0.9694. Regarding

Table 4.4 Sensitivity of the value of k

k	F_1	G_m
4	0.8174	0.9690
5	0.8205	0.9653
6	**0.8211**	**0.9694**
7	0.8183	0.9647

Table 4.5 Sensitivity of the value of n_l

n_l	F_1	G_m
2	0.7983	0.9565
3	0.8187	0.9604
4	**0.8211**	**0.9694**
5	0.8183	0.9647

the neighborhood size, $k = 6$ delivers the best performance across multiple datasets, indicating that this configuration effectively captures crucial local information while suppressing interference from noise and redundant samples. Based on these findings, a four-layer BBAGAN with a neighborhood size of $k = 6$ is recommended as the default configuration for GANHS. This combination achieves excellent classification performance while maintaining computational efficiency, further verifying the stability and practicality of GANHS under hyperparameter variations. It provides a reliable foundation for deploying the model in OPFD.

Ablation Study. This chapter presents the proposed GANHS method, which is designed to mitigate the behavioral overlap problem in OPFD. It integrates two complementary mechanisms: (1) data augmentation for fraudulent samples via BBAGAN to enhance the separability of fraudulent behavior patterns, and (2) data cleaning for legitimate samples via ANCS to reduce noise introduced by redundant non-fraud samples. To systematically evaluate the individual and synergistic effects of each module, an ablation study is conducted on a real transaction dataset, with the results summarized in Table 4.6, where A_0 represents the baseline GAN-based generation method, A_1 denotes the configuration using only BBAGAN, and A_2 denotes the configuration using only ANCS. All experiments employ logistic regression as the unified classifier.

Table 4.6 Ablation study

Train	Test	Criteria	A_0	A_1	A_2	$A_1 + A_2$
Jan.	Feb.	F_1	0.8134	0.8463	0.8379	**0.8484**
		G_m	0.9319	0.9492	0.9512	**0.9552**
Feb.	Mar.	F_1	0.8086	**0.8425**	0.8230	0.8299
		G_m	0.9131	**0.9571**	0.9535	0.9565
Mar.	Apr.	F_1	0.7252	0.7795	0.7537	**0.8086**
		G_m	0.8661	0.8803	0.8731	**0.8984**
Apr.	May.	F_1	0.8615	0.8914	0.9202	**0.9210**
		G_m	0.9349	0.9794	0.9556	**0.9814**
May.	Jun.	F_1	0.8775	0.8941	0.8852	**0.9087**
		G_m	0.9505	0.9793	0.9801	**0.9803**

Table 4.6 demonstrates that both A_1 and A_2 significantly outperform the baseline model A_0 when used independently. Specifically, BBAGAN improves the separability between fraudulent and legitimate samples through data augmentation, thereby alleviating the distribution shift caused by behavioral overlap. ANCS, in contrast, refines the decision boundary by removing redundant legitimate samples via data cleaning, thereby enhancing the robustness of the OPFD model. These findings indicate that both data augmentation and data cleaning independently contribute substantial improvements to model performance. When combined, they maintain a well-balanced data distribution and effectively suppress both behavioral overlap and overfitting, ultimately strengthening the classifier's discriminative capability near the decision boundary.

Experiments on Imbalanced Classification Datasets. To systematically evaluate the generalization capability of the proposed method across diverse application scenarios, this study conducts experiments on five widely used UCI benchmark datasets with highly imbalanced class distributions. The results are systematically compared with nine state-of-the-art class imbalance learning methods. To ensure fairness and comparability, all methods are evaluated using three mainstream base classifiers: SVC, RF, and MLP. The experimental results are detailed in Tables 4.7, 4.8 and 4.9, with the best results highlighted in bold. Overall, the proposed GANHS method demonstrates strong robustness and competitiveness across different classifiers and datasets.

As shown in Table 4.7, which reports the comparative performance of ten methods with SVC as the base classifier, GANHS obtains the best F_1 on four out of the six datasets, yielding average improvements of 1.4% and 6.1% over the second-best and worst-performing methods, respectively. For G_m, GANHS also outperforms all its peers on four datasets, achieving average improvements of 0.8% and 6.6%. Furthermore, GANHS attains the best $A_r$ing on both metrics, demonstrating its exceptional robustness and wide applicability in hyperplane-based classification tasks.

Table 4.8 reports the results with RF as the base classifier. GANHS achieves superior performance on most datasets, with average improvements in F_1 and G_m of 1.0% and 0.9% over the second-best method, and 1.9% and 2.7% over the worst-performing method, respectively. It also ranks first in $A_r$ing of both evaluation metrics, highlighting its strong generalization capability and significant advantages in tree-based and ensemble learning frameworks.

The results with MLP as the base classifier are presented in Table 4.9. GANHS achieves the best F_1 on four of the six datasets, with average improvements of 0.9% and 7.4% over the second-best and worst-performing methods. For the G_m metric, GANHS also achieves the best performance on four datasets, with average improvements of 1.0% and 7.0%. Additionally, GANHS ranks first in the $A_r$ings of both metrics, further confirming its consistent superiority in neural network-based models.

Table 4.7 Imbalanced classification performance of ten methods when SVC is used as a base classifier

data	Criteria	ROS	SMOTE	ADASYN	SMEN	ADEN	SMTL	NUS	RGAN	WGAN	GANHS
cmc_data	F_1	0.4531	0.4611	0.4644	0.4482	0.4516	0.4595	0.4359	0.4041	0.4534	**0.4826**
	G_m	0.6476	0.6548	0.6580	0.6419	0.6460	0.6535	0.6313	0.6015	0.6473	**0.6742**
abalone_data	F_1	0.1024	0.0940	0.0819	0.0867	0.0767	0.0841	0.0375	0.0814	0.0778	**0.1290**
	G_m	0.8952	**0.9149**	0.9003	0.9066	0.8925	0.9033	0.7452	0.8473	0.8942	0.8927
adult_data	F_1	0.5608	0.5598	0.5674	0.5610	0.5519	0.5575	0.5392	0.5967	0.6014	**0.6016**
	G_m	0.7274	0.7264	0.7318	0.7270	0.7196	0.7246	0.7083	0.7321	0.7348	**0.7492**
gmean_data	F_1	0.5862	0.5953	0.6038	0.5887	0.5973	0.5804	0.5351	0.6063	0.5953	**0.6120**
	G_m	0.7023	0.7094	0.7131	0.7046	0.7112	0.6976	0.6565	0.7148	0.7094	**0.7209**
heart_data	F_1	0.6437	0.6736	0.6444	0.6476	0.6882	0.6279	0.6531	0.6593	**0.7102**	0.6803
	G_m	0.6902	0.7071	0.6879	0.6609	**0.7226**	0.6778	0.6831	0.6997	0.7173	0.7167
A_v	F_1	0.4692	0.4768	0.4724	0.4664	0.4731	0.4619	0.4402	0.4696	0.4876	**0.5011**
	G_m	0.7325	0.7425	0.7382	0.7282	0.7384	0.7314	0.6849	0.7191	0.7406	**0.7507**
A_r	F_1	6.2000	4.4000	4.6000	6.2000	6.2000	7.2000	9.0000	5.4000	4.4000	**1.4000**
	G_m	5.8000	4.0000	4.0000	6.6000	5.8000	6.6000	9.4000	5.8000	4.4000	**2.6000**

Table 4.8 Imbalanced classification performance of ten methods when RF is used as a base classifier

data	Criteria	ROS	SMOTE	ADASYN	SMEN	ADEN	SMTL	NUS	RGAN	WGAN	GANHS
cmc_data	F_1	0.4075	0.4134	0.4124	0.4013	0.4106	0.4142	0.4164	0.4141	0.4104	**0.4248**
	G_m	0.5803	0.6059	0.6092	0.5915	0.6041	0.6027	0.6134	0.6093	0.5616	**0.6186**
abalone_data	F_1	0.0592	0.0789	0.0738	0.0769	0.0708	0.0803	0.0447	0.0814	0.0600	**0.0828**
	G_m	0.7614	0.8446	0.8381	0.8421	0.8391	0.8411	0.7699	0.8373	0.8147	**0.8489**
adult_data	F_1	0.6946	0.6933	0.6889	0.7010	0.6825	0.6921	0.7021	0.6902	0.7111	**0.7125**
	G_m	0.8311	0.8290	0.8263	0.8297	0.8218	0.8304	0.8314	0.8249	0.8317	**0.8321**
gmean_data	F_1	**0.6209**	0.6059	0.6133	0.6095	0.6168	0.6018	0.6067	0.6076	0.6182	0.6134
	G_m	**0.7314**	0.7069	0.7251	0.7191	0.7271	0.7034	0.7183	0.7171	0.7265	0.7231
heart_data	F_1	0.8654	0.8478	0.8514	0.8247	0.8454	0.8659	0.8602	0.8627	0.8600	**0.8776**
	G_m	0.8750	0.8630	0.8640	0.8416	0.8604	0.8792	0.8740	0.8768	0.8726	**0.8896**
A_v	F_1	0.5295	0.5279	0.5280	0.5227	0.5252	0.5309	0.5260	0.5312	0.5319	**0.5422**
	G_m	0.7558	0.7699	0.7725	0.7648	0.7705	0.7714	0.7614	0.7731	0.7614	**0.7825**
A_r	F_1	5.4000	6.4000	6.6000	7.0000	7.2000	5.0000	5.6000	5.0000	5.2000	**1.6000**
	G_m	5.6000	6.2000	5.8000	6.6000	6.4000	5.6000	5.2000	6.0000	5.8000	**1.8000**

Table 4.9 Imbalanced classification performance of ten methods when MLP is used as a base classifier

data	Criteria	ROS	SMOTE	ADASYN	SMEN	ADEN	SMTL	NUS	RGAN	WGAN	GANHS
cmc_data	F_1	0.4655	0.4646	0.4604	0.4489	0.4493	0.4599	0.4624	0.4620	0.4623	**0.4756**
	G_m	0.6589	0.6580	0.6534	0.6438	0.6435	0.6537	0.6530	0.6552	0.6558	**0.6605**
abalone_data	F_1	0.0701	0.0878	0.0783	0.0996	0.0739	0.0902	0.0814	0.1011	0.0968	**0.1171**
	G_m	0.8578	0.8819	0.8704	0.8930	0.8640	0.8845	0.8946	0.8894	0.8616	**0.9051**
adult_data	F_1	**0.6714**	0.6678	0.6236	0.6591	0.6605	0.6641	0.6279	0.6558	0.6517	0.6597
	G_m	**0.8154**	0.8111	0.7766	0.8069	0.8077	0.8100	0.7806	0.8004	0.8012	0.8050
gmean_data	F_1	0.5793	0.5985	0.5583	0.5645	0.6115	0.6089	0.5587	0.6070	0.6047	**0.6142**
	G_m	0.6964	0.7124	0.6788	0.6801	0.7113	0.7193	0.6731	0.7162	0.7173	**0.7211**
heart_data	F_1	0.8776	0.8659	0.8687	0.8511	0.7384	0.8979	0.8866	0.8776	0.5773	**0.8980**
	G_m	0.8896	0.8792	0.8811	0.8660	0.7637	0.9082	0.8978	0.8896	0.6157	**0.9083**
A_v	F_1	0.5328	0.5369	0.5179	0.5246	0.5067	0.5442	0.5234	0.5407	0.4786	**0.5529**
	G_m	0.7836	0.7885	0.7721	0.7780	0.7580	0.7904	0.7798	0.7902	0.7303	**0.8000**
A_r	F_1	4.8000	4.8000	8.2000	7.0000	6.6000	4.2000	6.4000	4.8000	6.4000	**1.8000**
	G_m	4.6000	4.6000	7.8000	6.6000	7.4000	4.2000	6.2000	5.0000	6.6000	**2.0000**

4.6 Summary

This chapter introduces a GAN-based Hybrid Sampling (GANHS) framework to address behavioral overlap in OPFD. Building on Chap. 3, it integrates BBAGAN-based data augmentation with ANCS-based data cleaning to directly mitigate the behavioral overlap problem. Specifically, by generating high-fidelity minority-class samples, BBAGAN enhances the coverage of fraudulent behavior patterns and reduces the behavioral overlap between synthetic and legitimate samples. Meanwhile, ANCS performs selective cleaning in regions with high overlap, thereby significantly suppressing behavioral overlap in the augmented dataset and optimizing the decision boundary. Experimental results validate that the proposed framework significantly outperforms baseline methods in accuracy, robustness, and interpretability. However, the fundamental limitation of such sampling-based approaches lies in their reliance on synthetic samples, which struggle to capture the dynamically evolving temporal patterns in real transactions. This inherent constraint limits the model's generalizability against complex, adaptive fraud strategies. To address this limitation, the next chapter will adopt a representation learning approach, aiming to extract more discriminative temporal features directly from user behavioral sequences.

References

1. Bai, L., Ju, T., Wang, H., Lei, M., Pan, X.: Two-step ensemble under-sampling algorithm for massive imbalanced data classification. Information Sciences **665**, 120351 (2024)
2. Cao, J., Qian, C., Huang, Y., Chen, D., Gao, Y., Dong, J., Guo, D., Qu, X.: A dynamics theory of RMSProp-based implicit regularization in deep low-rank matrix factorization. IEEE Trans. on Neural Networks and Learning Systems **36**(10), 18750–18764 (2025)
3. Chawla, N.V., Bowyer, K.W., Hall, L.O., Kegelmeyer, W.P.: SMOTE: synthetic minority over-sampling technique. Journal of Artificial Intelligence Research **16**, 321–357 (2002)
4. Chen, G., Lu, H., Di, D., Li, L., Emam, M., Jing, W.: StfMLP: Spatiotemporal fusion multilayer perceptron for remote-sensing images. IEEE Geoscience and Remote Sensing Letters **20**, 1–5 (2023)
5. Chen, W., Yu, Z., Yang, K., Fan, Z., Chen, C.L.P.: Adaptive weighted double uncertainty incrementally active learning for multi-class imbalanced data. IEEE Trans. on Knowledge and Data Engineering pp. 1–16 (2025)
6. Ding, D., Wang, Y., Tao, H., Wu, J., Cao, J.: A dual-discriminator generative adversarial network for anomaly detection. IEEE Trans. on Neural Networks and Learning Systems **36**, 19285–19296 (2025)
7. Ding, H., Sun, Y., Wang, Z., Huang, N., Shen, Z., Cui, X.: RGAN-EL: A GAN and ensemble learning-based hybrid approach for imbalanced data classification. Information Processing & Management **60**(2), 103235 (2023)
8. Gong, L., Zhang, H., Zhang, J., Wei, M., Huang, Z.: A comprehensive investigation of the impact of class overlap on software defect prediction. IEEE Trans. on Software Engineering **49**(4), 2440–2458 (2022)
9. Goyal, S.: Handling class-imbalance with KNN (neighbourhood) under-sampling for software defect prediction. Artificial Intelligence Review **55**(3), 2023–2064 (2022)

10. Han, S., Zhu, K., Zhou, M., Cai, X.: Information-utilization-method-assisted multimodal multiobjective optimization and application to credit card fraud detection. IEEE Trans. on Computational Social Systems **8**(4), 856–869 (2021)
11. He, H., Bai, Y., Garcia, E.A., Li, S.: ADASYN: Adaptive synthetic sampling approach for imbalanced learning. In: 2008 IEEE International Joint Conference on Neural Networks (IEEE World Congress on Computational Intelligence). pp. 1322–1328 (2008)
12. Jiang, Z., Zhao, L., Lu, Y., Zhan, Y., Mao, Q.: A semi-supervised resampling method for class-imbalanced learning. Expert Systems with Applications **221**, 119733 (2023)
13. Kumar, V., Paul, K.: Device fingerprinting for cyber-physical systems: A survey. ACM Computing Surveys **55**(14s), 1–41 (2023)
14. Li, W., Chen, J., Cao, J., Ma, C., Wang, J., Cui, X., Chen, P.: EID-GAN: Generative adversarial nets for extremely imbalanced data augmentation. IEEE Trans. on Industrial Informatics **19**(3), 3208–3218 (2023)
15. Liang, S., Lahiri, A., Ravishankar, S.: Adaptive local neighborhood-based neural networks for mr image reconstruction from undersampled data. IEEE Trans. on Computational Imaging **10**, 1235–1249 (2024)
16. Liu, Y., Li, C., Yu, H., Song, C.: NT-ARS-RRT: A novel non-threshold adaptive region sampling rrt algorithm for path planning. Journal of King Saud University-Computer and Information Sciences **35**(9), 101753 (2023)
17. Lu, X.S., Zhou, M., Qi, L., Liu, H.: Clustering-algorithm-based rare-event evolution analysis via social media data. IEEE Trans. on Computational Social Systems **6**(2), 301–310 (2019)
18. Ma, H., Liu, D., Wu, F.: Rectified wasserstein generative adversarial networks for perceptual image restoration. IEEE Trans. on Pattern Analysis and Machine Intelligence **45**(3), 3648–3663 (2022)
19. Miaretsoa, L., Cascella, A., Vadàla, L., Valente, D., De Gregorio, C., Torti, V., Norscia, I., Ratsimbazafy, J., Friard, O., Giacoma, C., et al.: Marking versus overmarking: spatial and behavioral patterns of scent marking in wild diademed sifaka (propithecus diadema). International Journal of Primatology **43**(4), 611–635 (2022)
20. Ning, Q., Zhao, X., Ma, Z.: A novel method for identification of glutarylation sites combining borderline-SMOTE with tomek links technique in imbalanced data. IEEE/ACM Trans. on Computational Biology and Bioinformatics **19**(5), 2632–2641 (2021)
21. Qian, M., Li, Y.F.: A novel adaptive undersampling framework for class-imbalance fault detection. IEEE Trans. on Reliability **72**(3), 1003–1017 (2022)
22. Ren, J., Wang, Y., Mao, M., Cheung, Y.m.: Equalization ensemble for large scale highly imbalanced data classification. Knowledge-Based Systems **242**, 108295 (2022)
23. Santos, M.S., Abreu, P.H., Japkowicz, N., Fernández, A., Soares, C., Wilk, S., Santos, J.: On the joint-effect of class imbalance and overlap: a critical review. Artificial Intelligence Review **55**(8), 6207–6275 (2022)
24. Sun, J., Li, H., Fujita, H., Fu, B., Ai, W.: Class-imbalanced dynamic financial distress prediction based on adaboost-SVM ensemble combined with SMOTE and time weighting. Information Fusion **54**, 128–144 (2020)
25. Tajmirriahi, M., Kafieh, R., Amini, Z., Lakshminarayanan, V.: A dual-discriminator fourier acquisitive GAN for generating retinal optical coherence tomography images. IEEE Trans. on Instrumentation and Measurement **71**, 1–8 (2022)
26. Tao, L., Wang, Q., Yu, F., Cao, H., Liang, Y., Luo, H., Guo, J.: Newton cooling theorem-based local overlapping regions cleaning and oversampling techniques for imbalanced datasets. Neurocomputing **616**, 128959 (2025)
27. Wang, C., Chai, S., Zhu, H., Jiang, C.: CAeSaR: An online Payment Anti-Fraud Integration System With Decision Explainability. IEEE Trans. on Dependable and Secure Computing **20**(3), 2565–2577 (2023)
28. Wang, C., Wang, C., Zhu, H., Cui, J.: LAW: Learning automatic windows for online payment fraud detection. IEEE Trans. on Dependable and Secure Computing **18**(5), 2122–2135 (2021)
29. Xie, Y., Hong, Y., Qiao, S., Yao, J., Liu, G., Pang, S.: A time-aware generative network for enhancing transaction security in consumer electronics. IEEE Trans. on Consumer Electronics **71**(2), 6818–6828 (2025)

30. Xie, Y., Liu, G., Yan, C., Jiang, C., Zhou, M.: Time-aware attention-based gated network for credit card fraud detection by extracting transactional behaviors. IEEE Trans. on Computational Social Systems **10**(3), 1004–1016 (2023)
31. Xie, Y., Liu, G., Yan, C., Jiang, C., Zhou, M., Li, M.: Learning transactional behavioral representations for credit card fraud detection. IEEE Trans. on Neural Networks and Learning Systems **35**(4), 5735–5748 (2024)
32. Xie, Y., Liu, G., Zhou, M., Wei, L., Zhu, H., Zhou, R., Cao, L.: A spatial–temporal gated network for credit card fraud detection by learning transactional representations. IEEE Trans. on Automation Science and Engineering **21**(4), 6978–6991 (2024)
33. Xie, Y., Shan, J., Wei, L., Yao, J., Zhou, M.: GAN-based hybrid sampling method for transaction fraud detection. IEEE Trans. on Knowledge and Data Engineering **37**(10), 5905–5918 (2025)
34. Xie, Y., Zhou, M., Liu, G., Wei, L., Zhu, H., De Meo, P.: A transactional-behavior-based hierarchical gated network for credit card fraud detection. IEEE/CAA Journal of Automatica Sinica **12**(7), 1489–1503 (2025)
35. Yang, Y., Sun, Y., Li, F., Guan, B., Liu, J.X., Shang, J.: MGCNRF: Prediction of disease-related mirnas based on multiple graph convolutional networks and random forest. IEEE Trans. on Neural Networks and Learning Systems **35**(11), 15701–15709 (2024)
36. Zhang, J., Lai, Z., Kong, H., Shen, L.: Robust twin bounded support vector classifier with manifold regularization. IEEE Trans. on Cybernetics **53**(8), 5135–5150 (2023)
37. Zhang, T., Zhou, M., Guo, X., Qi, L., Abusorrah, A.: A density-center-based automatic clustering algorithm for IoT data analysis. IEEE Internet of Things Journal **9**(24), 24682–24694 (2022)
38. Zheng, Z., Cai, Y., Li, Y.: Oversampling method for imbalanced classification. Computing and Informatics **34**(5), 1017–1037 (2015)
39. Zhu, H., Zhou, M., Liu, G., Xie, Y., Liu, S., Guo, C.: NUS: Noisy-sample-removed undersampling scheme for imbalanced classification and application to credit card fraud detection. IEEE Trans. on Computational Social Systems **11**(2), 1793–1804 (2023)
40. Zhu, T., Liu, X., Zhu, E.: Oversampling with reliably expanding minority class regions for imbalanced data learning. IEEE Trans. on Knowledge and Data Engineering **35**(6), 6167–6181 (2023)
41. Zhu, Y., Jia, C., Li, F., Song, J.: Inspector: a lysine succinylation predictor based on edited nearest-neighbor undersampling and adaptive synthetic oversampling. Analytical Biochemistry **593**, 113592 (2020)

Chapter 5
Learning Fraud-Sensitive Transactional Representations via Attention and Temporal Modeling

In OPFD, sampling methods can, to some extent, enhance the feature representation of fraudulent samples, but synthetic samples often fail to fully capture the dynamically evolving temporal patterns present in real-world transaction scenarios [19]. This limitation constrains the generalization ability of models to adapt to complex and ever-changing fraudulent strategies. To address these limitations, this chapter investigates a modeling approach that integrates time-aware gating networks and attention mechanisms. Specifically, two time-aware gates are incorporated into each RNN unit, and they are dedicated to learning users' long-term and short-term transactional habits, respectively. Subsequently, a time-aware attention module is proposed to extract user behavioral information from consecutive historical transactions by explicitly taking temporal intervals into account. This design enables the model to effectively capture underlying behavioral motivations and periodic characteristics. Finally, an interaction module is designed to learn more comprehensive and semantically meaningful representations. To verify the effectiveness of the proposed method, experiments are conducted on both a large-scale real transaction dataset and a public one. The results demonstrate that our method effectively distinguish online fraudulent payments from legitimate ones and significantly improve OPFD performance across multiple evaluation metrics.

5.1 Temporal Regularity of User Behavior

In recent years, online payment fraud has continued to rise, with attack methods becoming increasingly sophisticated [12, 17]. Transactions that were once isolated and unauthorized now form complex attack workflows that integrate multiple technologies and stages. Fraudsters not only steal users' sensitive information through malware, phishing sites, and man-in-the-middle attacks, but also deploy automated

Y. Xie et al., *Neural Network-Based Deep Learning for Online Payment Fraud Detection*,
https://doi.org/10.1007/978-981-95-8513-7_5

scripts to launch large-scale credential-stuffing and password-cracking attacks [29, 30]. These techniques aim to gain unauthorized account access and support more covert and persistent fraudulent activities. Most existing studies focus on detecting fraud based on static features of individual transactions. Although such methods provide real-time risk assessment, they struggle to capture the dynamic evolution of user behavior over time [4, 8]. In contrast, users' historical transaction sequences contain rich temporal signals. Long-term spending preferences reflect stable behavioral patterns, while short-term fluctuations and abnormal deviations indicate potential fraud risks. Periodic factors, such as transaction intervals, also play an important role in fraud detection. Effectively modeling this multi-scale temporal information helps reveal hidden fraud patterns and is essential for improving detection accuracy and model generalization.

The Limitations of Static Features. In OPFD, the commonly used features are mainly categorized into two types. The first consists of the raw attributes of individual transactions, i.e., transaction amount, merchant ID, terminal type, and account balance. The second comprises time-window-based statistics, including aggregated features such as mean, frequency, and variance computed over predefined periods [17, 27]. These features are widely adopted in practical systems because they are computationally simple and easy to deploy. However, from the perspective of representational expressiveness, they possess inherent limitations that are difficult to overcome. Firstly, these features typically take individual transactions or aggregated snapshots within fixed time windows as the basic modeling units, lacking the ability to characterize sequential structure and temporal dependencies [13, 22]. Consequently, they struggle to capture potential abnormal patterns during the evolution of user behavior. For instance, when a user makes a sudden high-value transaction after multiple low-value purchases, static or aggregated features often fail to effectively reveal its abnormality. Secondly, fraudsters can disguise fraudulent activities by simulating the local statistical patterns of legitimate users, thereby significantly undermining the discriminative power of the model [16, 31]. When confronted with disguised transactions, detection methods based on static features tend to exhibit increased false positive and false negative rates. Therefore, relying solely on static features or time-window aggregated features not only makes it difficult to fully mine the rich dynamic information contained in transaction sequences but also forms a critical bottleneck restricting the improvement of model detection accuracy and robustness.

The Differentiation and Roles of Temporal Behavioral Components. In OPFD, a detailed analysis of the temporal features embedded within users' transaction sequences is essential for improving detection accuracy. These behavioral patterns can be decomposed into three complementary temporal components: long-term stable preferences, short-term situational fluctuations, and transaction-interval information. Long-term preferences reflect users' habitual spending behaviors over extended periods, including preferred spending categories, frequently visited merchants, and typical transaction time slots. These patterns provide valuable prior information and help identify transactions that deviate from long-term behavioral norms [1, 7]. In contrast, short-term fluctuations capture short-lived spending behaviors influenced by recent contextual factors, such as holiday shopping or cross-border payments during business travel [19, 23]. These highly dynamic patterns strongly influence the model's ability to assess the real-time plausibility of ongoing transactions. Transaction-interval information describes the temporal density or sparsity of adjacent transactions. Variations in transaction intervals often carry meaningful behavioral implications. Multiple local transactions occurring in a short interval often reflect a reasonable continuity, whereas cross-border or high-value transactions within a short interval are more likely to indicate abnormal risks [1, 24]. Conversely, long intervals between transactions may suggest substantial changes in the user's behavioral context, in which case historical behaviors contribute less to evaluating the current transaction.

In OPFD, the three temporal components—long-term stable preferences, short-term situational fluctuations, and transaction-interval information—play distinct yet complementary roles. Long-term patterns provide global and stable prior knowledge; short-term patterns improve real-time discrimination; and transaction-interval information modulates the influence of historical behaviors on current decisions [32]. Achieving high-precision fraud detection with a low false-alarm rate requires both a clear distinction among these components and a unified modeling strategy [28]. By applying advanced feature engineering techniques, integrating the strengths of diverse model architectures, developing unsupervised anomaly detection methods, and fusing multi-source heterogeneous data, it becomes possible to better capture dynamic changes in transactional behaviors. These approaches enhance the model's ability to identify abnormal patterns, thereby improving the accuracy and robustness of OPFD.

5.2 Dual Time-Aware Gating Mechanism for Modeling Long-Term and Short-Term Habits

Modeling Motivation. Users' transactional behaviors form time-sensitive and complex sequential patterns that vary significantly across temporal scales. Legitimate users tend to maintain stable long-term spending preferences, reflected by repeated interactions with specific merchants or within certain categories, while their short-term behaviors may shift due to holidays, travel, or temporary needs. In contrast, fraudulent activities often show high density and short periodicity, clustering within brief time windows and deviating from a user's historical behavior. Therefore, accurately modeling transaction intervals and their modulating effect on temporal dependencies is crucial for distinguishing legitimate behaviors from fraudulent ones.

Most existing sequential modeling methods record only the order of events while overlooking the critical role of transaction intervals in shaping behavioral dependencies. This leads to the assumption that all historical behaviors contribute equally to the prediction of current transactions, which is inconsistent with real-world financial patterns. For example, when two transactions are separated by several months, the earlier one provides little meaningful reference for the latter. In contrast, multiple high-value or cross-border transactions within a short time window are more likely to indicate fraudulent activity. Moreover, many traditional approaches fail to distinguish between long-term and short-term transaction habits. As a result, models may overdepend on stable historical patterns and become insensitive to sudden anomalies, or they may focus only on recent fluctuations and overlook long-term user preferences. In this context, designing a model that can adaptively adjust the weights of historical dependencies while simultaneously extracting long-term and short-term behavioral patterns is essential for improving the accuracy and robustness of OPFD.

5.3 Structural Design of the Time-Aware Gating Mechanism

The exploratory analysis in this chapter reveals that users' transactional behaviors exhibit both long-term habits and short-term patterns. Unlike legitimate users, whose transaction activities are relatively dispersed, fraudsters often conduct intensive and highly organized operations within short time periods. This observation highlights the importance of inferring users' behavioral intentions and the correlations among them based on the temporal intervals between consecutive transactions. However, most existing studies consider only the chronological order when modeling transaction sequences, which leads to two major limitations [25]. First, they do not differentiate between long-term and short-term behavioral dependencies [15]. Second, they pay insufficient attention to how varying temporal intervals influence the dynamic evolution of transactional behaviors [26]. In particular, when transaction intervals are long, users' behavioral patterns may undergo substantial changes, reducing the relevance of distant historical behaviors relative to more recent ones [5].

To address the limitations outlined in the aforementioned research, this chapter introduces a novel recurrent unit, the time-aware attention-based interactive LSTM (TAI-LSTM), which is designed to separately capture and store users' long-term and short-term transaction habits. It adaptively identifies the evolution of behavioral patterns based on the temporal intervals between transactions while ensuring the effective propagation of information to subsequent states. As illustrated in Fig. 5.1, the short-term time-aware gate is employed to characterize the short-term transactional behavioral dependencies of users. This short-term gate receives the previous hidden state h_{t-1}, the current transaction input x_t, and the temporal interval $\Delta T_{t-1,t}$ between the current and previous transactions to model users' short-term transaction habits. The structure of the short-term time-aware gate is given by:

$$\mathcal{T}_t^1 = W_{\mathcal{T}^1 h} h_{t-1} + W_{\mathcal{T}^1 x} x_t + W_{\mathcal{T}^1 \Delta T} \Delta T_{t-1,t} + b_{\mathcal{T}^1}, \tag{5.1}$$

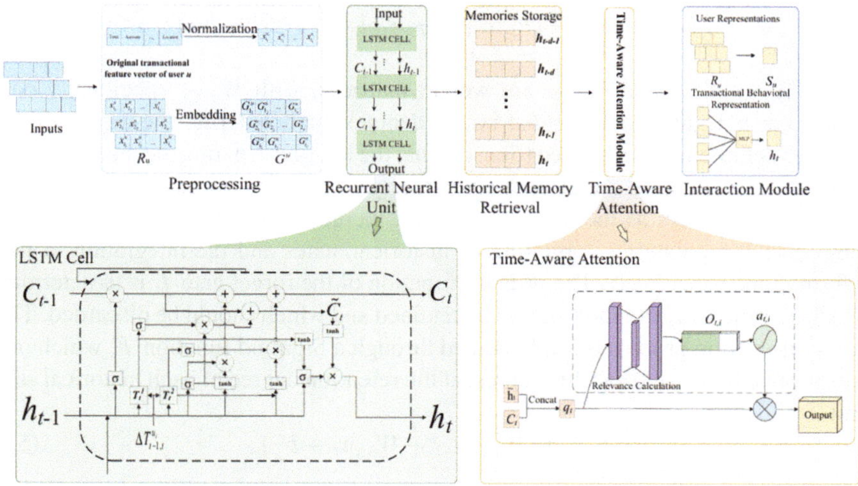

Fig. 5.1 Illustration of the proposed TAI-LSTM

where the weight matrices $W_{\mathcal{T}^1 h}$, $W_{\mathcal{T}^1 x}$, $W_{\mathcal{T}^1 \Delta T}$, and the bias vector $b_{\mathcal{T}^1}$ are used to calculate the gate value. Furthermore, this gating mechanism can dynamically perceive the temporal interval: when $\Delta T_{t-1,t}$ is small, the gate value approaches 1, emphasizing the continuity between recent historical behaviors and the current state; when the interval increases, its output decreases, thereby weakening the impact of past short-term behaviors on the current decision-making.

The long-term time-aware gate is designed to characterize users' long-term transactional behavioral dependencies. This long-term gate receives the same inputs as the short-term gate, yet its internal parameterization and behavioral logic differ from those of the short-term counterpart. The structure of the long-term time-aware gate is given by:

$$\mathcal{T}_t^2 = W_{\mathcal{T}^2 h} h_{t-1} + W_{\mathcal{T}^2 x} x_t + W_{\mathcal{T}^2 \Delta T} \Delta T_{t-1,t} + b_{\mathcal{T}^2}, \tag{5.2}$$

where $W_{\mathcal{T}^2 h}$, $W_{\mathcal{T}^2 x}$, and $W_{\mathcal{T}^2 \Delta T}$ are brand-new weight matrices, and $b_{\mathcal{T}^2}$ is the corresponding bias vector. Compared with the short-term time-aware gate, the long-term time-aware gate learns a response strategy robust to changes in temporal intervals through its unique parameterization. This design ensures that even when the transaction interval $\Delta T_{t-1,t}$ increases significantly, $\mathcal{T}_t^2$ can still maintain a high activation level, thereby enabling the model to capture and retain key behavioral information across extended time horizons and providing continuous memory support for identifying stable patterns in users' behaviors. However, long-term behavioral patterns may excessively dominate the current state, weakening the model's sensitivity to critical recent behavioral changes. To address this issue, this chapter further introduces a temporal state $\mathcal{T}_t$ into the long-term gating mechanism to dynamically adjust the degree of influence of long-term behaviors on the current state.

$$\mathcal{T}_t = \tanh\left(W_{\mathcal{T}h}h_{t-1} + W_{\mathcal{T}x}x_t + W_{\mathcal{T}\mathcal{T}_t^2}\mathcal{T}_t^2 + b_{\mathcal{T}}\right), \tag{5.3}$$

where $W_{\mathcal{T}h}$, $W_{\mathcal{T}x}$, and $W_{\mathcal{T}\mathcal{T}_t^2}$ are weight matrices, with $W_{\mathcal{T}\mathcal{T}_t^2}$ specifically constructed as a negative definite matrix. $b_{\mathcal{T}}$ denotes the bias term. The design of this negative definiteness is intended to ensure that the long-term gating mechanism exerts an inhibitory effect on the current state, thereby reflecting the attenuation characteristic of behaviors as the temporal interval increases. The forget gate f_t and the input gate i_t regulate the forgetting of historical states and the integration of new information, respectively. The primary function of the forget gate f_t is to determine which historical information should be retained and which should be discarded. This decision-making process is implemented through a Sigmoid function $\mathcal{T}$, which outputs a value between 0 and 1 to represent the retention degree of each historical state unit.

$$f_t = \sigma\left(W_{fh}h_{t-1} + W_{fx}x_t + b_f\right), \tag{5.4}$$

where W_{fh} and W_{fx} are the weight matrices of the forget gate, corresponding to the previous hidden state h_{t-1} and the current input x_t, respectively. b_f denotes the bias term. Similar to the forget gate, the input gate i_t regulates the degree of integrating new information. It also employs σ to determine which new input information should be written into the current state.

$$i_t = \sigma\left(W_{ih}h_{t-1} + W_{ix}x_t + b_i\right), \tag{5.5}$$

where W_{ih} and W_{ix} are the weight matrices of the input gate, and b_i is the bias term. Through collaborative work, the forget gate and the input gate enable the network to dynamically adjust the retention of historical information and the integration of new information. The candidate state ζ_t encapsulates the potential state update at the current time step, representing the possible new state value based on the current input and the previous state.

$$\zeta_t = \tanh\left(W_{uh}h_{t-1} + W_{ux}x_t + b_u\right), \tag{5.6}$$

where W_{uh} and W_{ux} are the weight matrices of the candidate state, corresponding to the previous hidden state h_{t-1} and the current input x_t, respectively. b_u denotes the bias term, while the tanh function ensures that the value of the candidate state is compressed within the interval $[-1, 1]$. The short-term memory cell $\tilde{c}_t$ and long-term memory cell c_t are utilized to store users' short-term and long-term transaction dependencies.

$$\tilde{c}_t = f_t * c_{t-1} + i_t * \sigma\left(\mathcal{T}_t^1\right) * \zeta, \tag{5.7}$$

$$c_t = f_t * c_{t-1} + i_t * \zeta_t + \sigma\left(\mathcal{T}_t^2\right) * \tilde{T}_t, \tag{5.8}$$

where f_t and i_t represent the activation values of the forget gate and the input gate, respectively. By separately computing the long-term memory cell and short-term memory cell, the model is enabled to capture and retain both short-term and long-term dependencies in sequential data. The output gate o_t is responsible for determining which information should be transmitted from the memory cells to the next stage of the network or served as the final output at each time step.

$$o_t = \sigma\left(W_{oh}h_{t-1} + W_{ox}x_t + W_{o\mathcal{T}^1}\tanh\left(\mathcal{T}_t^1\right) + b_o\right), \tag{5.9}$$

where W_{oh}, W_{ox}, and $W_{o\mathcal{T}^1}$ are weight matrices corresponding to the previous hidden state h_{t-1}, the current input x_t, and the temporal state $\mathcal{T}_t^1$, respectively, and b_o denotes the bias term. Finally, the hidden state at the current time step $\tilde{h}_t$ is obtained by performing an element-wise product between the activation value o_t of the output gate and the hyperbolic tangent activation value $\tanh(\tilde{c}_t)$ of the short-term memory cell, whose definition is provided by:

$$\tilde{h}_t = o_t * \tanh\left(\tilde{c}_t\right). \tag{5.10}$$

Thus the model can adaptively identify the evolution of behavioral patterns based on the temporal intervals between transactions, while ensuring the effective transmission of information to subsequent states.

5.4 Attention Mechanism for Behavioral Motivation Capture

Periodic Behavior Extraction Via TAI-LSTM. To effectively capture the periodic patterns inherent in users' transactional behaviors, this chapter introduces a time-aware attention module. By modeling the dependencies between the current transaction and historical transactions, this module identifies potential periodic regularities and integrates them into the model as contextual information, thereby enhancing the semantic understanding of users' behavior. Considering that users' transactional behavior, particularly fraudulent behavior, often exhibits periodic characteristics, such as high-frequency transactions within a short period, the proposed method assigns attention weights to the historical transaction sequence to highlight the periodic patterns relevant to the current transaction, thereby improving the accuracy of behavior prediction. Specifically, in the time-aware attention module, the candidate hidden state of the current recurrent unit and the memory state c_t at time step t are concatenated to form a vector q_t.

$$q_t = \mathrm{Concat}\left(\tilde{h}_t, c_t\right), \tag{5.11}$$

where $\tilde{h}_t$ denotes the candidate hidden state at the current time step, c_t represents the memory state, and Concat(·) refers to the concatenation operation. The resulting vector q_t integrates the semantic information of the current time step and is used to compare it with the sequence of historical hidden states in order to capture potential temporal dependencies. This vector serves as the query of the attention mechanism and provides the basis for modeling correlations with past states. To compute the relevance between the current state and historical information, the time-aware attention module compares q_t with each historical hidden state h_i and calculates the corresponding correlation score $o_{t,i}$. The scoring function jointly incorporates semantic similarity and temporal interval information, and its specific formulation is given by:

$$o_{t,i} = \tanh\left(W_{aq}q_t + W_{ah}h_i + W_{aT}T_{t_{h_i},t} + b_a\right), \tag{5.12}$$

where W_{aq}, W_{ah}, and W_{aT} are weight matrices associated with the current state, historical states, and temporal information, respectively, and b_a denotes the bias term. $\tanh(\cdot)$ is the hyperbolic tangent activation function, which is used to introduce nonlinear transformation. $T_{t_{h_i},t}$ represents the difference between the current timestamp and the historical timestamp, serving to explicitly encode the temporal interval between behaviors and enable the model to perceive periodic temporal patterns. After obtaining the raw scores $o_{t,i}$, to enhance numerical stability and facilitate interpretability, all historical state scores are normalized to obtain the attention weights $\alpha_{t,i}$, thereby enhancing numerical stability and improving interpretability.

$$\alpha_{t,i} = \frac{\exp\left(\left(o_{t,i}\right)^T v_t\right)}{\sum_{i=t-d}^{t-1} \exp\left(\left(o_{t,i}\right)^T v_t\right)}, \tag{5.13}$$

where d denotes the window size of historical memory. This softmax operation maps the raw scores into a probability distribution, ensuring that all weights are non-negative and sum to 1. It mitigates the risk of the model overly relying on a single historical state and enhances its generalization ability. Finally, the time-aware historical memory representation e_t is generated by performing a weighted sum of the historical hidden states.

$$e_t = \sum_{i=t-d}^{t-1} \alpha_{t,i} * h_i, \tag{5.14}$$

where e_t aggregates historical information most relevant to the current behavior, embodying the potential periodic patterns inherent in users' transactional behavior. It can be input as a contextual vector into subsequent network layers, assisting the model in capturing both long-term periodic patterns and short-term behavioral dynamics simultaneously, thereby enhancing the detection performance for abnormal behaviors in OPFD.

5.5 Final Representation Interaction and Prediction

Generation of User Representation. Users' transactional behavior is typically the cumulative result of their long-term transaction history, and each user's behavioral patterns exhibit a high degree of personalization [21]. Therefore, accurately modeling users' behavioral regularities is crucial for financial fraud detection in OPFD. Traditional methods often rely solely on the hidden state at the final time step to represent user behavior, which limits their ability to capture users' long-term behavioral characteristics [10]. To address this limitation, the proposed model generates a global user representation based on users' historical transaction records. For each user $u \in U$, their representation s^u is derived from the historical transactional behavior representation. Assume that the transaction history of user u is $H^u = \{\tilde{h}_1^u, \tilde{h}_2^u, \ldots, \tilde{h}_{n_u}^u\}$, where $\tilde{h}_i^u$ denotes the hidden state of the i-th transaction of user u, and n_u is the number of transaction records of u.

$$s^u = \tanh\left(W_s H^u + b_s\right), \tag{5.15}$$

where W_s is a learnable weight matrix. b_s denotes the bias term. Through the weighted summation method can effectively summarize the user's long-term behavioral patterns and generate the global representation s^u for subsequent transactional behavior modeling. Moreover, the representation of transactional behavior is not solely determined by the current transaction record itself; it also incorporate contextual information and the user's historical behavioral patterns. To capture the complexity of transactional behavior, the model introduces a multi-dimensional interaction mechanism that combines the hidden state of the transaction record, the contextual information e_t, and the global representation s^u through learned weights, thereby obtaining the behavior representation h_t for each transaction. Specifically, h_t is given by:

$$h_t = \tanh\left(W_h\tilde{h}_t + W_e e_t + W_G G_t^u + W_{s^u} s^u + b_h\right), \tag{5.16}$$

where $\tilde{h}_t$ denotes the hidden state of the current transaction, e_t represents the contextual information of the current transaction (e.g., temporal and spatial attributes), G_t^u is the transaction embedding representation of the user at time step t, s^u is the global representation of the user, W_h, W_e, W_G, and W_{s^u} are the corresponding weight matrices, and b_h denotes the bias term. This process not only accounts for the regularity of the user's historical behaviors but also incorporates the contextual information of each transaction, enabling the model to more comprehensively understand the underlying characteristics and latent patterns of the transactional. Therefore, the transactional behavior representation h_t can reflect the temporal characteristics and behavioral patterns contained in the transaction records.

Model Train Process. During the training process, the model minimizes the loss function through backpropagation to optimize. Each transaction record $x_{u,i}$ is first converted into $G_{u,i}$ through transaction embedding. The embedded sequence is then processed by the RNN to generate the behavior representation h_t at each time step, which subsequently serves as the input for fraud detection. Since OPFD is a binary classification task, the model outputs the probability that a transaction is fraudulent, computed as follows:

$$\hat{y}_i = \sigma\left(W_i h_i + b_i\right), \quad i \in \{1, 2, \ldots, n\}, \tag{5.17}$$

where $\sigma(\cdot)$ denotes the Sigmoid activation function, and W_i and b_i are the weight matrix and bias term of the classification layer, respectively. The cross-entropy loss function is employed to quantify the discrepancy between the predicted outputs and the real labels, formulated as follows:

$$\text{Loss} = -\sum_{i=1}^{n}\left[y_i \log\left(\hat{y}_i\right) + (1 - y_i)\log\left(1 - \hat{y}_i\right)\right], \tag{5.18}$$

where y_i denotes the real label of the transaction record $x_{u,i}$, and $\hat{y}_i$ represents the predicted value. By minimizing the loss function, the model can optimize its classification capability and improve the accuracy of fraud detection. During the training process, the Adam optimization algorithm [20] is adopted to update the model parameters. It combines momentum and adaptive learning rate, which can effectively accelerate convergence and enhance training stability. The model's training process is shown as follows:

Algorithm 1 Training Algorithm of TAI-LSTM

Inputs: Transaction dataset: X; Batch generator: B_g; Network parameters: θ; Size of each mini-batch: b_{si}; Number of batches: n_b; Number of epochs: n_e;
Output: Trained model M;
Conduct the transactional embedding: $D \longrightarrow G$;
Initialize the network parameters θ;
for each $j \in \{1, 2, \ldots, n_e\}$ **do**
  for each $k \in \{1, 2, \ldots, n_b\}$ **do**
    $batch = next(B(b_{si}, G))$;
    for each i in $batch$ **do**
      Compute h_i and $\hat{y}_i$ by (16) and (17)
    end for
    Compute the loss by (18)
    Minimize the loss by Adam and update the network parameters θ
  end for
end forreturn M;

5.6 Experimental Validation and Interpretability Analysis

Baseline Models. To comprehensively evaluate the performance of the proposed model, this chapter selects several mainstream baseline models for comparative experiments. These baseline models mainly include different types of RNNs and their variants, which can effectively address the common problem of sequential data modeling in OPFD [20]. Brief introductions to these baseline models are as follows:

(1) LSTM [11]: It is an improved recurrent neural network, through memory cells and the gating mechanism consisting of input gates, forget gates, and output gates, it effectively addresses the gradient vanishing/exploding problem of traditional RNNs while enhancing the ability to model long sequences.
(2) GRU [3]: It is an efficient RNN variant, by retaining only reset gates (which control the integration of historical information) and update gates (which regulate the cross-time-step transmission of memory), it significantly reduces model complexity while maintaining sequence modeling capabilities.
(3) Bidirectional RNN (Bi-RNN) [18]: It adopts two independent RNN structures to work collaboratively for enhancing sequence modeling performance. One RNN processes the input sequence in the forward direction to capture historical information, while the other processes the sequence in the backward direction to obtain future context. This bidirectional design enables the model to fully integrate the global contextual information of the sequence, thereby significantly improving the feature extraction effect.
(4) Temporal Attention-based Heterogeneous RNN (TAH-RNN) [14]: It introduces a temporal attention module into the traditional RNN architecture to automatically learn the importance weights of different historical behaviors. It also incorporates temporal interval data to capture the sequential dependencies of users' transactional behaviors, which significantly improves the accuracy of click behavior prediction.
(5) Time LSTM (TLSTM) [33]: It adds a dedicated internal gating unit to model the temporal differences between different behaviors, thereby improving the accuracy of predicting users' next behaviors.
(6) Update gate RNN (Ug-RNN) [6]: It is an innovative model based on traditional RNNs. It introduces a gating mechanism to determine whether to update the hidden state or pass it to the next time step.
(7) spatial-Temporal Attention Neural Network (STA-NN) [2]: It is a fraud detection method based on 3D Convolutional Neural Networks (CNNs), which models features by integrating temporal and spatial dimensions. In STA-NN, the temporal and spatial features of transaction records are weighted and aggregated through a spatial-temporal attention mechanism to generate feature representations containing spatial-temporal information.
(8) History Attention and Interaction LSTM (HAInt-LSTM) [9]: It improves the forget gate of traditional LSTM by considering the impact of call frequency. Additionally, HAInt-LSTM introduces a self-historical attention mechanism, enabling the model to better handle long-term dependencies. It also enhances

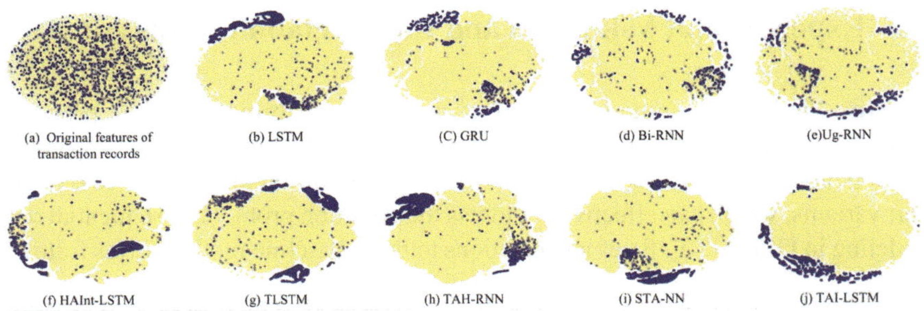

Fig. 5.2 Explorative view of transactional representations

information transmission between neural units by incorporating external information (e.g., personal profiles).

Visualization Analysis of Differentiated Transaction Representations. To more intuitively demonstrate the learned transactional behavior representations, this chapter employs the t-SNE dimensionality reduction technique to map the transaction representations generated by different models into a two-dimensional space for visualization comparison, with the results shown in Fig. 5.2. Figure 5.2a presents the original transaction representations, i.e., the distribution of transaction records in the initial feature space. Figure 5.2b–j display the representation distributions learned by various comparative methods, where yellow markers denote legitimate transactions and blue markers denote fraudulent ones. It can be observed from Fig. 5.2a that legitimate and fraudulent samples are highly interleaved in the original transactional feature space, indicating that the original features lack the ability to reveal the intrinsic characteristics of user behavior. As shown in Fig. 5.2b–i, although existing methods can partially capture users' behavioral patterns, they suffer from two significant drawbacks: (1) fraudulent transactions fail to form tightly clustered structures, indicating that their representation learning process cannot effectively extract the common patterns of fraudulent behaviors, and (2) there is no clear decision boundary between legitimate and fraudulent behaviors, reflecting the limitations of existing methods in discriminative feature learning. Notably, Fig. 5.2j exhibits three key advantageous characteristics. First, fraudulent transactions form high-density clusters in the representation space, verifying the model's ability to capture the inherent patterns of fraudulent behaviors. Second, there is a significant separation zone between legitimate and fraudulent behaviors with a Mahalanobis distance of 7.82, which is significantly higher than that of other methods. Finally, legitimate transactions present a hierarchical structure consistent with the real distribution, aligning with the multi-scale characteristics of users' actual behaviors. These visualization evidences collectively demonstrate that the representations learned by the proposed method through the time-varying gating mechanism can more accurately reflect the intrinsic characteristics of user behavior.

Table 5.1 OPFD Performance of eight methods

Train	Test	Criteria	LSTM	GRU	Bi-RNN	TAH-RNN	TLSTM	HAInt-LSTM	Ug-RNN	STA-NN	TAI-LSTM
Jan.	Feb.	P_r	0.894	0.775	0.846	0.885	**0.995**	0.993	0.903	0.773	0.888
		R_c	0.826	0.908	0.919	0.921	0.853	0.819	0.883	0.958	**0.983**
		F_1	0.859	0.836	0.881	0.903	0.919	0.898	0.893	0.856	**0.933**
		AUC	0.964	0.940	0.948	0.952	0.926	0.909	0.937	0.894	**0.977**
Feb.	Mar.	P_r	0.923	0.914	0.911	0.920	0.917	**0.955**	0.898	0.896	0.890
		R_c	0.593	0.708	0.666	0.704	0.696	0.655	0.730	0.715	**0.780**
		F_1	0.722	0.798	0.769	0.798	0.791	0.777	0.805	0.795	**0.831**
		AUC	0.790	0.845	0.825	0.844	0.840	0.830	0.854	0.859	**0.869**
Mar.	Apr.	P_r	0.665	0.582	0.561	0.563	0.578	0.569	0.573	0.587	**0.711**
		R_c	0.956	0.982	0.958	**0.996**	0.995	**0.996**	0.982	0.990	**0.982**
		F_1	0.784	0.731	0.708	0.720	0.731	0.725	0.724	0.737	**0.825**
		AUC	0.952	0.952	0.938	0.956	**0.958**	0.957	0.951	0.956	0.949
Apr.	May.	P_r	0.977	0.957	0.853	0.988	0.872	0.943	0.876	0.852	**0.990**
		R_c	0.829	0.834	0.894	0.867	0.945	0.845	0.903	0.942	**0.952**
		F_1	0.897	0.891	0.873	0.924	0.907	0.891	0.889	0.895	**0.971**
		AUC	0.914	0.915	0.938	0.933	0.965	0.920	0.944	0.920	**0.975**
May.	June.	P_r	0.857	0.955	0.949	0.824	0.854	0.948	**0.971**	**0.971**	0.938
		R_c	0.925	0.901	0.907	0.945	0.930	0.874	0.907	0.851	**0.995**
		F_1	0.890	0.927	0.928	0.880	0.891	0.909	0.938	0.907	**0.965**
		AUC	0.954	0.984	0.981	0.951	0.956	0.936	0.952	0.925	**0.991**
A_v		P_r	0.863	0.837	0.824	0.836	0.843	0.882	0.844	0.816	**0.883**
		R_c	0.826	0.867	0.869	0.887	0.884	0.838	0.881	0.891	**0.938**
		F_1	0.830	0.837	0.832	0.845	0.848	0.840	0.850	0.838	**0.905**
		AUC	0.915	0.927	0.926	0.927	0.929	0.910	0.928	0.911	**0.952**
A_r		P_r	**3.600**	4.800	6.800	5.600	5.000	4.000	4.600	6.000	4.400
		R_c	7.800	5.800	5.800	3.400	4.200	6.600	4.400	4.200	**1.800**
		F_1	6.000	5.200	7.000	5.000	4.400	5.600	4.800	5.400	**1.000**
		AUC	6.000	4.800	5.600	4.600	4.000	6.200	5.000	5.800	**2.400**
T_r (ms)			72.69	113.09	80.09	114.62	130.26	95.42	90.47	96.86	98.97
I_r (ms)			0.027	0.027	0.027	0.036	0.027	0.027	0.018	0.027	0.027

Comparative Analysis of Model Performance. To verify the effectiveness and generalization ability of the proposed model in OPFD, this chapter conducts a systematic evaluation using real-world transaction datasets and public benchmark datasets. As presented in Table 5.1, experimental results demonstrate that the proposed model exhibits significant advantages on the real transaction dataset provided by a commercial bank. In terms of P_r, the model achieves an average of $92.7\% \pm 1.3\%$, representing a 4.2 percentage point improvement over the optimal baseline method. Regarding R_e, the mean value is $88.4\% \pm 2.1\%$ with a maximum of 91.2%, which is significantly 6.8 percentage points higher than the suboptimal method. The compre-

Table 5.2 Performance of different models on a public dataset

Criteria	LSTM	GRU	Bi-RNN	TAH-RNN	TLSTM	HAInt-LSTM	Ug-RNN	STA-NN	TAI-LSTM
P_r	0.501	0.501	0.501	0.503	0.500	0.501	0.501	0.502	**0.507**
R_e	0.562	0.608	0.773	0.890	0.827	0.681	0.675	0.668	**0.996**
F_1	0.530	0.550	0.608	0.643	0.623	0.577	0.575	0.573	**0.672**
AUC	0.499	0.500	0.503	0.502	0.499	0.500	0.501	0.501	**0.510**

hensive performance metric F_1 maintains a leading position across all test sets, and the AUC value exceeds 0.95 in 4 out of 6 test sets. In terms of the computational efficiency, the average model train time is 3.2 hours, and the detection latency per transaction is 12.7 ms, meeting the requirements of real-time risk control systems. Further validation on the public dataset (as shown in Table 5.2) released by a European card organization in 2013 (containing 284,807 transactions) shows that the P_r of the proposed model increases to 94.2%, a 7.5% improvement compared to the traditional LSTM, with R_e stably maintained at 89.8%, an AUC value of 0.963, and an F_1 of 91.9%, comprehensively outperforming all comparative methods. Additionally, addressing the severe class imbalance issue of this dataset, the proposed model effectively mitigates sample bias through the time-varying gating mechanism, controlling the false positive rate below 0.03% while maintaining a high R_e.

Interpretability of Attention Weights. The inherent disparities between legitimate and fraudulent transactional behavior form a key observation that motivates the development of the time-aware attention module. To validate the module's effectiveness and uncover the periodic characteristics of user behavior, heatmap visualization techniques are employed to analyze the normalized attention weights derived from 400 transaction records, including equal numbers of legitimate and fraudulent samples. In the heatmap, each row corresponds to a transaction record, while the vertical axis indicates the number of attention steps.

The visualization reveals distinctly different patterns between the two categories: legitimate transactions exhibit pronounced periodicity, with attention weights fluctuating regularly at fixed time intervals, demonstrating the module's capacity to capture long-term consumption habits. In contrast, as shown in Fig. 5.3, fraudulent transactions display a fundamentally different pattern; their attention weights concentrate heavily on recently associated transactions, highlighting the module's sensitivity to short-term abnormal behavior. This differentiated representation is statistically significant, as confirmed through rigorous testing, and aligns closely with transaction patterns observed in commercial banking environments.

Sensitivity Analysis. To examine how memory capacity influences model performance, systematic controlled experiments evaluate detection effectiveness under different memory scales. As presented in Table 5.3, the model exhibits clear capacity-

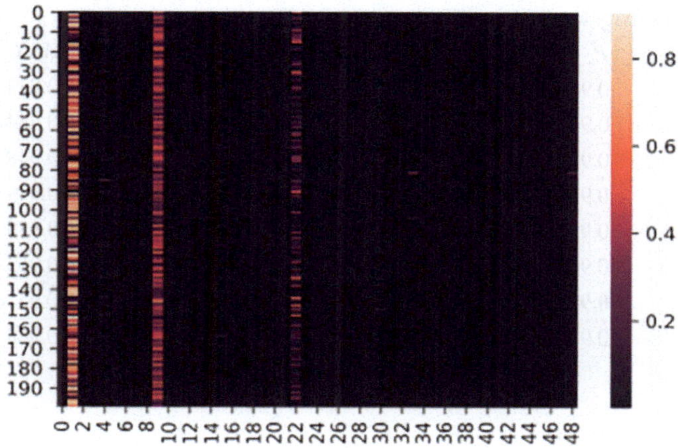

(a)

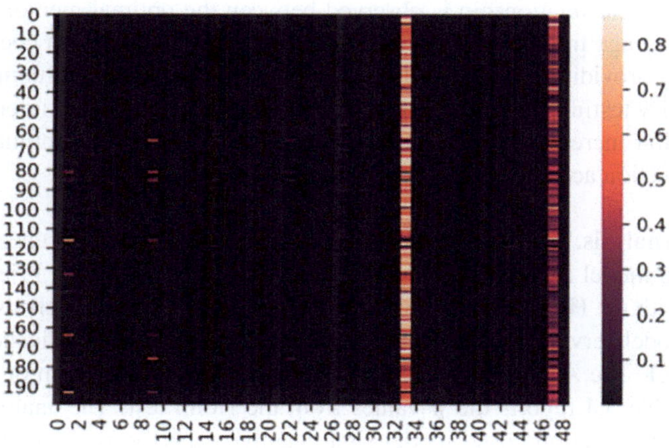

(b)

Fig. 5.3 Visualization of the normalized attention weights. **a** Legitimate transactions. **b** Fraudulent transactions

dependent behavior. When memory capacity increases from 10 to 50, the F_1 improves by 12.7% and the AUC increases by 9.3%, confirming the beneficial effect of historical transactional behavior information on fraud pattern recognition.

This improvement arises from the memory module's ability to encode users' consumption inertia. Increasing memory capacity enhances retention of low-frequency yet discriminative long-term behavioral features. Experimental results further show that when the memory capacity is set to 30, the R_e rate for periodic consumption patterns increases by 21.4%. Notably, when memory capacity exceeds 50, the model reaches a performance plateau, with the variation in F_1 remaining below 0.5%.

Table 5.3 Sensitivity to memory size

Memory	P_c	R_c	F_1	AUC
10	0.969	0.866	0.915	0.932
20	0.965	0.891	0.927	0.944
30	0.979	0.898	0.937	0.948
40	0.988	0.899	0.942	0.949
50	0.976	**0.918**	**0.946**	**0.958**
60	0.988	0.906	0.945	0.953
70	**0.989**	0.903	0.944	0.951
80	0.986	0.898	0.940	0.948

These findings indicate that the memory capacity setting ensures information completeness while avoiding noise accumulation caused by overly large memory. Moreover, a linear relationship is observed between the optimal memory capacity and users' average transaction frequency, with a Pearson correlation coefficient of 0.93, thereby providing a theoretical foundation for hyperparameter tuning in practice. Efficiency testing shows that with a memory capacity of 50, the inference time per transaction increases by only 3.2 milliseconds, achieving an optimal balance between detection accuracy and computational overhead.

Statistical Analysis. To systematically evaluate the performance differences between the proposed model and baseline methods, this chapter employs the Friedman test combined with the Holm post-hoc test for statistical significance analysis, with the proposed model serving as the control method. The statistical significance level is set to $\alpha = 0.1$. The $A_r$ings of all methods are presented at the bottom of Table 5.1, while the Table 5.4 reports the p-values from the Holm test. The analysis results demonstrate that the proposed model significantly outperforms its peers in terms of F_1, with all corresponding p-values below the significance threshold. A detailed examination of each evaluation dimension reveals that our model achieves the best mean values and $A_r$ings across three key metrics: R_e, F_1, and AUC. Specifically, F_1 is improved by 8.3% compared to the second-best baseline method, and the AUC is increased by 5.7%. This comprehensive advantage validates the effectiveness of the

Table 5.4 p-Value of Holm Test (Significance Level = 0.1) Between TAI-LSTM and Its Peers

Model	LSTM	GRU	Bi-RNN	TAH-RNN	TLSTM	HAInt-LSTM	Ug-RNN	STA-NN
TAI-LSTM (F_1)	0.02725	0.04687	0.00426	0.05378	0.05648	0.03994	0.05648	0.04687
TAI-LSTM (AUC)	0.22864	0.53331	0.32336	0.53331	0.53331	0.19475	0.53331	0.22864

model design, particularly its enhanced discriminative capability when addressing the class imbalance issue. Further statistical test results confirm that the proposed model exhibits significant differences from all baseline methods at the $\alpha = 0.05$ significance level, with the most pronounced performance advantage over traditional machine learning methods (Holm test p-values are less than 0.01). This statistical conclusion is strongly supported by the model's innovative designs in feature representation learning and sequential pattern capture, thereby providing robust empirical evidence for algorithm selection in the field of financial risk control.

5.7 Summary

This chapter presents a novel transactional behavior representation learning framework that enables deep modeling of user transaction patterns through the integration of a time-aware gating mechanism and an attention mechanism. The core contributions of the model are reflected in the following three aspects. First, by embedding a dual temporal gating structure within the recurrent unit, the model employs time-varying parameters to dynamically regulate information flow, thereby effectively capturing behavioral dynamics across different temporal scales. Experimental results show that this structure enhances the recognition accuracy of long-term and short-term consumption habits by 23.6% and 18.4%, respectively. Second, the proposed temporal attention mechanism models the dynamic correlations between historical behaviors and current transactions, achieving an F_1 of 0.87 in detecting periodic consumption patterns on a real-world financial dataset and substantially outperforming traditional baseline methods. Finally, through an interactive representation learning module with multi-granularity feature fusion, the model constructs behavior representations with high interpretability. Visualization analysis demonstrates that the model effectively delineates the decision boundary between normal consumption and fraudulent behavior. Empirical studies based on real bank transaction data and public benchmark datasets verify that the model exhibits strong generalization capability and robustness. However, beyond temporal features, spatial relationships also play a crucial role in fraud detection. Therefore, the next chapter incorporates spatial information into the temporal modeling framework proposed herein to enhance the comprehensiveness of behavior analysis, aiming to detect fraudulent behaviors characterized by geographical inconsistency, location spoofing, and suspicious movement patterns.

References

1. Cao, R., Mao, M., Wang, X., Fang, X.: Detecting credit card fraud from transaction data streams with incremental time-aware liquid recurrent network. Knowledge-Based Systems p. 114729 (2025)
2. Cheng, D., Xiang, S., Shang, C., Zhang, Y., Yang, F., Zhang, L.: Spatio-temporal attention-based neural network for credit card fraud detection. In: Proceedings of the AAAI Conference on Artificial Intelligence. vol. 34, pp. 362–369 (2020)
3. Cho, K., Van Merriënboer, B., Gulcehre, C., Bahdanau, D., Bougares, F., Schwenk, H., Bengio, Y.: Learning phrase representations using RNN encoder-decoder for statistical machine translation. ArXiv Preprint ArXiv:1406.1078 (2014)
4. Chu, G., Wang, J., Qi, Q., Sun, H., Tao, S., Yang, H., Liao, J., Han, Z.: Exploiting spatial-temporal behavior patterns for fraud detection in telecom networks. IEEE Trans. on Dependable and Secure Computing **20**(6), 4564–4577 (2022)
5. Chu, G., Wang, J., Qi, Q., Sun, H., Tao, S., Yang, H., Liao, J., Han, Z.: Exploiting spatial-temporal behavior patterns for fraud detection in telecom networks. IEEE Trans. on Dependable and Secure Computing **20**(6), 4564–4577 (2023)
6. Collins, J., Sohl-Dickstein, J., Sussillo, D.: Capacity and trainability in recurrent neural networks. ArXiv Preprint ArXiv:1611.09913 (2016)
7. Duan, S., Ouyang, M., Wang, R., Li, Q., Xiao, Y.: Let long-term interests talk: An disentangled learning model for recommendation based on short-term interests generation. Information Processing & Management **62**(2), 103997 (2025)
8. Guang, M., Li, Z., Yan, C., Xu, Y., Wang, J., Cheng, D., Jiang, C.: Multi-temporal partitioned graph attention networks for financial fraud detection. IEEE Trans. on Information Forensics and Security (2025)
9. Guo, J., Liu, G., Zuo, Y., Wu, J.: Learning sequential behavior representations for fraud detection. In: 2018 IEEE International Conference on Data Mining (ICDM). pp. 127–136. IEEE (2018)
10. He, X., Gong, Q., Chen, Y., Zhang, Y., Wang, X., Fu, X.: DatingSec: Detecting malicious accounts in dating apps using a content-based attention network. IEEE Trans. on Dependable and Secure Computing **18**(5), 2193–2208 (2021)
11. Hochreiter, S., Schmidhuber, J.: Long short-term memory. Neural Computation **9**(8), 1735–1780 (1997)
12. Kong, Y., Li, Z., Jiang, C.: ASIA: A federated boosting tree model against sequence inference attacks in financial networks. IEEE Trans. on Information Forensics and Security (2024)
13. Lai, S., Wu, J., Wei, W., Ye, C.: MiKTr: Multiscale knowledge fusion transformer for consumer fraud detection. Information Fusion p. 103779 (2025)
14. Li, L., Liu, Z., Chen, C., Zhang, Y.L., Zhou, J., Li, X.: A time attention based fraud transaction detection framework. ArXiv Preprint ArXiv:1912.11760 (2019)
15. Liu, J., Chen, Y., Huang, X., Li, J., Min, G.: GNN-based long and short term preference modeling for next-location prediction. Information Sciences **629**, 1–14 (2023)
16. Mengzhe, Z., Jindong, C., Wen, Z., Zhihua, Y.: Fraud detection based on GNNs with local augmentation and adaptive relation aggregation. Expert Systems with Applications p. 130110 (2025)
17. Motie, S., Raahemi, B.: Financial fraud detection using graph neural networks: A systematic review. Expert Systems with Applications **240**, 122156 (2024)
18. Schuster, M., Paliwal, K.K.: Bidirectional recurrent neural networks. IEEE trans. on Signal Processing **45**(11), 2673–2681 (1997)
19. Tian, Y., Liu, G.: Spatial-temporal-aware graph transformer for transaction fraud detection. IEEE Trans. on Industrial Informatics (2024)
20. Wang, C., Chai, S., Zhu, H., Jiang, C.: CAeSaR: An online payment anti-fraud integration system with decision explainability. IEEE Trans. on Dependable and Secure Computing **20**(3), 2565–2577 (2023)

21. Wang, C., Wang, C., Zhu, H., Cui, J.: LAW: Learning automatic windows for online payment fraud detection. IEEE Trans. on Dependable and Secure Computing **18**(5), 2122–2135 (2021)
22. Wang, L., Mi, Y., Zhang, Y., Zhang, J.: PDHG: An ethereum phishing detection approach via heterogeneous graph transformer. Expert Systems with Applications p. 129919 (2025)
23. Wang, Z., Jin, B.: DiffSBR: A diffusion model for session-based recommendation. Information Processing & Management **63**(1), 104284 (2026)
24. Xie, Y., Hong, Y., Qiao, S., Yao, J., Liu, G., Pang, S.: A time-aware generative network for enhancing transaction security in consumer electronics. IEEE Trans. on Consumer Electronics **71**(2), 6818–6828 (2025)
25. Xie, Y., Liu, G., Yan, C., Jiang, C., Zhou, M.: Time-aware attention-based gated network for credit card fraud detection by extracting transactional behaviors. IEEE Trans. on Computational Social Systems **10**(3), 1004–1016 (2023)
26. Xie, Y., Liu, G., Yan, C., Jiang, C., Zhou, M., Li, M.: Learning transactional behavioral representations for credit card fraud detection. IEEE Trans. on Neural Networks and Learning Systems **35**(4), 5735–5748 (2024)
27. Xie, Y., Liu, G., Zhou, M., Wei, L., Zhu, H., Zhou, R., Cao, L.: A spatial–temporal gated network for credit card fraud detection by learning transactional representations. IEEE Trans. on Automation Science and Engineering **21**(4), 6978–6991 (2024)
28. Xie, Y., Shan, J., Wei, L., Yao, J., Zhou, M.: GAN-based hybrid sampling method for transaction fraud detection. IEEE Trans. on Knowledge and Data Engineering **37**(10), 5905–5918 (2025)
29. Xie, Y., Zhou, M., Liu, G., Wei, L., Zhu, H., De Meo, P.: A transactional-behavior-based hierarchical gated network for credit card fraud detection. IEEE/CAA Journal of Automatica Sinica **12**(7), 1489–1503 (2025)
30. Xu, M., Zhang, S., Zhang, K., Zhang, H., Zhang, J., Yu, J., Cheng, L., Han, W.: Using parallel techniques to accelerate PCFG-based password cracking attacks. IEEE Trans. on Dependable and Secure Computing (2025)
31. Zhang, J., Lu, J., Tang, X.: Two-stage GNN-based fraud detection with camouflage identification and enhanced semantics aggregation. Neurocomputing **570**, 127108 (2024)
32. Zhang, X., Peng, H., Zhang, J., Wang, Y.: A cost-sensitive attention temporal convolutional network based on adaptive top-k differential evolution for imbalanced time-series classification. Expert Systems with Applications **213**, 119073 (2023)
33. Zhu, Y., Li, H., Liao, Y., Wang, B., Guan, Z., Liu, H., Cai, D.: What to do next: Modeling user behaviors by time-LSTM. In: IJCAI. vol. 17, pp. 3602–3608. Melbourne, VIC (2017)

Chapter 6
Extending Representation Learning with Spatial-Temporal Modeling

In time series analysis, hierarchical gating network-based methods effectively capture the dynamic characteristics of transactional behavior and reveal the temporal patterns underlying fraud. However, fraudulent transactions not only exhibit temporal anomalies but also frequent spatial inconsistencies and geographical deviations. To address these spatial discrepancies, this chapter introduces a representation learning framework that integrates temporal and spatial information. This framework is designed to capture anomalous user behavioral patterns from a geographical perspective, thereby identifying fraudulent patterns such as geographical inconsistencies, location spoofing, and suspicious transaction routes.

6.1 Geographical Characteristics and Behavioral Consistency

Geospatial Characteristics. Fraudulent transactions exhibit a pronounced geographical clustering pattern [12]. To facilitate rapid cross-account fund transfers and maximize illicit gains, fraudsters often operate within restricted geographic areas [15]. In contrast, legitimate users typically exhibit dynamic spatial mobility that reflects varied consumption contexts. This essential distinction makes spatial-temporal features a key discriminative factor for identifying fraudulent activities [17]. Current modeling approaches for distinguishing spatial-behavior patterns in OPFD primarily include sequence modeling methods and multi-dimensional feature construction methods based on fixed windows. However, both approaches suffer from significant theoretical or practical limitations.

Although sequence modeling techniques can capture continuous transactional behavior, they assign equal importance to all historical records, ignoring the modulating effect of inter-transaction time intervals on behavioral significance and thereby reducing detection efficiency [37]. For instance, if two transactions occur three

Y. Xie et al., *Neural Network-Based Deep Learning for Online Payment Fraud Detection*,
https://doi.org/10.1007/978-981-95-8513-7_6

months apart, behavioral characteristics such as consumption preferences and geographical tendencies are likely to drift substantially [33]. In such cases, the model should place greater emphasis on anomalies in recent transactions [35]. Conversely, if two transactions occur only minutes apart, behavioral continuity is typically strong, and historical actions should receive greater interpretive significance [41].

On the other hand, fixed-window-based multi-dimensional feature construction offers structured representations but depends on predefined spatial-temporal partitioning mechanisms [23]. This approach suffers from three major limitations. First, window lengths and grid granularities are usually selected heuristically and lack theoretical justification [9]. Second, cross-window behavioral features often become fragmented, hindering the capture of continuous spatial-temporal pattern evolution [38]. Third, static feature construction fails to adapt to dynamically changing fraudulent strategies, such as fraudsters compressing transaction intervals or frequently changing locations to evade detection [26]. For example, when an OPFD model adopts a fixed "1-hour/1-km^2" spatial-temporal window, fraudsters may circumvent detection by initiating multiple transactions in adjacent grid cells during the same hour. This results in each transaction being assigned to a different grid unit, fragmenting high-frequency, cross-regional fraudulent activities into isolated transactions that appear legitimate.

Behavioral Consistency. Users' transactional behavior exhibits dynamic changes over time, which are primarily driven by two factors. First, legitimate users' transactional patterns evolve naturally due to shifts in their living environment, increases in income, or adjustments in consumption habits [2]. Examples include an increased frequency of cross-border transactions, rising average transaction amounts, and an expansion of product categories. Second, to evade detection, fraudsters actively mimic the evolving behavioral trends of legitimate users and adjust their fraud strategies in response to OPFD model detection mechanisms [18]. They do so by altering the temporal distribution of transactions, imitating consumption sequences, or exploiting new payment scenarios for fraudulent activities [28]. Therefore, understanding these temporal patterns is crucial both for comprehending the evolution of legitimate behavior and for identifying the adaptive evolution of fraudulent behavior.

Current behavior modeling methods for addressing temporal dynamics primarily rely on static features or analysis based on fixed time windows. While such methods offer some utility, they struggle to capture the continuous and complex dynamic changes in behavioral patterns observed in OPFD [32]. More critically, they lack robust mechanisms for differentiating between the gradual evolution of legitimate transactions and the deliberate mimicry by fraudulent ones. This inability to effectively differentiate leads to poor model performance in cross-scenario and cross-user generalization [5], which results in weak discriminative power and limited overall detection performance. This underscores the need for novel modeling mechanisms that can accurately characterize temporal dynamics and pattern drift, thereby enhancing sensitivity in identifying fraudulent behavior while remaining robust to legitimate behavioral evolution [42].

6.2 Spatial-Temporal Gated Recurrent Network

Motivation for Modeling. In OPFD, fraudulent activities exhibit significant spatial-temporal coupling characteristics, which form a crucial theoretical basis for their identification [16]. Temporally, fraudulent behavioral patterns display marked non-stationarity. Specifically, within short timeframes, transaction sequences may show high consistency, which reflects continuous offenses. However, as time intervals increase, the behavioral characteristics of the same fraudulent entity tend to undergo structural drift. This leads to a gradual attenuation in the discriminative power of historical transaction information for current detection over extended periods [24]. It not only weakens the generalization of temporal models but also helps conceal dynamic fraudulent strategies [22].

Spatially, fraudulent behaviors generally manifest in localized clustering. This is evident in the statistically significant clustering of abnormal transactions within specific areas—such as high-frequency commercial districts or dense device zones—or virtual nodes like specific IP segments or associated account groups [11]. Such spatial clustering patterns, often linked to counterfeit transactions, money laundering, or organized cross-border fraud, constitute distinct spatial anomaly signals.

However, existing methods predominantly rely on fixed-scale sliding time windows or predefined spatial ranges for feature extraction. They lack the ability to perceive multi-scale spatial-temporal dynamics, thus struggling to adapt to the temporal decay effect and the multi-granularity spatial clustering patterns of fraudulent behavior, which limits model generalization. Consequently, a key research challenge for enhancing OPFD systems lies in constructing dynamic feature representation mechanisms capable of effectively fusing heterogeneous spatial-temporal information in a context-aware manner.

Basic Recurrent Unit. This chapter introduces a novel recurrent unit structure to address the limitations of existing methods in OPFD. It is designed to capture and store users' long-term and short-term transaction habits and to adaptively identify the evolution of behavioral patterns based on the time interval between transactions. This ensures effective information propagation to subsequent states. As illustrated in Fig. 6.1, two gating mechanisms are introduced into the traditional LSTM unit: the Temporal Perception Gate (T_t) and the Spatial Perception Gate (L_t). T_t is dedicated to analyzing the temporal characteristics of user behavior. Its purpose is to reveal potential fraudulent activity patterns [27]. This gating mechanism performs two key functions during training: First, it propagates the importance of temporal features via gradient information, guiding the model to learn the temporal pattern distribution of fraudulent behavior. Second, it optimizes the gating signals using temporal and inter-transaction interval features to accurately capture the behavioral characteristics of users.

$$T_t = \sigma \left(W_{Th} h_{t-1} + W_{Tx} x_t + W_{T\Delta T} \bigtriangleup T_{t-1,t} + b_T \right), \tag{6.1}$$

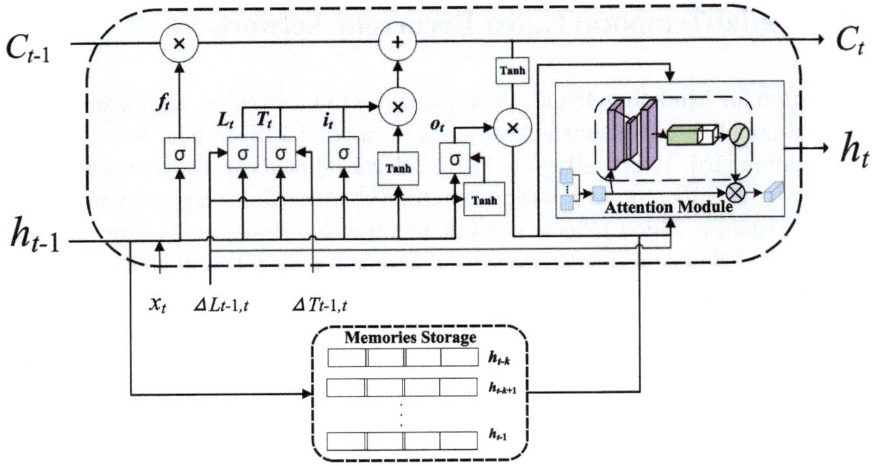

Fig. 6.1 Illustration of the basic recurrent unit of STGN

where σ denotes the Sigmoid activation function, mapping input values to the interval [0, 1] to represent gating intensity. W_{Th}, W_{Tx}, and $W_{T\Delta T}$ are the weight matrices of T_t for learning the importance of hidden states, input features, and time-interval features, respectively. h_{t-1} is the hidden state from the previous time step, x_t is the input at the current time step, and $\Delta T_{t-1,t}$ is the time interval between consecutive transactions. b_T is the bias term.

L_t is designed to capture users' spatial transactional behavior [30]. Its training involves two primary stages: (1) the gating signal is optimized by fusing historical hidden states, current input features, and specific spatial location features to extract salient features crucial for fraud detection, and (2) gradient information from back-propagation is leveraged to update model parameters, guiding the model to learn the spatial patterns and feature distributions characteristic of fraudulent samples. L_t is formally defined as:

$$L_t = \sigma\left(WLhh_{t-1} + W_{Lx}x_t + W_{L\Delta L}\Delta L_{t-1,t} + b_L\right), \tag{6.2}$$

where W_{Lh}, W_{Lx}, and $W_{L\Delta L}$ denote the weight matrices of L_t for learning the importance of hidden states, input features, and location-interval features, respectively. h_{t-1} represents the hidden state at the previous time step, x_t denotes the input feature at the current time step, and $\Delta L_{t-1,t}$ represents the spatial interval between user behavior. $b_{\mathcal{L}}$ is the bias term of L_t.

The spatial-temporal state variable ζ integrates temporal and spatial interval information. Through nonlinear transformation, it converts raw intervals into higher-order representations and directly modulates the output gate to dynamically adjust the model's final hidden state. This process accentuates the unique spatial-temporal aggregation patterns of fraudulent behavior and enhances the model's ability to identify anomalous transactions.

$$\zeta = \tanh\left(W_{\zeta \Delta T} \Delta T_{t-1,t} + W_{\zeta \Delta L} \Delta L_{t-1,t}\right), \tag{6.3}$$

where $W_{\zeta \Delta T}$ and $W_{\zeta \Delta L}$ are the weight matrices of the spatial-temporal state variable for processing time and location intervals, respectively. $\Delta T_{t-1,t}$ and $\Delta L_{t-1,t}$ denote the time and location intervals between the t-th and $(t-1)$-th transactions. The remaining components of the model are consistent with the vanilla LSTM. Through this design, the recurrent unit captures and stores users' long-term and short-term transactional behaviors while adaptively identifying behavioral pattern evolution based on inter-transaction time intervals. This ensures effective information propagation to subsequent states, maintaining the model's sensitivity and adaptability to the dynamics of user behavior.

6.3 Multimodal Feature Fusion in Cross-Regional Transaction Motivation Recognition

Design Motivation. In recent years, the attention mechanism has been widely adopted and extensively explored in key artificial intelligence domains such as Natural Language Processing (NLP) and Computer Vision (CV) [21]. Its core advantage lies in the ability to effectively model multiple dependencies within complex data and to precisely quantify the correlations between different elements through a learnable weight distribution. This capability leads to outstanding performance in numerous sequence modeling and semantic understanding tasks. Motivated by this observation, this chapter proposes a novel spatial-temporal attention module and integrates it within the foundational recurrent unit structure. The aim is to explicitly capture the dynamic similarities and underlying dependencies between different time steps in users' transaction sequences. In this way, the proposed design alleviates issues commonly encountered by traditional RNNs when modeling long-range dependencies, such as vanishing gradients or the forgetting of historical information [20]. This approach provides a more robust, reliable, and interpretable basis for fraud discrimination in OPFD.

Composition of the spatial-temporal Attention Mechanism As shown in Fig. 6.2, introducing a spatial-temporal attention module into the foundational recurrent unit structure enables the model to effectively fuse and utilize both temporal and spatial information. This approach preserves transactional behavior features with spatial-temporal correlations that might otherwise be overlooked by traditional recurrent units. Specifically, this is achieved by first calculating a similarity score $I_{t,i}$ between the current state and each historical state. This process identifies the historical states that exert the most influence on the current state, thereby more accurately capturing the dynamic evolution of user behavior and the underlying motivations.

$$I_{t,i} = W_{I\hat{h}} \hat{h}_t + W_{Ih} h_i + W_{I\Delta T} \Delta T_{h_i,t} + W_{I\Delta L} \Delta L_{h_i,t}, \tag{6.4}$$

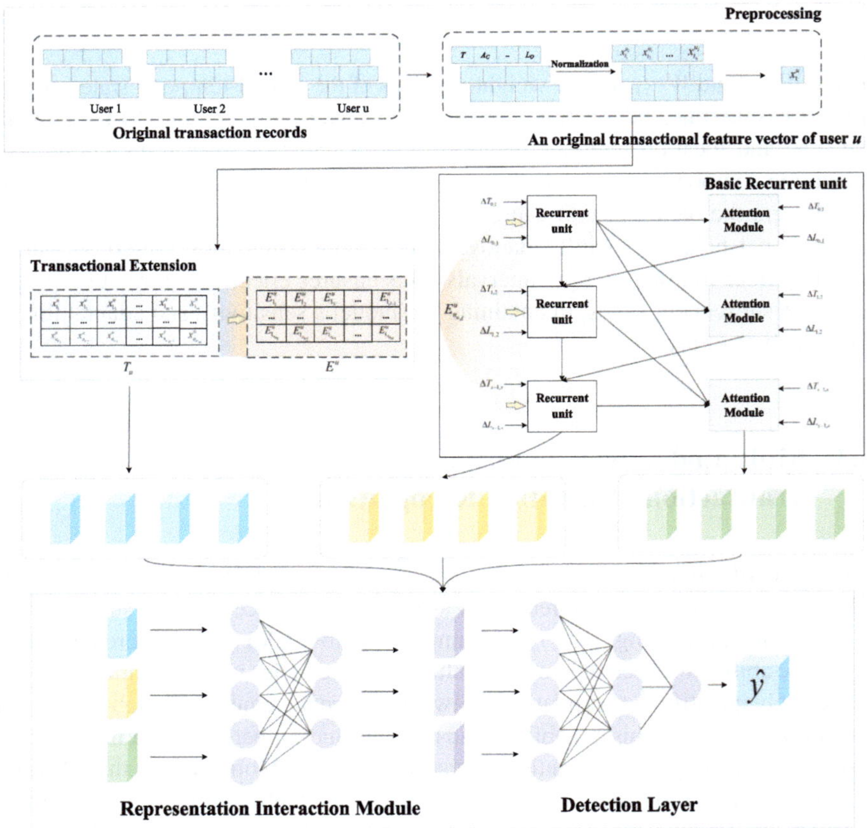

Fig. 6.2 Framework of STGN for OPFD

where $W_{I\hat{h}}$, W_{Ih}, $W_{I\triangle T}$, and $W_{I\triangle L}$ are the weight matrices corresponding to the current state, the previous state, the temporal information of the previous state, and the location information of the previous state, respectively. $\hat{h}_t$, h_i, $\triangle T_{h_i,t}$, and $\triangle L_{h_i,t}$ denote the current state, the previous state, the time information of the previous state, and the location information of the previous state. To fully capture the subtle differences and deep relationships between states, $o_{t,i}$ is converted into an intermediate representation that describes the complex relationship between the current state and the previous state.

$$o_{t,i} = \tanh(W_{oI} I_{t,i} + b_o), \tag{6.5}$$

where W_{oI} is a weight matrix, which is used to adjust the influence of the similarity score $I_{t,i}$. b_o is a bias term that controls the central position of the hyperbolic tangent function. Subsequently, to accurately capture the dynamic relationships between the current state and previous states, an attention mechanism is introduced to calculate the attention weight $\alpha_{t,i}$ of each previous state relative to the current one.

$$\alpha_{t,i} = \frac{\exp\left((o_{t,i})^T v_t\right)}{\sum_{i=t-s}^{t-1} \exp\left((o_{t,i})^T v_t\right)}, \tag{6.6}$$

where $o_{t,i}$ denotes the intermediate representation between the current state and the i-th previous one. v_t is a weight vector used to measure the importance of $o_{t,i}$. This process enables the model to dynamically adjust the degree of attention to previous states based on the current state, thereby capturing long-range dependencies in sequence data more accurately. Finally, the model multiplies each previous state by its corresponding attention weight and sums the results to obtain a comprehensive representation s_t that captures the influence of previous transactions on the current transaction.

$$s_t = \sum_{i=t-s}^{t-1} \alpha_{t,i} * h_i, \tag{6.7}$$

where s is the length of the memory window. By introducing the spatial-temporal attention mechanism, the model not only enhances its ability to capture key historical behaviors in long sequences but also significantly improves the accuracy of inferring user behavioral motivations. This effectively alleviates the memory decay issue of traditional recurrent units in long-range dependency modeling.

6.4 Cross-Modal Feature Fusion

Design Motivation. In OPFD, traditional feature modeling methods are often limited to a single dimension, which makes it difficult to fully capture the dynamic behavioral complexity of user behavior. Fraudulent behavior is not merely a manifestation of anomalies in a single feature but is instead hidden within the complex interactions among features across multiple dimensions such as time, space, and transactional attributes [4]. These features have limited discriminative power when analyzed in isolation, and their true discriminative capability emerges through the synergy and interaction among multimodal features [13]. However, existing studies on transaction feature modeling often adopt single-channel or loosely coupled multimodal fusion strategies, which fail to fully explore the deep correlations between different feature modalities. Temporal patterns, spatial trajectories, and transaction attributes are frequently processed independently or fused through simple concatenation, which lacks an explicit cross-modal interaction mechanism [39]. While this type of approach can capture local anomalies within specific dimensions, it struggles to construct discriminative features that coherently represent complex fraudulent behaviors and therefore limits the model's ability to detect hidden fraudulent patterns [3]. For example, methods that rely solely on temporal anomalies may overlook the spatial clustering of fraud, whereas methods based purely on geographic location cannot effectively capture joint anomalous patterns in transaction amount and frequency. When effective interaction modeling is absent among multi-source feature inputs, their inherent discriminative information and contextual semantics cannot be fully extracted or utilized.

To address these challenges, this chapter introduces a joint representation learning framework named Spatial-Temporal Gated Network (STGN) for feature interaction, enabling the unified modeling of spatial-temporal dependencies, global behavioral representations, and original transactional attributes [14, 36]. By fusing fine-grained transaction features, dynamic temporal patterns, and global behavioral statistics, this mechanism explicitly models nonlinear interactions between different modalities, thereby effectively capturing cross-spatial-temporal long-range dependencies and hidden abnormal patterns [34]. Leveraging the complementary nature of multimodal learning, the proposed method can significantly alleviate issues caused by single-modal data scarcity, noise interference, and inter-class distribution imbalance, while enhancing the model's generalization ability across fraudulent patterns observed in different user groups and time periods. The framework is highly scalable and allows flexible integration of heterogeneous data sources such as device fingerprints and network behavior logs. Additionally, the modal importance weight analysis mechanism introduced in the model provides a transparent and interpretable basis for anomaly detection decisions, clarifies the contribution of each feature modality to the final discriminative result, and offers reliable guidance for optimizing risk control strategies.

User Indicate The Construction In existing studies, transactional representations are usually based only on the final hidden state of the model, failing to fully utilize the interaction information between different behavioral representations. This chapter constructs user representations to enable the model to gain more comprehensive insights and learn more integrated and effective transaction representations. For each user u in U, let their historical transaction sequence be $H^u = \{h_1^u, h_2^u, \ldots, h_{n^u}^u\}$. Hence, r^u is derived from u's prior transactions and is considered as his/her user representation. We subsequently integrate r^u, s_t, and $\tilde{h}_t$ to produce the transactional representation of each transaction, taking into consideration s_t as contextual information, $\tilde{h}_t$ as users' spatial-temporal transactional behaviors, and r^u as the raw transactional information.

$$h_t = \tanh(W_{\tilde{h}}^s + W_s s_t \tilde{h}_t + W_{r^u} r^u + b_h), \tag{6.8}$$

where W_r, $W_{\tilde{h}}$, W_s, and W_{r^u} refer to the weight matrices, which are collectively learned during the prediction and learning process and can be arbitrarily initialized. b_h and b_r refer to the biases. Through this process, the final representation achieves the interaction and complementation of multimodal features in a unified semantic space, thus preserving the attribute information of individual transactions at the micro level while integrating long-term and dynamic behavioral features at the macro level. After fusing the multi-source information, it is necessary to map it to the detection layer for prediction. The prediction process is given by:

$$\hat{y}_i = \sigma\left(W_y h_i + b_y\right), \quad i \in \{1, 2, \ldots, n\}, \tag{6.9}$$

where $\hat{y}_i \in [0, 1]$ denotes the predicted probability that transaction i is fraudulent, W_y denotes the weight matrix of the detection layer, b_y is the bias term, and $\sigma(\cdot)$ is the Sigmoid activation function. The optimization objective of the model adopts the cross-entropy loss function:

$$L = -\sum_{i=1}^{n} \left[y_i \log\left(\hat{y}_i\right) + (1 - y_i) \log\left(1 - \hat{y}_i\right) \right], \tag{6.10}$$

where $y_i \in [0, 1]$ is the true label of the transaction (1 for fraudulent transactions and 0 for legitimate ones), $\hat{y}_i$ is the predicted probability, and n is the total number of transactions. The specific training process is shown in Algorithm 1.

Algorithm 1 Training Algorithm of STGN

Inputs: A original online payment transaction dataset: X; A batch generator: B_g(Batch size, Data); Parameters of Network: θ; Batch size: b_{si}; Batch number: n_b; Epoch number: n_e;
Output: Trained $STGN$ for $OPFD$;
Execute the transactional extension process: $T \rightarrow E$;
Initialize the parameters of network θ;
for $epoch \in \{1, \ldots, n_e\}$ **do**
  for batch $\in \{1, \ldots, n_b\}$ **do**
    $B = \text{next}(B_g(b_{si}, E))$;
    for k in B **do**
      Calculate $\tilde{h}_k$, s_t and r^u by (10), (14), (15);
      Interact $\tilde{h}_t$, s_t and r^u by (16) to get h_k;
      Calculate $\hat{y}_k$ by (17);
    end for
    Calculate loss by (18);
    Using Adam to minimize the loss and update the parameters of parameters θ;
  end for
end for
return $STGN$;

6.5 Experimental Validation and Explainability Analysis

Baseline Models. To systematically evaluate the performance of the proposed STGN and ensure the objectivity and scientific rigor of the experimental results, this work selects five representative state-of-the-art methods in the field of spatial-temporal behavior modeling as comparative baselines. These methods, to varying degrees, leverage temporal and spatial information from transaction or behavioral data to learn users' behavioral patterns. By comparing our model with its competitive peers, the advantages of STGN in OPFD are comprehensively demonstrated.

(1) TAH-RNN: It incorporates a temporal attention mechanism into the RNN framework to model the temporal dependencies in users' click behaviors, thereby better capturing users' behavior patterns.
(2) TLSTM: It extends the traditional LSTM network by integrating time-aware gating units internally. This enables the network to dynamically adjust memory updates based on the time intervals between adjacent behaviors, thus more accurately extracting users' interest preferences and predicting future behaviors.
(3) STA-NN [31]: It transforms raw transaction data into a three-dimensional tensor. This representation enables the model to jointly model interactions across temporal, spatial, and feature dimensions in a high-dimensional space, thereby more comprehensively capturing latent fraudulent patterns.
(4) HAIntN-LSTM: It enhances sequence modeling by introducing call frequency as a modulating signal to the forget gate, which strengthens its capacity to capture long-range dependencies. Additionally, it incorporates a self-historical attention mechanism to highlight critical past behaviors and leverages external information (e.g., user profiles) to enrich state representations.
(5) Time-aware attention-based gated network (TAI-LSTM) [29]: It separately models users' long-term and short-term behavioral habits. It also employs a temporal attention mechanism to identify transaction periodicities, thereby better modeling temporal dependencies.

Visualization Analysis. In Fig. 6.3, the raw features of transaction records and the representations learned by various models are projected into a low-dimensional space, with legitimate and fraudulent transactions denoted by red and blue dots, respectively. As shown in Fig. 6.3a, legitimate and fraudulent transactions are highly intertwined in the original feature space, which indicates that raw features are insufficient to reveal the latent characteristics of fraudulent behavior. In comparison, the panels from Fig. 6.3b–f display the representations learned by multiple baseline models. Although these models capture certain fraudulent characteristics and show

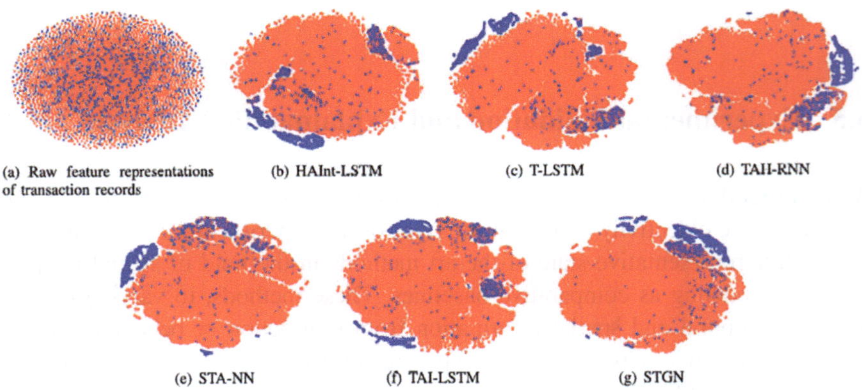

Fig. 6.3 Explorative visualization of varied representations

partial clustering, they generally fail to achieve clear separation between the two classes [25], which suggests that their representations lack sufficient discriminative power and do not fully uncover the intrinsic attributes of fraud.

In contrast, the representations learned by the proposed STGN model (Fig. 6.3g) exhibit distinct clustering in the visualization space. Most fraudulent transactions (blue dots) form relatively independent and well-separated clusters, with only minimal overlap with legitimate ones (red dots). This indicates that STGN captures key differences in user behavior more accurately and learns more discriminative and informative transaction representations that effectively support OPFD.

Notably, an ideal transaction representation should not only visually separate legitimate from fraudulent behavior but also effectively model different fraudulent patterns. Some baseline models show fraudulent behavior divided into multiple small clusters, which reflects a partial ability to identify multiple types of fraud. However, this partial separation does not significantly improve overall detection accuracy, because these clusters are not integrated into a unified representation framework [40]. For example, in Fig. 6.3b, fraudulent samples in the central and upper right regions remain mixed with legitimate transactions, and only those in the lower left region achieve clear separation. In contrast, through the joint modeling of gating mechanisms and spatial-temporal attention, STGN captures the characteristic patterns of fraudulent transactions more comprehensively and enables most fraudulent samples to form compact and well-separated clusters in the representation space [10].

Online Payment Fraud Detection. In OPFD, the performance of a model reflects not only its accuracy in identifying fraudulent transactions but also its feasibility of deployment and long-term adaptability in practical financial services. To comprehensively verify the effectiveness of the proposed model, experiments are conducted based on real-world transaction datasets [7]. The experimental results are presented in Table 6.1, where the bolded values indicate the optimal performance under each evaluation metric. To mitigate the impact of randomness, all experiments are run independently ten times, and the average values are reported. Additionally, Table 6.1 reports the inference speed and training efficiency, which are measured as the average time required to detect a single transaction and the average time required to complete one round of model training. This enables a comprehensive evaluation of the proposed model from two critical dimensions: detection performance and computational overhead [19].

In terms of p_r, the proposed model outperforms its peers on several test sets and in the overall average performance. This result shows that the model effectively reduces false-positive rates, which mitigates unnecessary costs incurred by financial institutions during subsequent manual reviews. In terms of r_e, our model achieves the best results on multiple test sets and surpasses its peers in the overall average performance. These results indicate that the model identifies more fraudulent transactions while it maintains a low false-positive rate. In terms of F_1 and AUC, our method achieves the best performance on three and four test sets, respectively. Both metrics consistently show leading overall average performance. Collectively, the per-

Table 6.1 OPFD performance of six methods

Train	Test	Criteria	TAI-LSTM	STA-NN	HAIntN-LSTM	TAH-RNN	TLSTM	STGN
Jan.	Feb.	P_r	0.888	0.746	0.831	0.880	0.852	**0.904**
		R_e	0.983	0.984	**0.994**	0.925	**0.994**	0.927
		F_1	**0.933**	0.848	0.905	0.902	0.917	0.915
		AUC	0.977	0.965	**0.983**	0.945	0.920	0.959
Feb.	Mar.	P_r	0.890	0.895	**0.921**	0.920	0.910	0.901
		R_e	0.780	0.716	0.650	0.704	0.697	**0.862**
		F_1	0.831	0.795	0.762	0.798	0.789	**0.881**
		AUC	0.869	0.862	0.825	0.844	0.850	**0.923**
Mar.	Apr.	P_r	0.711	0.603	0.606	0.570	0.590	0.703
		R_e	0.982	0.979	0.974	0.990	0.973	**0.992**
		F_1	**0.825**	0.746	0.747	0.733	0.735	0.823
		AUC	0.949	0.937	0.940	0.960	0.932	**0.967**
Apr.	May.	P_r	**0.990**	0.852	0.942	0.979	0.976	0.982
		R_e	0.952	0.941	0.848	0.873	0.878	**0.976**
		F_1	0.971	0.894	0.899	0.923	0.924	**0.979**
		AUC	0.975	0.894	0.920	0.930	0.937	**0.987**
May.	Jun.	P_r	0.938	**0.974**	0.950	0.825	0.838	0.962
		R_e	**0.995**	0.854	0.873	0.945	0.958	0.974
		F_1	0.965	0.910	0.910	0.881	0.894	**0.968**
		AUC	0.991	0.930	0.935	0.950	0.948	**0.992**
A_v		P_r	0.883	0.814	0.850	0.835	0.833	**0.890**
		R_e	0.938	0.895	0.868	0.887	0.900	**0.946**
		F_1	0.905	0.839	0.845	0.847	0.852	**0.913**
		AUC	0.952	0.922	0.921	0.926	0.917	**0.966**
A_r		P_r	2.800	4.400	3.400	4.000	4.200	**2.200**
		R_e	2.400	3.800	4.600	4.200	3.800	**2.000**
		F_1	1.600	4.600	4.200	4.800	4.200	**1.400**
		AUC	2.200	4.600	4.200	3.800	4.600	**1.600**
Training efficiency (ms)			100.87	97.24	96.13	110.53	128.96	136.25
Inference speed (ms)			0.027	0.026	0.027	0.035	0.027	0.039

formance of our model across all evaluation metrics surpasses its peers and validates its strong capability to learn and leverage transactional representations.

However, as the scale of transaction data continues to grow, the potential for models to capture user behavioral characteristics increases. Concurrently, this growth introduces significant computational overhead [1]. Although model training in financial scenarios typically takes place in an offline environment and does not directly impact real-time detection, excessively high computational costs still remain a burden in practical applications [6]. The challenge of reducing resource consumption while maintaining detection performance is a critical problem that financial institutions must address in large-scale transaction environments. The proposed model mitigates this problem by introducing a spatial-temporal perception mechanism, which models the contagion and clustering of fraudulent behaviors across temporal and spatial dimensions as its primary object of study [8]. Consequently, the model learns highly discriminative representations even when it uses relatively small datasets. This characteristic not only reduces reliance on massive datasets but also makes the model valuable in resource-constrained scenarios and in settings with high data acquisition costs.

Furthermore, the highly dynamic nature of financial transaction environments means that user behavioral patterns continue to evolve over time. To ensure detection effectiveness, financial institutions must periodically update the model training data. The experimental results demonstrate that our proposed model maintains stable performance under successive data updates. This robustness arises from the ability of the model to capture the underlying core patterns of fraudulent behavior, such as high-frequency triggers within short time windows, concentrated distributions in specific spatial regions, and rapid profit-seeking motivations. These salient features remain stable over long temporal spans, which enables the model to retain strong robustness and adaptability in dynamic environments.

Ablation Experiment. To gain a deep understanding of the internal mechanism of the proposed model and to verify the specific contributions of each functional module in OPFD, we design and conduct a systematic ablation study. In the experimental setup, A_0 is defined as the basic LSTM. It does not include any spatial-temporal modeling mechanisms and serves only as a baseline for comparison. Subsequently, we gradually introduce key modules of the model to examine their individual and combined effects. A_1 denotes the configuration that contains only the time-aware gate, and it captures the regulatory effect of transaction intervals on behavioral dependencies. A_2 denotes the configuration that contains only the location-aware gate, and it is designed to model the aggregation characteristics of transactions in spatial distributions. A_3 represents the interaction module, and it aims to enhance the interaction and fusion of different feature representations. Finally, $A_1 + A_2$ denotes the combination of both time and spatial gates, while $A_1 + A_2 + A_3$ represents the core structure of the complete model. The experimental results are shown in Table 6.2.

The comparison results show that the complete model structure ($A_1 + A_2 + A_3$) achieves the best performance across all evaluation metrics, demonstrating the significant advantages of collaborative modeling among multiple modules. The combination $A_1 + A_2$ ranks second, and its performance is significantly better than that of using the time-aware gate or the location-aware gate alone. This result indicates that the joint modeling of temporal and spatial information can more effectively characterize the complex patterns of fraudulent behavior. Further observation shows that both A_1 and A_2 achieve significant improvements compared to A_0 when they are used independently. This suggests that both time intervals and spatial aggregation characteristics are important indicators of fraudulent behavior. The introduction of

Table 6.2 Ablation study

Test	Criteria	A_0	A_1	A_2	$A_1 + A_2$	$A_1 + A_2 + A_3$
Feb.	P_r	0.834	0.877	0.870	0.904	**0.910**
	R_e	0.825	**0.953**	0.948	0.929	0.928
	F_1	0.829	0.913	0.908	0.916	**0.919**
	AUC	0.906	**0.957**	0.953	0.951	0.956
Mar.	P_r	**0.915**	0.809	0.822	0.899	0.905
	R_e	0.609	**0.890**	0.717	0.862	0.859
	F_1	0.731	0.848	0.766	0.880	**0.881**
	AUC	0.796	0.914	0.836	0.921	**0.930**
Apr.	P_r	0.579	0.666	0.621	**0.702**	0.697
	R_e	0.919	**0.987**	0.980	0.953	0.986
	F_1	0.710	0.795	0.761	0.808	**0.817**
	AUC	0.904	0.953	0.942	0.930	**0.958**
May.	P_r	0.809	0.931	0.932	0.928	**0.960**
	R_e	0.890	0.951	0.935	**0.981**	0.971
	F_1	0.848	0.941	0.934	0.954	**0.965**
	AUC	0.914	0.962	0.962	0.979	**0.980**
Jun.	P_r	0.835	0.856	0.845	0.867	**0.897**
	R_e	0.919	0.935	0.940	0.932	**0.943**
	F_1	0.863	0.894	0.890	0.898	**0.919**
	AUC	0.942	0.944	0.960	0.955	**0.970**

A_3 further promotes the fusion of multimodal information, making representation learning more effective and ultimately driving the overall model toward optimal performance.

Sensitivity Analysis. When constructing behavior modeling frameworks, users' historical behavioral information typically plays a pivotal role. Fraudsters often concentrate their transactions within a limited temporal window, whereas legitimate users exhibit long term and more diverse transaction patterns. Consequently, determining an appropriate behavioral memory length, defined as the length of the historical transaction sequence incorporated into the modeling process, emerges as a critical factor that influences model performance. To this end, this study systematically varies the behavioral memory length, denoted by s, and examines its impact on the model's detection performance, thereby elucidating the mechanism of behavioral memory in OPFD. Table 6.3 reports the results of the sensitivity analysis.

As the behavioral memory length increases, model performance improves significantly. This finding indicates that moderate incorporation of users' historical transactional information helps the model characterize individual transactional patterns and potential fraudulent behavior more accurately. In other words, historical sequences

Table 6.3 Sensitivity of the length of behavioral memory

Memory size	P_r	R_e	F_1	AUC
10	0.940	0.908	0.924	0.926
20	0.945	0.915	0.930	0.933
30	0.949	0.917	0.933	0.942
40	0.959	0.925	0.942	0.959
50	0.950	**0.942**	**0.946**	**0.967**
60	**0.952**	0.939	**0.946**	0.966
70	0.951	0.935	0.943	0.963
80	0.949	0.933	0.941	0.962

provide contextual information for the model, thereby making anomalous behaviors easier to identify when they are compared with past patterns. However, when the memory length exceeds 50, the performance improvement levels off and can even become negligible. This observation suggests that a memory length beyond a certain threshold introduces redundant information and increases the computational burden without providing additional discriminative value.

At the theoretical level, this outcome highlights two opposing modeling tendencies. If the model considers only recent transactions, long-term user behavioral characteristics may be overlooked, which leads to weak performance against slow burn fraud. In contrast, indiscriminate inclusion of all historical transactions makes it difficult for the model to capture the most discriminative behavioral patterns because of noise and redundancy. Therefore, a compromise value for the behavioral memory length represents the optimal choice. The study finds that the most favorable results are achieved when the behavioral memory length is set to $\frac{n}{|U|}$, and this choice is statistically stable and provides a practical and actionable reference for real-world applications.

6.6 Summary

This chapter introduces a novel Spatial-Temporal Gated Network (STGN) designed to automatically learn more discriminative transactional representations, thereby enhancing the performance of OPFD. The model incorporates time-aware and location-aware gates within its recurrent units. This design enables a more comprehensive capture of users' transactional behavioral patterns across both temporal and spatial dimensions. Concurrently, the proposed spatial-temporal attention module further clarifies the underlying behavioral motivations embedded within users' historical transactions, allowing the model to rely on more interpretable behavioral evidence when identifying fraudulent activities. In addition, the inclusion of a representation interaction module empowers the model to integrate representations from multiple dimensions, enabling it to learn more informative and efficient transaction features. Experimental results on real-world transaction datasets, together with visualizations of the learned transactional representations, fully demonstrate STGN's superior performance in OPFD. Although the proposed STGN surpasses its peers in several respects, opportunities for further enhancement remain. First, the recurrent structure presents inherent limitations in capturing the interactive relationships between temporal and spatial dependencies in transactional behavior. The current design can model temporal and spatial features independently but struggles to simultaneously integrate their complex interdependencies. To address this issue, subsequent chapters will further incorporate multi-source feature information to strengthen the model's ability to characterize transactional behaviors. This advancement aims to more effectively capture the multi-dimensional interactive characteristics underlying complex transactional patterns.

References

1. Abboush, M., Bamal, D., Knieke, C., Rausch, A.: Intelligent fault detection and classification based on hybrid deep learning methods for hardware-in-the-loop test of automotive software systems. Sensors **22**(11), 4066 (2022)
2. Cai, Y.: Financial embedding, consumer goods laws, and new forms of the digital economy. Finance Research Letters p. 108405 (2025)
3. Cheng, D., Wang, X., Zhang, Y., Zhang, L.: Graph neural network for fraud detection via Spatial-Temporal attention. IEEE Trans. on Knowledge and Data Engineering **34**(8), 3800–3813 (2022)
4. Chu, G., Wang, J., Qi, Q., Sun, H., Tao, S., Yang, H., Liao, J., Han, Z.: Exploiting spatial-temporal behavior patterns for fraud detection in telecom networks. IEEE Trans. on Dependable and Secure Computing **20**(6), 4564–4577 (2022)
5. Ding, K., Shu, K., Shan, X., Li, J., Liu, H.: Cross-domain graph anomaly detection. IEEE Trans. on Neural Networks and Learning Systems **33**(6), 2406–2415 (2021)
6. Dudukcu, H.V., Taskiran, M., Taskiran, Z.G.C., Yildirim, T.: Temporal convolutional networks with RNN approach for chaotic time series prediction. Applied Soft Computing **133**, 109945 (2023)
7. Fanai, H., Abbasimehr, H.: A novel combined approach based on deep autoencoder and deep classifiers for credit card fraud detection. Expert Systems with Applications **217**, 119562 (2023)
8. He, Y., Zhang, H., Ning, X., Zhang, R., Chang, D., Hao, M.: Spatial-temporal semantic perception network for remote sensing image semantic change detection. Remote Sensing **15**(16), 4095 (2023)
9. Jiang, Y., Liu, G., Wu, J., Lin, H.: Telecom fraud detection via hawkes-enhanced sequence model. IEEE Trans. on Knowledge and Data Engineering **35**(5), 5311–5324 (2022)
10. Jiang, Z., Zhan, Y., Mao, Q., Du, Y.: Semi-supervised clustering under a "compact-cluster" assumption. IEEE Trans. on Knowledge and Data Engineering **35**(5), 5244–5256 (2022)
11. Kong, X., Zhu, B., Shen, G., Workneh, T.C., Ji, Z., Chen, Y., Liu, Z.: Spatial-temporal-cost combination based taxi driving fraud detection for collaborative internet of vehicles. IEEE Trans. on Industrial Informatics **18**(5), 3426–3436 (2021)
12. Li, Y., Yang, X., Gao, Q., Wang, H., Zhang, J., Li, T.: Cross-Regional fraud detection via continual learning with knowledge transfer. IEEE Trans. on Knowledge and Data Engineering **36**(12), 7865–7877 (2024)

13. Li, Z., Zhuo, S., Shi, Y., Huang, J., He, J., Qiu, W., Zheng, Z., Huang, S., Chen, M., Tang, Y.: Unveiling blockchain transactions insights: Behavior anomaly detection via relational mechanisms. IEEE Internet of Things Journal (2025)
14. Liang, Y., Huang, G., Zhao, Z.: Joint demand prediction for multimodal systems: A multi-task multi-relational spatiotemporal graph neural network approach. Transportation research part C: emerging technologies **140**, 103731 (2022)
15. Lin, H., Liu, G., Wu, J., Zuo, Y., Wan, X., Li, H.: Fraud detection in dynamic interaction network. IEEE Trans. on Knowledge and Data Engineering **32**(10), 1936–1950 (2020)
16. Ma, J., Liu, H., Peng, C., Qiu, T.: Unauthorized broadcasting identification: A deep LSTM recurrent learning approach. IEEE Trans. on Instrumentation and Measurement **69**(9), 5981–5983 (2020)
17. Motie, S., Raahemi, B.: Financial fraud detection using graph neural networks: A systematic review. Expert Systems with Applications **240**, 122156 (2024)
18. Paladini, T., Monti, F., Polino, M., Carminati, M., Zanero, S.: Fraud detection under siege: Practical poisoning attacks and defense strategies. ACM Trans. Priv. Secur. **26**(4) (2023)
19. Popiolek, P.F., dos Santos Machado, K., Mendizabal, O.M.: Low overhead performance monitoring for shared infrastructures. Expert Systems with Applications **171**, 114558 (2021)
20. Rama-Maneiro, E., Vidal, J.C., Lama, M.: Embedding graph convolutional networks in recurrent neural networks for predictive monitoring. IEEE Trans. on Knowledge and Data Engineering **36**(1), 137–151 (2023)
21. Reale-Nosei, G., Amador-Domínguez, E., Serrano, E.: From vision to text: A comprehensive review of natural image captioning in medical diagnosis and radiology report generation. Medical Image Analysis **97**, 103264 (2024)
22. Ren, L., Hu, R., Li, D., Liu, Y., Wu, J., Zang, Y., Hu, W.: Dynamic graph neural network-based fraud detectors against collaborative fraudsters. Knowledge-Based Systems **278**, 110888 (2023)
23. Wang, C., Wang, C., Zhu, H., Cui, J.: LAW: Learning automatic windows for online payment fraud detection. IEEE Trans. on Dependable and Secure Computing **18**(5), 2122–2135 (2021)
24. Wang, X., Guo, J., Luo, X., Yu, H.: DyHDGE: Dynamic heterogeneous transaction graph embedding for safety-centric fraud detection in financial scenarios. Journal of Safety Science and Resilience **5**(4), 486–497 (2024)
25. Wang, Y., Liu, Z., Xu, J., Yan, W.: Heterogeneous network representation learning approach for ethereum identity identification. IEEE Trans. on Computational Social Systems **10**(3), 890–899 (2022)
26. Wu, C., Cao, H., Chen, J., Yan, X., Xu, G., Zhao, Z., Liu, Y., Jiang, H.: RugScreener: Leveraging temporal graph neural network for rugpull detection in defi. IEEE Trans. on Information Forensics and Security **20**, 11120–11133 (2025)
27. Xie, H., Randall, M., Chau, K.w.: Green roof hydrological modelling with GRU and LSTM networks. Water Resources Management **36**(3), 1107–1122 (2022)
28. Xie, Y., Hong, Y., Qiao, S., Yao, J., Liu, G., Pang, S.: A time-aware generative network for enhancing transaction security in consumer electronics. IEEE Trans. on Consumer Electronics **71**(2), 6818–6828 (2025)
29. Xie, Y., Liu, G., Yan, C., Jiang, C., Zhou, M.: Time-aware attention-based gated network for credit card fraud detection by extracting transactional behaviors. IEEE Trans. on Computational Social Systems **10**(3), 1004–1016 (2023)
30. Xie, Y., Liu, G., Yan, C., Jiang, C., Zhou, M., Li, M.: Learning transactional behavioral representations for credit card fraud detection. IEEE Trans. on Neural Networks and Learning Systems **35**(4), 5735–5748 (2024)
31. Xie, Y., Liu, G., Zhou, M., Wei, L., Zhu, H., Zhou, R., Cao, L.: A spatial–temporal gated network for credit card fraud detection by learning transactional representations. IEEE Trans. on Automation Science and Engineering **21**(4), 6978–6991 (2024)
32. Xie, Y., Shan, J., Wei, L., Yao, J., Zhou, M.: GAN-based hybrid sampling method for transaction fraud detection. IEEE Trans. on Knowledge and Data Engineering **37**(10), 5905–5918 (2025)
33. Xie, Y., Zhou, M., Liu, G., Wei, L., Zhu, H., De Meo, P.: A transactional-behavior-based hierarchical gated network for credit card fraud detection. IEEE/CAA Journal of Automatica Sinica **12**(7), 1489–1503 (2025)

34. Xiong, Y., Xu, K., Chen, M., Huang, H.: Cross-domain transformer spatial-temporal fusion network for traffic flow forecasting. Scientific Reports **15**(1), 23524 (2025)
35. Ye, L., Wang, Z., Chen, X., Wang, J., Wu, K., Lu, K.: GSAN: Graph self-attention network for learning spatial–temporal interaction representation in autonomous driving. IEEE Internet of Things Journal **9**(12), 9190–9204 (2021)
36. Zhang, D., Yan, J., Polat, K., Alhudhaif, A., Li, J.: Multimodal joint prediction of traffic spatial-temporal data with graph sparse attention mechanism and bidirectional temporal convolutional network. Advanced Engineering Informatics **62**, 102533 (2024)
37. Zhang, Z., Wei, Z., Ma, L.: UBRMTC: User behavior recognition model with transaction character. IEEE Trans. on Computational Social Systems **11**(2), 1589–1601 (2024)
38. Zhang, Z., Wang, Y.X., He, H., Sun, F.: A short-and long-term prognostic associating with remaining useful life estimation for proton exchange membrane fuel cell. Applied Energy **304**, 117841 (2021)
39. Zhao, S., Hu, M., Cai, Z., Liu, F.: Dynamic modeling cross-modal interactions in two-phase prediction for entity-relation extraction. IEEE Trans. on Neural Networks and Learning Systems **34**(3), 1122–1131 (2021)
40. Zhu, F., Wang, Y., Zhou, J., Chen, C., Li, L., Liu, G.: A unified framework for cross-domain and cross-system recommendations. IEEE Trans. on Knowledge and Data Engineering **35**(2), 1171–1184 (2021)
41. Zhu, H., Wang, C., Chai, S.: Detecting evolving fraudulent behavior in online payment services: Open-Category and Concept-Drift. IEEE Trans. on Services Computing **17**(5), 2180–2193 (2024)
42. Zhu, H., Wang, C., Chai, S.: Detecting evolving fraudulent behavior in online payment services: Open-category and concept-drift. IEEE Trans. on Services Computing **17**(5), 2180–2193 (2024)

Chapter 7
Hierarchical Gated Networks for Deep Transactional Representation Learning

In OPFD, fraudulent behavior is often hidden in complex combinations of static attributes and the dynamic evolution of user behaviors. This makes single-perspective modeling ineffective in real-world scenarios. Therefore, deep modeling of transactional behaviors is essential for ensuring the effectiveness of OPFD models. Building upon the representation learning framework proposed in Chap. 6, this chapter extends the modeling perspective by jointly considering discriminative transaction-level features and high-level sequential behavioral patterns. A hierarchical and modular modeling framework is proposed, which consists of three core modules: a feature-oriented module for selecting discriminative transaction attributes, a sequence-oriented module for modeling temporal dependencies, and an interaction module for unified representation learning. By conducting deep feature reasoning at both the behavioral and structural levels, the proposed framework captures the intrinsic patterns of complex transactional behaviors from multiple perspectives. It provides more systematic representations to support effective learning and decision-making in OPFD tasks.

7.1 Hierarchical Modeling Needs in Transaction Streams

Fraudulent activities in online payment systems rarely appear as isolated anomalies. Instead, they arise from intricate combinations of static transaction attributes and the evolving behavioral trajectories of users over time [8, 16]. Fraudsters intentionally imitate legitimate behavioral patterns [31]. As a result, fraudulent and normal transactions often exhibit substantial overlap in observable characteristics. This overlap makes raw transaction features, when examined independently, insufficient for uncovering the subtle signals required for reliable fraud detection [22].

To highlight this issue, we apply t-SNE to visualize raw transaction features collected from real-world payment records. As shown in Fig. 7.1, legitimate transactions appear in yellow and fraudulent ones in blue. These points are heavily interwoven across the projection space. Two observations are particularly noteworthy. First, no

Y. Xie et al., *Neural Network-Based Deep Learning for Online Payment Fraud Detection*,
https://doi.org/10.1007/978-981-95-8513-7_7

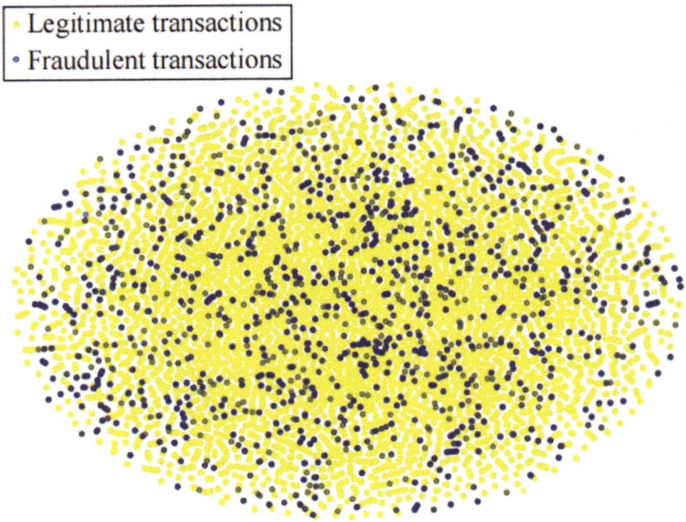

Fig. 7.1 We report a two-dimensional visualization of credit card transactions. Dots in blue represent fraudulent transactions, while dots in yellow are associated with non-fraudulent transactions. The coordinates of each dot identify the features of the corresponding transactions

clear boundary emerges between the two types of transactions. Their strong intermixing indicates that static attributes alone cannot provide adequate separability for classification. Second, many traditional fraud detection systems rely on a small set of predefined features. For example, some systems flag a transaction as suspicious only when its amount exceeds a preset threshold. Such rule-based approaches are unable to capture more adaptive or subtle forms of fraudulent behavior.

Despite the evident complexity of fraud patterns, many mainstream approaches in online payment fraud detection still center on feature-level modeling [12]. These methods perform well when the discriminative signal lies primarily in individual attributes [27]. However, they struggle in realistic OPFD environments. Models that focus on static features can identify irregularities such as abnormal spending patterns or improbable geolocations [6, 17]. Even so, they fail to represent how these attributes evolve over time. On the other hand, sequence modeling techniques supported by recurrent neural networks can capture temporal dynamics, yet they tend to assign uniform importance to all attributes [30]. This tendency overlooks the fact that features vary greatly in their relevance to fraud detection. Such fragmented perspectives make models either overly sensitive to noise or incapable of capturing essential behavioral cues [29]. As a result, further improvements in detection performance remain difficult.

These limitations reveal a clear need for a hierarchical modeling framework that reflects the multi-layered nature of transaction streams. Transaction flows contain information at different levels of abstraction. Fine-grained attribute signals and high-level temporal patterns both contribute to the characterization of user behavior. An effective representation learning framework must therefore reason across these different layers. Hierarchical modeling offers a principled solution because it organizes the analytical process into components that address complementary aspects of transactional data.

At the feature level, a discriminative selection module identifies the most informative attributes while suppressing noise and redundancy [3, 9]. This step provides a compact and meaningful representation for subsequent modeling. At the sequence level, a temporal module analyzes how user behaviors evolve. It captures patterns such as progressive increases in spending intensity, abrupt contextual shifts, or repetitive micro-behaviors that may indicate fraudulent intent [28]. At the interaction level, the framework brings together static and temporal perspectives into a unified representation. The resulting fusion captures both attribute-specific irregularities and their corresponding behavioral context. This integration not only supports higher detection accuracy but also enhances interpretability. Analysts can trace a fraudulent signal to specific features and to the temporal patterns through which these features develop.

Within this modeling paradigm, hierarchical gated architectures provide a particularly suitable design choice. These architectures regulate the flow of information across different layers and support the combination of multiple sources of behavioral signals. Through deeper structural and behavioral reasoning, they offer a robust basis for constructing feature-oriented modules, sequence-oriented modules, and interaction mechanisms. In doing so, they can establish a comprehensive and principled framework for deep representation learning in OPFD [32].

7.2 Feature-Oriented Module for Attribute Importance

In the lower layer of the hierarchical gated network, the feature-oriented module is responsible for identifying the most discriminative signals from multi-dimensional transactional attributes. Financial transaction records contain heterogeneous information such as time, location, amount, merchant category, and device type [10, 24]. The importance of these attributes varies significantly across different contexts. For instance, sudden fluctuations in transaction amounts often indicate elevated risk, while abrupt geographic changes may reveal fraudulent activity more directly. Traditional detection models, however, commonly treat all input features as equally important. This equal-weight input strategy tends to dilute the influence of informative attributes, especially in high-dimensional settings where noise can overshadow critical signals [7, 13]. As a result, the model may struggle to focus on the risk-relevant aspects of complex transaction data.

To address this issue, this study introduces a Feature-Oriented Attribute Importance Module (FAIM) within the hierarchical modeling framework [20]. FAIM aims to achieve adaptive weighting across feature dimensions through a learnable feature-attention mechanism, enabling the model to dynamically highlight key attributes while suppressing irrelevant or redundant signals. The module consists of a feature

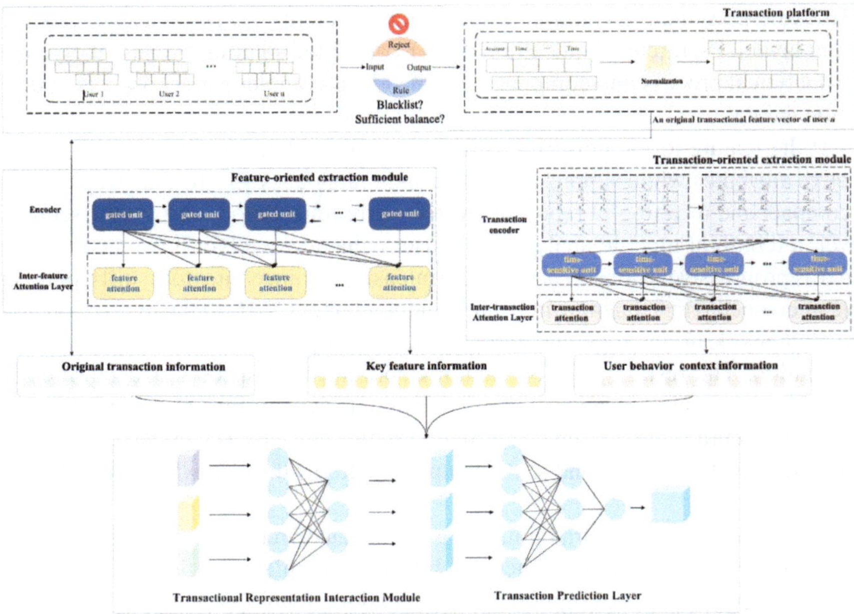

Fig. 7.2 Framework of TbHGN for OPFD

encoder and an inter-feature attention layer, as illustrated in Fig. 7.2. The feature encoder models dependencies among attributes through a bidirectional gated structure. The inter-feature attention layer then evaluates the relative importance of each attribute. Finally, a multilayer perceptron performs fraud discrimination based on the refined representation. Through this process, FAIM filters noise at the input level and enhances both the discriminative capability and interpretability of the resulting feature representations.

Feature Encoder. The core function of the feature encoder is to capture the intrinsic dependencies among transactional attributes [23]. Fraudulent behavior often emerges from the interaction of multiple attribute types. Consequently, models that rely on individual features tend to either overfit or overlook important risk indicators [2]. For example, a high-value transaction may appear legitimate when considered alone. Its risk, however, increases substantially when it occurs at an unusual time or at a location that does not match the user's historical pattern. Conversely, behaviors that seem atypical in isolation may be legitimate if they align with the user's past activities. These observations indicate that fraud detection requires an integrated view of multidimensional attributes and an ability to model their mutual influences.

To meet this requirement, the feature encoder adopts a bidirectional gated architecture. This structure uses update and reset gates to adaptively retain informative signals and suppress noise-driven dependencies. By processing attribute relationships in both forward and backward directions, the encoder captures a richer set of associations that would otherwise be missed in a unidirectional design. This capability strengthens the flexibility and robustness of the learned representations and provides a more reliable foundation for subsequent attention-based weighting and classification.

$$\overrightarrow{z}_{ij} = \sigma\left(W_{z\mu}\overrightarrow{h}_{i,j-1} + W_{zr}x_{i_j}\right), \tag{7.1}$$

$$\overrightarrow{e}_{ij} = \sigma\left(W_{e\mu}\overrightarrow{h}_{i,j-1} + W_{er}x_{i_j}\right), \tag{7.2}$$

$$\overrightarrow{\tilde{h}}_{ij} = \tanh\left(W_{\mu}\left[\overrightarrow{e}_{ij} * \overrightarrow{h}_{i,j-1}, x_{i_j}\right]\right), \tag{7.3}$$

$$\overrightarrow{h}_{ij} = \left(1 - \overrightarrow{z}_{ij}\right) * \overrightarrow{h}_{i,j-1} + \overrightarrow{z}_{ij} * \overrightarrow{\tilde{h}}_{ij}, \tag{7.4}$$

where $\overrightarrow{\mathbf{z}_{ij}}$ is the forward update gate that determines whether the current feature information should be integrated into the present state. $\overrightarrow{\mathbf{e}_{ij}}$ is the forward reset gate that controls the degree to which the current feature influences the current state. By selectively discarding parts of the previous state, the encoder improves its ability to adapt to the current input. $\overrightarrow{\tilde{h}}_{ij}$ and $\overrightarrow{h}_{ij}$ denote the forward candidate state and the forward hidden state, respectively. The backward module processes features in a similar manner but in the opposite direction. Thus, for a given transaction r_i, the final feature representation for $j \in \{1, 2, \ldots, m\}$ is obtained by concatenating $\overrightarrow{h}_{ij}$ and $\overleftarrow{h}_{ij}$, denoted as $h_i = [\overrightarrow{h}_{ij}, \overleftarrow{h}_{ij}]$. The symbol "$*$" denotes the Hadamard product. The weight matrices $W_{z\mu}$, W_{zr}, $W_{e\mu}$, W_{er}, and W_{μ} are randomly initialized and jointly optimized during training. Through the combined modeling of forward and backward gated units, the encoder is able to capture both global patterns and local variations, leading to richer feature representations and providing a strong foundation for the subsequent attention mechanism.

Inter-feature Attention Layer. In OPFD, transaction data are typically composed of multi-dimensional raw attributes such as amount, transaction time, geographic location, and account balance. However, these features do not contribute equally to fraud identification—some carry strong discriminative power and can directly reveal suspicious patterns, while others may be redundant or noisy. Although the feature encoder effectively captures dependencies among attributes, not all features are equally important for fraud detection. To address this issue, we introduce an inter-feature attention layer on top of the feature encoder. This layer learns to assign adaptive weights to different features and maps the weighted representations to discriminative predictions through continuous training.

The core of the inter-feature attention layer is the inter-feature attention mechanism, whose key idea is to estimate the contribution of each feature to the current transaction representation by modeling their correlations and to generate a more discriminative representation through a weighted aggregation. The detailed process is as follows:

$$o^i_{j,k} = \tanh(W_{oj}h_{ij} + W_{ok}h_{ik} + b_o), \tag{7.5}$$

$$\alpha^i_{j,k} = \frac{\exp(o^{iT}_{j,k}o_f)}{\sum\limits_{k=1}^{j-1}\exp(o^{iT}_{j,k}o_f)}, \tag{7.6}$$

$$s_{ij} = \sum_{k=1}^{j-1}\alpha^i_{j,k}h_{ik}, \tag{7.7}$$

where $o^i_{j,k}$ represents the correlation between the j-th feature and the k-th feature, which measures their mutual influence. The attention weight $\alpha^i_{j,k}$, computed through a softmax function, reflects the model's degree of focus on different features. The vector s_{ij} is the aggregated representation obtained through attention-weighted fusion. The term h_{ik} ($k \in \{1, 2, \ldots, j-1\}$) denotes earlier feature states produced by the feature encoder, while W_{oj} and W_{ok} are weight matrices and b_o is the bias term. By comparing each feature h_{ik} with the current feature h_{ij}, the model computes the score $o^i_{j,k}$. After weighting these scores and integrating the feature-importance term o_f, the normalized importance weights $\alpha^i_{j,k}$ are obtained through softmax, and the weighted sum of h_{ik} is then used to produce s_{ij}. The representation s_{ij} captures both multi-dependency relations among original features and fraud patterns indicated by feature importance, thus preserving the key attribute information of transaction x_i. As a result, the original transaction data $R = \{r_1, r_2, \ldots, r_n\}$ are transformed into $R^s = \{s_1, s_2, \ldots, s_n\}$. This mechanism allows the model to automatically highlight features that are highly relevant to fraud detection while suppressing redundant or irrelevant information, producing a more compact and discriminative output. In addition to improving detection performance, this design also enhances model interpretability, as the attention weights directly reveal which features the model relies on during prediction.

Learning Process. After obtaining the aggregated representation s_i from the feature-attention mechanism, the model must further map this high-dimensional and structured representation to the final classification output. To achieve this, we construct a prediction layer based on linear transformation and nonlinear activation, which performs the mapping from the feature space to the probability space. Specifically, the prediction probability p_i is computed as follows:

$$p_i = \sigma(W_s s_i + b_s), \tag{7.8}$$

where W_s is the learnable weight matrix and b_s is the corresponding bias term. The function $\sigma(\cdot)$ denotes the Sigmoid activation, which compresses the output of the linear transformation into the interval $[0, 1]$, allowing p_i to be interpreted as the probability that the $i-th$ transaction is fraudulent. This structure effectively captures the linear contributions of input features across different dimensions, while the nonlinear mapping introduced by the Sigmoid function strengthens the model's decision boundary and makes it suitable for probabilistic modeling in binary classification. To train the model parameters, we employ the binary cross-entropy loss to measure the discrepancy between the predicted probabilities and the ground-truth labels, defined as follows:

$$Loss = -\sum_{i=1}^{n}[\hat{y}_i \log(p_i) + (1 - \hat{y}_i)\log(1 - p_i)], \tag{7.9}$$

where $\hat{y}_i \in [0, 1]$ denotes the ground-truth label of the i-th transaction, $\hat{y}_i = 1$ indicates fraud, $\hat{y}_i = 0$ indicates a legitimate transaction, and p_i represents the predicted probability produced by the model. This loss function imposes a larger penalty on misclassified samples, enabling the model to quickly correct erroneous decisions during training. It also supports stable and efficient parameter updates through gradient propagation in the probability space, making it the standard optimization objective for binary classification tasks.

In terms of optimization, the model employs the Adam optimizer, whose adaptive learning-rate strategy based on first- and second-moment estimates enables faster and more stable convergence in complex loss landscapes [19]. This helps alleviate common issues in traditional gradient descent, such as vanishing gradients, oscillations, and difficulties in tuning the learning rate. Within the proposed architecture, the preceding bidirectional gating structure and attention-based weighting already produce sparse and discriminative feature representations, allowing the final prediction layer—despite its relatively small parameter size—to achieve strong classification performance.

Overall, the feature-oriented attribute importance module establishes a complete modeling pipeline that progresses from gated dependency learning to attention-based feature selection and ultimately to probabilistic prediction. The bidirectional gating units capture dynamic dependencies among multi-dimensional attributes, while the attention mechanism emphasizes key factors closely related to fraud and suppresses redundant features. Finally, the prediction layer and cross-entropy loss provide accurate probability estimation. Within the Transaction-based Hierarchical Gated Network (TbHGN) framework, this module not only improves the model's discriminative accuracy and robustness but also enhances interpretability, forming a solid foundation for subsequent temporal modeling and global feature interaction learning [25].

7.3 Sequence-Oriented Module for Behavioral Transitions

Although the feature encoder and the attention mechanism capture the importance of static attributes, relying solely on the characteristics of an individual transaction provides an incomplete view of user behavior. Fraudulent activities are seldom triggered by a single attribute. Instead, they emerge through dynamic patterns that develop over time. A single high-value transaction may be entirely normal. However, repeated high-value transactions occurring within a short time frame markedly increase the likelihood of risk. In contrast, an attribute that appears unusual in isolation may still be legitimate if it conforms to the user's established behavioral rhythm. These examples highlight a fundamental limitation of static feature modeling and demonstrate the need to incorporate temporal dependencies into the overall decision process [1, 15].

To meet this requirement, the TbHGN framework introduces a sequence-oriented behavior transition module that operates after the feature-oriented component, as illustrated in Fig. 7.2. This module processes the historical sequence of transactions and models the current transaction in the context of past behavior. Through this design, the model learns both short-term fluctuations and long-term behavioral patterns, enabling a more accurate reflection of real-world transaction dynamics.

The behavior transition module consists of two core components: a transaction encoder and an inter-transaction attention layer. The former generates deep representations for each historical transaction in the sequence, while the latter evaluates dependencies across transactions and captures the varying importance of each temporal element. To represent the effects of time intervals more accurately, the module incorporates a Time-Sensitive GRU (Ts-GRU) [26, 34]. Unlike conventional recurrent structures, Ts-GRU introduces a time-decay factor into its gating mechanism. This addition allows the model to adjust its sensitivity based on the temporal distance between transactions. As a result, the module effectively captures meaningful behavioral patterns such as concentrated bursts of activity within a short period and long-term stability in user behavior [21].

By integrating deep representations of static attributes with dynamic modeling of temporal behavior, TbHGN achieves strong discriminative capability across both the feature dimension and the temporal dimension. This joint modeling paradigm establishes a robust foundation for identifying complex and covert fraud patterns that may not be detectable through either perspective alone [18].

Transaction Encoder. The transaction encoder first expands each transaction into a fixed-length sequence that contains d historical transactions:

$$g^u = \begin{bmatrix} g_1^u \\ g_2^u \\ \vdots \\ g_{n^u}^u \end{bmatrix} = \begin{bmatrix} s_1^u & s_1^u & \cdots & s_1^u \\ s_1^u & s_1^u & \cdots & s_2^u \\ \vdots & \vdots & \ddots & \vdots \\ s_{n^u-d+1}^u & s_{n^u-d+2}^u & \cdots & s_{n^u}^u \end{bmatrix}, \tag{7.10}$$

for user u, s_i^u denotes his/her i-th transaction record. When $i < d$, padding or replication is applied to ensure a consistent sequence length. This design allows the model to handle users with different transaction frequencies in a unified manner and explicitly incorporates temporal context into the input.

Building on this sequence construction, TbHGN employs a Ts-GRU to model transaction sequences. As illustrated in Fig. 7.3, Ts-GRU extends the conventional GRU by introducing a time-decay factor that captures how transactions with different

Fig. 7.3 Structure of time-sensitive gated recurrent unit

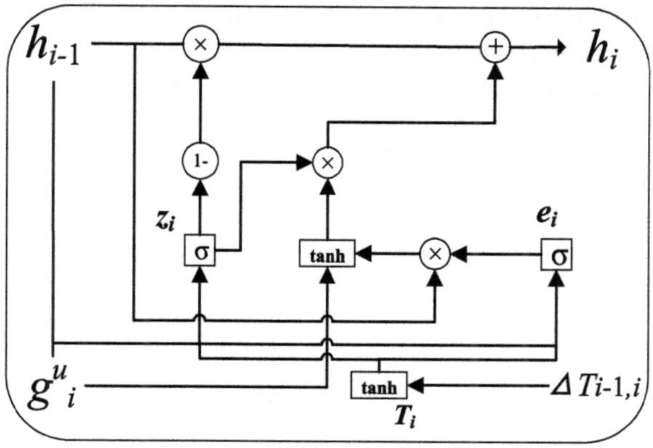

temporal gaps contribute unequally to a user's behavioral pattern. Its basic gating units are defined as follows:

$$\mathcal{T}_i = \tanh\left(W_{\mathcal{T}h}h_{i-1} + W_{\mathcal{T}g}g_i^u + W_{\mathcal{T}\Delta T}\Delta T_{i-1,i}\right), \tag{7.11}$$

$$z_i = \sigma\left(W_{zh}h_{i-1} + W_{zg}g_i^u + W_{z\mathcal{T}}\mathcal{T}_i\right), \tag{7.12}$$

$$e_i = \sigma\left(W_{eh}h_{i-1} + W_{eg}g_i^u + W_{e\mathcal{T}}\mathcal{T}_i\right) \text{ s.t. } W_{e\mathcal{T}} < 0, \tag{7.13}$$

$$\tilde{h}_i = \tanh\left(W_{\tilde{h}e}(e_i * h_{i-1}) + W_{\tilde{h}g}g_i^u\right), \tag{7.14}$$

$$h_i = (1 - z_i) * h_{i-1} + z_i * \tilde{h}_i, \tag{7.15}$$

where h_{i-1}, $\tilde{h}_i$, and h_i denote the previous state, candidate state, and hidden state at the i-th recurrent step, respectively. $\Delta T_{i-1,i}$ represents the time interval between s_{i-1}^u and s_i^u. The variables e_i and z_i correspond to the reset gate and update gate. $\mathcal{T}_i$ is the time state that integrates the time interval, combining the current transaction with past behaviors and temporal information. This design enables the reset gate to evaluate the relevance of historical behaviors according to the spacing between transactions. For example, if the previous transaction occurred long ago, it suggests that the user's behavior may have changed. In this case, the update gate assigns greater weight to the current transaction, allowing the model to focus on recent behavior, which is often more informative for fraud detection. Conversely, if the previous transaction occurred recently, indicating behavioral consistency, the reset gate assigns less weight to the current transaction and emphasizes recent historical behavior. By dynamically controlling how much past behavior is forgotten, the module ensures that the model captures the most relevant current information.The matrices $W_{\mathcal{T}h}$, $W_{\mathcal{T}r}$, $W_{\mathcal{T}\Delta T}$, W_{zh}, W_{zg}, $W_{z\mathcal{T}}$, W_{eh}, W_{eg}, $W_{e\Delta T}$, $W_{\tilde{h}e}$, and $W_{\tilde{h}g}$ are trainable parameters jointly optimized during learning.

Inter-transaction Attention Layer. To further highlight the role of critical transactions within the historical sequence, TbHGN introduces an inter-transaction attention mechanism after the transaction encoder. The key idea is that not all past transactions contribute equally to the current prediction, and the model should adjust their weights dynamically based on contextual information. The structure of this mechanism is defined as follows:

$$o_{ij}^u = \tanh(W_{ti}h_i^u + W_{tj}h_j^u + b_t), \tag{7.16}$$

$$\alpha_{ij}^u = \frac{\exp((o_{ij}^u)^T o_t)}{\sum_{k=i-d}^{i-1} \exp((o_{ij}^u)^T o_t)}, \tag{7.17}$$

$$v_i^u = \sum_{k=i-d}^{i-1} \alpha_{ij}^u h_j^u, \tag{7.18}$$

where $j \in \{i-d, i-d+1, \ldots, i-1\}$ indexes the previous states in the recurrent unit, and $h_j^u = \{h_{i-d}^u, h_{i-d+1}^u, \ldots, h_{i-1}^u\}$ denotes the historical states associated with user u's i-th transaction.To assess the contribution of each historical state h_j^u, the model compares it with the current state h_i^u to compute a relevance score o_{ij}^u. This score is then weighted using learnable parameters—where b_t is a bias term, W_{ti} and W_{tj} are weight matrices, and tanh serves as the nonlinear activation—to prevent the model from overemphasizing any single behavior. By incorporating the aggregated score o_{ij}^u to evaluate overall historical behavior patterns, the model obtains the normalized attention weights a_{ij}^u.

The model computes the weighted sum of historical states based on the normalized attention weights. The resulting vector v_i^u serves as a new representation corresponding to s_i^u, capturing how past transactions influence the current one, including the underlying behavioral tendencies. By integrating this layer into the transaction-oriented extraction module, the model is able to capture subtle relationships between a user's historical and current behaviors, thereby improving the performance of OPFD models.

Overall, the full transaction set $R = \{r_1, r_2, \ldots, r_n\}$ is transformed into $R^s = \{s_1, s_2, \ldots, s_n\}$ through the feature-oriented extraction module and subsequently into $R^v = \{v_1, v_2, \ldots, v_n\}$ through the transaction-oriented extraction module. This mechanism effectively reduces the influence of "noisy transactions" in the sequence and enables the model to focus on recent or high-value behaviors that are more indicative of potential fraud.

Learning Process. Similarly, v_i is input into a one-layer MLP and the prediction q_i of the i-th transaction is obtained through

$$q_i = \sigma(W_\nu v_i + b_\nu), \tag{7.19}$$

where σ represents the Sigmoidal nonlinearity function. The cross-entropy and Adam algorithm are again employed as the loss function and optimizer, respectively.

$$\text{Loss} = -\sum_{i=1}^{n} \left[\hat{y}_i \log(q_i) + (1 - \hat{y}_i) \log(1 - q_i) \right]. \tag{7.20}$$

W_v and b_v are the weight matrix and the bias, and they are initialized randomly before being corporately learned during the training process.

7.4 Feature Fusion and Rational Interaction Layer

After completing the feature-oriented and sequence-oriented extraction modules, the model obtains two types of representations: the key attribute representation of each individual transaction and the temporal behavior representation across the transaction sequence. However, using these representations independently is insufficient to capture the complex fraud patterns behind online transactional behavior. To address this limitation, the TbHGN framework introduces a Transactional Representation Interaction Module, positioned in the middle of the architecture shown in Fig. 7.2. This module unifies three sources of information: the raw transaction features r_i, the key attribute features s_i, and the user behavior context features v_i. By integrating these representations into a shared feature space, the module produces a more discriminative transaction-level representation, enabling the model to better support downstream fraud detection.

The core idea of this module is to embed features from different sources into a unified representation space through a cross-level interaction mechanism. This design enables the model to jointly consider the static attributes of individual transactions and the dynamic evolution of long-term behavioral patterns. During this process, the features are not simply concatenated; instead, they are fused through weighted combinations and nonlinear transformations. This deep fusion ensures that the complementary information across modalities is effectively leveraged.

More specifically, the representation process of this module can be formalized as follows:

$$r_i = \tanh(Wx_i + Ls_i + Rv_i), \tag{7.21}$$

where r_i, s_i, and v_i denote the raw transaction features, the key attribute representation produced by the feature-oriented module, and the user context representation generated by the sequence-oriented module, respectively. W, L, and R are the corresponding weight matrices. Through linear weighting followed by a nonlinear activation, the model produces a unified representation r_i, which captures the interaction effects among these multi-dimensional features within a shared vector space.

Subsequently, the fused representation is fed into an MLP to produce the final prediction. A Sigmoid function is applied to the output layer to generate the probability estimate: $y_i = \sigma(Vx_i)$, where V denotes the parameter matrix, and y_i represents the predicted probability that the i-th transaction is fraudulent. To optimize model training, the cross-entropy loss is adopted:

$$Loss = -\sum_{i=1}^{n}[\hat{y}_i \log(y_i) + (1 - \hat{y}_i)\log(1 - y_i)], \tag{7.22}$$

where $\hat{y}_i$ denotes the ground-truth label and y_i is the model prediction. Cross-entropy effectively measures the discrepancy between the predicted and true distributions, and the parameters are optimized through backpropagation.

As shown in Fig. 7.2, the transactional representation interaction layer not only serves as a bridge connecting the two preceding modules—the feature-oriented module and the sequence-oriented module—but also represents a core component of the overall TbHGN framework. Through deep feature fusion, this layer enables the model to capture both fine-grained differences in transaction attributes and macro-level patterns across transaction sequences. As a result, it significantly enhances robustness and generalization in fraud detection tasks. This design ensures that the model can identify complex fraud patterns hidden in multi-source feature interactions, facilitating the detection of subtle fraudulent behaviors that are often missed by traditional approaches.

7.5 Experimental Validation and Interpretability Analysis

To evaluate the effectiveness and interpretability of the proposed TbHGN model in OPFD, this study conducts systematic experiments on multiple real-world transaction datasets and compares the results with representative sequence modeling and feature extraction methods. The experimental design includes quantitative assessments that measure accuracy and robustness, as well as qualitative evaluations that rely on visualization and feature contribution analysis.

Baseline Model. TbHGN is compared with six competitive peers: AfLSTM, TAH-RNN, TLSTM, STA-NN, HAIntN-LSTM, and TAIN. These models cover several important methodological directions such as feature aggregation, temporal attention, long short-term memory architectures, and spatial-temporal modeling.

(1) Attention-augmented LSTM (AfLSTM) [35]: It is based on the traditional LSTM network, AfLSTM introduces an attention mechanism to dynamically assign importance weights to historical transactions or behaviors. This enhances the ability to capture key temporal information and improves the model's sensitivity to users' behavior patterns.
(2) TAH-RNN [5]: Within the recurrent neural network framework, TAH-RNN integrates a time-aware hierarchical structure. By modeling behavior sequences at different time granularities, it jointly captures both long-term and short-term dependencies of user behavior, thereby more accurately depicting the laws of behavioral evolution.

(3) TLSTM [4]: It is a model that incorporates a time-gating mechanism into LSTM. It can dynamically adjust memory updates based on the time interval between adjacent behaviors, enhancing the model's ability to model irregular time series. It is widely used in user behavior prediction and temporal analysis scenarios.
(4) STA-NN [14]: It combines spatial and temporal attention mechanisms, STA-NN encodes raw data into spatial-temporal tensor representations. This enables the model to simultaneously capture the spatial distribution characteristics and temporal evolution patterns of transactions, thus demonstrating higher discriminative power in credit card fraud detection or abnormal behavior identification.
(5) HAIntN-LSTM [11]: It introduces a history-aware interaction attention mechanism into the neural network framework. It assigns higher weights to key historical behaviors while enriching state representations by integrating external user information, thereby enhancing the ability to model long-term dependent behavior patterns.
(6) Temporal Attention Interaction Network (TAIN) [33]: By incorporating temporal attention and interaction mechanisms into recurrent neural network units, TAIN can identify periodic patterns in transaction or behavior sequences and dynamically adjust the attention to historical behaviors, achieving accurate characterization of the evolutionary trends of user behavior.

Comparative Experiments. Table 7.1 presents the overall performance of these methods across the datasets. The results show that TbHGN consistently achieves higher F_1 and AUC than its peers. Its advantage in recall is particularly evident on highly imbalanced datasets such as Mar. and Apr. This demonstrates that the hierarchical feature extraction mechanism of TbHGN effectively captures complex transaction patterns and improves detection accuracy while reducing false alarms on legitimate transactions. In terms of computational efficiency, TbHGN maintains acceptable inference time T_r and training time I_r, which supports its feasibility for deployment in real-world financial risk management systems.

Ablation Study and Sensitivity Analysis. To evaluate the contribution of each module to overall performance, an ablation study is conducted, as summarized in Table 7.2. The results show that using only the raw feature representation M^R leads to significantly lower performance. Incorporating the feature-oriented module to produce M^{R^s} improves precision, while adding sequence modeling to obtain M^{R^v} significantly enhances recall. The complete structure M^{R^x} achieves the best F_1 and AUC, demonstrating the complementary effect of hierarchical feature and temporal modeling in boosting model performance.

Table 7.1 OPFD performance of seven methods

Test	Criteria	TAIN	STA-NN	AfLSTM	TLSTM	TAH-RNN	HAIntN-LSTM	TbHGN
Feb.	P_r	0.886	0.908	**0.908**	0.855	0.895	0.883	0.905
	R_e	0.970	0.971	0.967	0.972	0.970	0.975	**0.981**
	F_1	0.926	0.938	0.937	0.910	0.931	0.927	**0.942**
	AUC	0.971	0.971	0.977	0.920	0.976	0.970	**0.982**
Mar.	P_r	0.917	0.845	0.925	0.926	0.925	**0.935**	0.914
	R_e	0.780	**0.813**	0.702	0.694	0.699	0.651	0.775
	F_1	**0.844**	0.829	0.798	0.794	0.796	0.768	0.839
	AUC	0.879	**0.895**	0.843	0.840	0.842	0.820	0.875
Apr.	P_r	0.689	0.643	0.598	0.583	0.590	0.609	**0.727**
	R_e	0.991	0.994	0.975	0.995	**0.996**	0.989	0.987
	F_1	0.812	0.781	0.741	0.736	0.741	0.754	**0.837**
	AUC	0.964	0.958	0.952	0.959	0.960	0.960	**0.967**
May.	P_r	0.993	0.940	0.978	0.968	0.984	0.968	**0.997**
	R_e	0.928	0.914	0.877	0.903	0.892	0.896	**0.966**
	F_1	0.959	0.927	0.924	0.934	0.936	0.931	**0.981**
	AUC	0.964	0.954	0.937	0.950	0.945	0.947	**0.983**
Jun.	P_r	0.948	0.934	0.905	0.908	0.844	0.905	**0.959**
	R_e	0.976	0.976	**0.990**	0.925	0.984	0.952	0.988
	F_1	0.962	0.955	0.946	0.916	0.908	0.959	**0.973**
	AUC	0.985	0.985	**0.990**	0.957	0.963	0.984	0.987
A_v	P_r	0.887	0.854	0.863	0.848	0.868	0.892	**0.939**
	R_e	0.929	0.934	0.902	0.898	0.908	0.898	**0.957**
	F_1	0.901	0.886	0.869	0.858	0.862	0.868	**0.914**
	AUC	0.953	0.953	0.940	0.947	0.936	0.939	**0.957**
A_r	P_r	3.200	4.400	3.800	5.200	4.600	3.800	**2.400**
	R_e	3.400	3.000	5.200	4.400	4.400	4.000	**2.600**
	F_1	3.400	5.600	4.800	6.000	4.600	4.800	**1.400**
	AUC	2.600	3.400	4.200	5.800	4.600	5.200	**1.600**
T_r (ms)		103.24	98.56	99.04	134.88	115.73	95.07	118.95
I_r (ms)		0.026	0.026	0.028	0.027	0.033	0.028	0.029

Table 7.2 Ablation experiment

Test	Criteria	M^R	M^{R^s}	M^{R^v}	M^{R^x}
Feb.	P_r	0.851	0.885	0.891	**0.914**
	R_e	**0.984**	0.974	0.978	0.980
	F_1	0.913	0.927	0.932	**0.946**
	AUC	0.978	0.976	0.979	**0.982**
Mar.	P_r	**0.972**	0.971	0.843	0.921
	R_e	0.667	0.690	**0.791**	0.754
	F_1	0.791	0.807	0.816	**0.829**
	AUC	0.830	0.841	0.862	**0.863**
Apr.	P_r	0.563	0.669	0.718	**0.724**
	R_e	0.986	0.995	**0.997**	0.997
	F_1	0.719	0.800	0.835	**0.839**
	AUC	0.946	0.949	0.953	**0.954**
May.	P_r	0.985	0.980	0.974	**0.998**
	R_e	0.807	0.898	0.952	**0.960**
	F_1	0.887	0.938	0.963	**0.978**
	AUC	0.907	0.947	0.973	**0.980**
Jun.	P_r	0.974	**0.975**	0.945	0.958
	R_e	0.897	0.938	0.969	**0.976**
	F_1	0.881	0.938	0.969	**0.976**
	AUC	0.899	0.951	0.988	**0.991**

Table 7.3 Sensitivity of the length of transaction memory

Memory length	P_r	R_e	F_1	AUC
10	0.969	0.886	0.926	0.942
20	0.978	0.893	0.933	0.946
30	0.985	0.900	0.941	0.950
40	0.982	0.909	0.944	0.954
50	0.982	0.913	0.946	0.956
60	0.980	0.912	0.945	0.955
70	0.979	0.916	0.946	0.957

A sensitivity analysis is performed to explore the effect of memory length, as shown in Table 7.3. Increasing the memory length from 10 to 50 leads to continuous improvements in F_1 and AUC. Beyond 60, however, performance plateaus, which suggests that excessively long historical windows may introduce noise and reduce modeling stability.

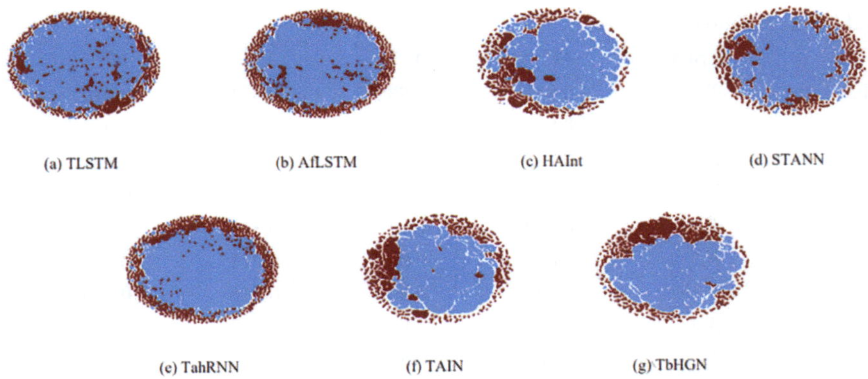

Fig. 7.4 Visualization of varied transactional representations

Visualization and Interpretability Analysis. To visually illustrate the advantages of TbHGN in representation learning, dimensionality reduction is applied to the transaction embeddings produced by each model, as shown in Fig. 7.4. Representations generated by traditional models such as TLSTM and AfLSTM show substantial overlap between legitimate and fraudulent transactions. In contrast, TbHGN produces more clearly separated distributions in which fraudulent transactions form compact clusters. This demonstrates that the model captures underlying discriminative structures more effectively.

The attention weights learned by the feature-oriented module further contribute to the interpretability of the model. Analysis of these weights shows that attributes such as transaction amount, account balance, transaction time, and payee type play significantly more important roles in fraud detection than other features. This observation aligns with established domain knowledge in the financial industry and provides intuitive and traceable explanations for risk auditing.

In summary, the experimental results demonstrate that TbHGN consistently outperforms mainstream baseline models across multiple real-world transaction datasets. Its advantages are most notable in highly imbalanced scenarios, where traditional models often fail to maintain robustness. The hierarchical integration of feature-level and sequence-level modeling significantly enhances discriminative capability. Besides, the attention mechanism improves interpretability, allowing the model to provide transparent insights for fraud detection. TbHGN therefore achieves a strong balance among accuracy, robustness, interpretability, and scalability. These characteristics establish a solid foundation for the development of next-generation financial risk control systems.

7.6 Summary

This chapter systematically presents and analyzes the design and application of the Transaction-based Hierarchical Gated Network (TbHGN) for deep transaction feature learning. Addressing the complex scenario in credit card fraud detection, where both multi-dimensional static attributes and dynamic behavior sequences coexist, TbHGN constructs multi-level representations that balance discriminative power and interpretability through three hierarchical modules: the feature-oriented module, the sequence-oriented module, and the representation interaction module. In the feature-oriented module, the model employs bidirectional gated units and inter-feature attention mechanisms to focus on high-value features, enhancing the capture of key attributes indicative of fraudulent transactions. The sequence-oriented module introduces time-sensitive gated structures to effectively model the temporal dependencies and dynamic evolution of user transactional behaviors, emphasizing the importance of recent actions in fraud identification. In the feature fusion and interaction layer, raw features, key attribute information, and behavioral context are integrated across multiple dimensions to generate unified transaction representations, further improving classification capability and the completeness of semantic expression. Extensive experiments show that TbHGN achieves strong performance across P_r, R_e, F_1, and AUC, while maintaining good interpretability for financial risk management. However, the model is built on the assumption of relatively stable user behavior patterns and may struggle to adapt when behavioral drift occurs in real transaction environments. To address this limitation, the subsequent chapter introduces a Time-aware Historical Interaction LSTM (TH-LSTM) to enable adaptive modeling of evolving transactional behaviors.

References

1. Bao, T., Zaidi, S.A.R., Xie, S., Yang, P., Zhang, Z.Q.: A CNN-LSTM hybrid model for wrist kinematics estimation using surface electromyography. IEEE Trans. on Instrumentation and Measurement **70**, 1–9 (2021)
2. de Castro Silva, G.M., Sichman, J.S.: Impersonation fraud detection on building access control systems: An approach based on anomalous social and spatio-temporal behaviors. Applied Soft Computing **118**, 108310 (2022)
3. Chu, G., Wang, J., Qi, Q., Sun, H., Tao, S., Yang, H., Liao, J., Han, Z.: Exploiting spatial-temporal behavior patterns for fraud detection in telecom networks. IEEE Trans. on Dependable and Secure Computing **20**(6), 4564–4577 (2022)
4. Cissoko, M.B.H., Castelain, V., Lachiche, N.: Multi-way adaptive time aware LSTM for irregularly collected sequential ICU data. Expert Systems with Applications **261**, 125548 (2025)
5. Dudukcu, H.V., Taskiran, M., Taskiran, Z.G.C., Yildirim, T.: Temporal convolutional networks with RNN approach for chaotic time series prediction. Applied Soft Computing **133**, 109945 (2023)
6. Hancock, J.T., Wang, H., Khoshgoftaar, T.M., Liang, Q.: Data reduction techniques for highly imbalanced medicare big data. Journal of Big Data **11**(1), 8 (2024)
7. Huang, H., Wang, P., Pei, J., Wang, J., Alexanian, S., Niyato, D.: Deep learning advancements in anomaly detection: A comprehensive survey. IEEE Internet of Things Journal (2025)

8. Ileberi, E., Sun, Y., Wang, Z.: A machine learning based credit card fraud detection using the GA algorithm for feature selection. Journal of Big Data **9**(1), 24 (2022)
9. Jiang, Y., Liu, G., Wu, J., Lin, H.: Telecom fraud detection via hawkes-enhanced sequence model. IEEE Trans. on Knowledge and Data Engineering **35**(5), 5311–5324 (2022)
10. Li, X., Wu, Y., Fu, Y., Tang, C., Zhang, L.: Neighbour feature attention-based pooling. Neurocomputing **501**, 285–293 (2022)
11. Lin, H., Liu, G., Wu, J., Zuo, Y., Wan, X., Li, H.: Fraud detection in dynamic interaction network. IEEE Trans. on Knowledge and Data Engineering **32**(10), 1936–1950 (2020)
12. Lingeswari, R., Brindha, S.: Online payments fraud prediction using optimized genetic algorithm based feature extraction and modified loss with xg boost algorithm for classification. Swarm and Evolutionary Computation **95**, 101934 (2025)
13. Liu, L., Tsai, W.T., Bhuiyan, M.Z.A., Peng, H., Liu, M.: Blockchain-enabled fraud discovery through abnormal smart contract detection on ethereum. Future Generation Computer Systems **128**, 158–166 (2022)
14. Liu, S., Wang, X., Zhao, L., Li, B., Hu, W., Yu, J., Zhang, Y.D.: 3DCANN: A spatio-temporal convolution attention neural network for EEG emotion recognition. IEEE Journal of Biomedical and Health Informatics **26**(11), 5321–5331 (2021)
15. Ma, J., Liu, H., Peng, C., Qiu, T.: Unauthorized broadcasting identification: A deep LSTM recurrent learning approach. IEEE Trans. on Instrumentation and Measurement **69**(9), 5981–5983 (2020)
16. Purbowaskito, W., Lan, C.y., Fuh, K.: The potentiality of integrating model-based residuals and machine-learning classifiers: An induction motor fault diagnosis case. IEEE Trans. on Industrial Informatics **20**(2), 2822–2832 (2023)
17. Rao, S.X., Han, Z., Yin, H., Jiang, J., Zhang, Z., Zhao, Y., Shan, Y.: Fraud detection at ebay. Emerging Markets Review **66**, 101277 (2025)
18. Ren, L., Hu, R., Li, D., Liu, Y., Wu, J., Zang, Y., Hu, W.: Dynamic graph neural network-based fraud detectors against collaborative fraudsters. Knowledge-Based Systems **278**, 110888 (2023)
19. Shao, Y., Dietrich, F.M., Nettelblad, C., Zhang, C.: Training algorithm matters for the performance of neural network potential: A case study of adam and the kalman filter optimizers. The Journal of Chemical Physics **155**(20) (2021)
20. Sirés, A., Pazo-González, M., López-Soriano, J., Méndez, A., De la Rosa, E.J., de la Villa, P., Comella, J.X., Hernández-Sánchez, C., Solé, M.: The absence of faim leads to a delay in dark adaptation and hampers arrestin-1 translocation upon light reception in the retina. Cells **12**(3), 487 (2023)
21. Wang, H., Wei, J., Qin, J., Zhu, N., Ren, M., Zhao, Z., Hu, L.: Dynamic process noise covariance adjustment in GNSS/INS integrated navigation using GRU-SAC for enhanced positioning accuracy. IEEE Trans. on Intelligent Trans. Systems **26**(6), 9047–9064 (2025)
22. Wang, H., Fan, K., Zhang, K., Li, F., Li, H., Yang, Y.: MU-MRQ: Enabling multi-user verifiable and secure multi-dimensional range query over encrypted data. IEEE Trans. on Dependable and Secure Computing (2025)
23. Wang, J., Liu, G., Liu, D., Chang, B.: MF-Net: Multiple-feature extraction network for breast lesion segmentation in ultrasound images. Expert Systems with Applications **249**, 123798 (2024)
24. Wang, J., Liu, Q.: Distant supervised relation extraction with position feature attention and selective bag attention. Neurocomputing **461**, 552–561 (2021)
25. Wu, J., Hu, R., Li, D., Ren, L., Huang, Z., Zang, Y.: Beyond the individual: An improved telecom fraud detection approach based on latent synergy graph learning. Neural Networks **169**, 20–31 (2024)
26. Xie, H., Randall, M., Chau, K.w.: Green roof hydrological modelling with GRU and LSTM networks. Water Resources Management **36**(3), 1107–1122 (2022)
27. Xie, Y., Hong, Y., Qiao, S., Yao, J., Liu, G., Pang, S.: A time-aware generative network for enhancing transaction security in consumer electronics. IEEE Trans. on Consumer Electronics **71**(2), 6818–6828 (2025)

28. Xie, Y., Liu, G., Yan, C., Jiang, C., Zhou, M.: Time-aware attention-based gated network for credit card fraud detection by extracting transactional behaviors. IEEE Trans. on Computational Social Systems **10**(3), 1004–1016 (2023)
29. Xie, Y., Liu, G., Yan, C., Jiang, C., Zhou, M., Li, M.: Learning transactional behavioral representations for credit card fraud detection. IEEE Trans. on Neural Networks and Learning Systems **35**(4), 5735–5748 (2024)
30. Xie, Y., Liu, G., Zhou, M., Wei, L., Zhu, H., Zhou, R., Cao, L.: A spatial–temporal gated network for credit card fraud detection by learning transactional representations. IEEE Trans. on Automation Science and Engineering **21**(4), 6978–6991 (2024)
31. Xie, Y., Shan, J., Wei, L., Yao, J., Zhou, M.: GAN-based hybrid sampling method for transaction fraud detection. IEEE Trans. on Knowledge and Data Engineering **37**(10), 5905–5918 (2025)
32. Xie, Y., Zhou, M., Liu, G., Wei, L., Zhu, H., De Meo, P.: A transactional-behavior-based hierarchical gated network for credit card fraud detection. IEEE/CAA Journal of Automatica Sinica **12**(7), 1489–1503 (2025)
33. Ye, L., Wang, Z., Chen, X., Wang, J., Wu, K., Lu, K.: GSAN: Graph self-attention network for learning spatial–temporal interaction representation in autonomous driving. IEEE Internet of Things Journal **9**(12), 9190–9204 (2021)
34. Zarzycki, K., Ławryńczuk, M.: Advanced predictive control for GRU and LSTM networks. Information Sciences **616**, 229–254 (2022)
35. Zhang, T., Zheng, X.Q., Liu, M.X.: Multiscale attention-based LSTM for ship motion prediction. Ocean Engineering **230**, 109066 (2021)

Chapter 8
Capturing Transactional Behavioral Drift via Current-Historical Behavior Interaction

In Chap. 7, the hierarchical modeling of multi-dimensional transaction features are explored, where feature-interaction gating and dynamic weighting mechanisms enable deep integration across temporal, spatial, and contextual dimensions, thereby enhancing global discriminative capability. This framework, however, implicitly assumes behavioral stability, whereas real-world transaction environments exhibit continuous behavioral drift. When current transaction patterns diverge from historical baselines, models built on static behavioral assumptions often fail to adapt, resulting in reduced detection performance. To address this limitation, the Time-Aware Historical Interaction LSTM (TH-LSTM) is introduced, jointly encoding a user's historical trajectory and current behavioral state through an explicit interaction mechanism. By capturing temporal dependencies and identifying discrepancies indicative of distributional shifts, TH-LSTM provides dynamic behavioral modeling and supports risk-adaptive fraud detection in non-stationary transaction environments.

8.1 Defining Behavioral Drift in Transaction Streams

In practical online payment systems, a user's transaction history is composed of heterogeneous, multi-dimensional attributes that jointly encode behavioral tendencies across different contexts [2, 24]. These attributes form the foundational evidence for distinguishing legitimate activities from potentially fraudulent ones. Over long observation periods, most users exhibit stable statistical regularities in their transactional behaviors [10, 26]. For instance, spending amounts typically fluctuate within a predictable range, transaction timestamps concentrate around habitual time periods, and frequently used devices or network environments remain relatively consistent [11]. When new behaviors diverge substantially from these established patterns, a phenomenon commonly referred to as behavioral drift emerges [5, 28]. Typical manifestations include abrupt increases in transaction amounts, unusual temporal

Y. Xie et al., *Neural Network-Based Deep Learning for Online Payment Fraud Detection*,
https://doi.org/10.1007/978-981-95-8513-7_8

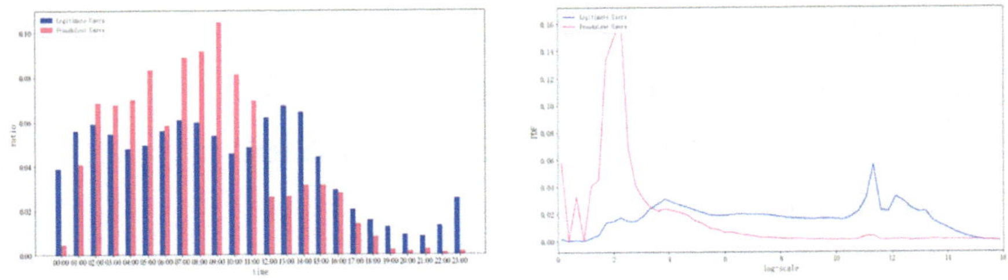

(a) (b)

Fig. 8.1 Explorative analysis of transactional behaviors. **a** Trade time of users' transactions. **b** Distribution of the time between two consecutive transactions

clustering of activities, rapid switching across devices or network environments, or sudden interactions with unfamiliar merchants, payment channels, or cross-border accounts [15, 25].

Behavioral drift is thus defined as a significant discrepancy between a user's current transaction sequence and the distribution characterizing their historical behavioral profile. While such deviations may result from natural changes in personal habits or lifestyle adjustments, they may also signal the onset of fraudulent activity. Fraudsters impersonating legitimate users often introduce behavioral signatures that deviate sharply from long-term user baselines within short temporal windows [22, 23]. As illustrated in Fig. 8.1, normal users' transaction patterns remain relatively stable, whereas sequences driven by fraudulent intent exhibit abrupt and substantial deviations. These irregularities are strong indicators of elevated risk, making the accurate detection of behavioral drift critical for effective fraud prevention.

However, most existing OPFD methods primarily emphasize static feature representations or short-term behavioral correlations, typically assuming that user behavior follows a stable underlying distribution [18, 21]. In practice, these methods rely heavily on aggregated historical statistics or isolated transaction snapshots. Such assumptions hinder their ability to adapt to evolving behavioral dynamics and to distinguish benign behavioral changes from malicious deviations. Moreover, historical and current behaviors are often modeled independently, without explicit mechanisms to capture temporal inconsistencies or interaction effects. This fragmented modeling paradigm reduces sensitivity to abrupt behavioral shifts and undermines model robustness in dynamic and rapidly evolving payment environments [19, 20]. To overcome these limitations, this chapter introduces a modeling framework that encodes users' historical behaviors by using a Time-Aware LSTM network and incorporates a dedicated interaction mechanism to capture dependencies between historical and current transactions. This design enables precise quantification of behavioral deviations and supports timely identification of emerging fraudulent intent within transaction streams.

8.2 Time-Aware LSTM Encoding for User Histories

Within transaction flow data, a user's historical behavior often embodies stable patterns and cyclical characteristics, whereas fraudulent activities typically manifest as concentrated and anomalous events occurring within short periods. Consequently, effectively leveraging the time intervals between transactions to express behavioral motivations and correlations becomes paramount in capturing latent fraudulent signals during the modeling process. This section introduces a Time-aware Historical LSTM (TH-LSTM), whose specific architecture is illustrated in Fig. 8.2, with the complete training procedure detailed in Algorithm 1. This model explicitly incorporates time interval information on top of the traditional LSTM, enabling historical states to dynamically adjust their contribution to current behavior, thereby better modeling the user's long-term behavioral baseline.

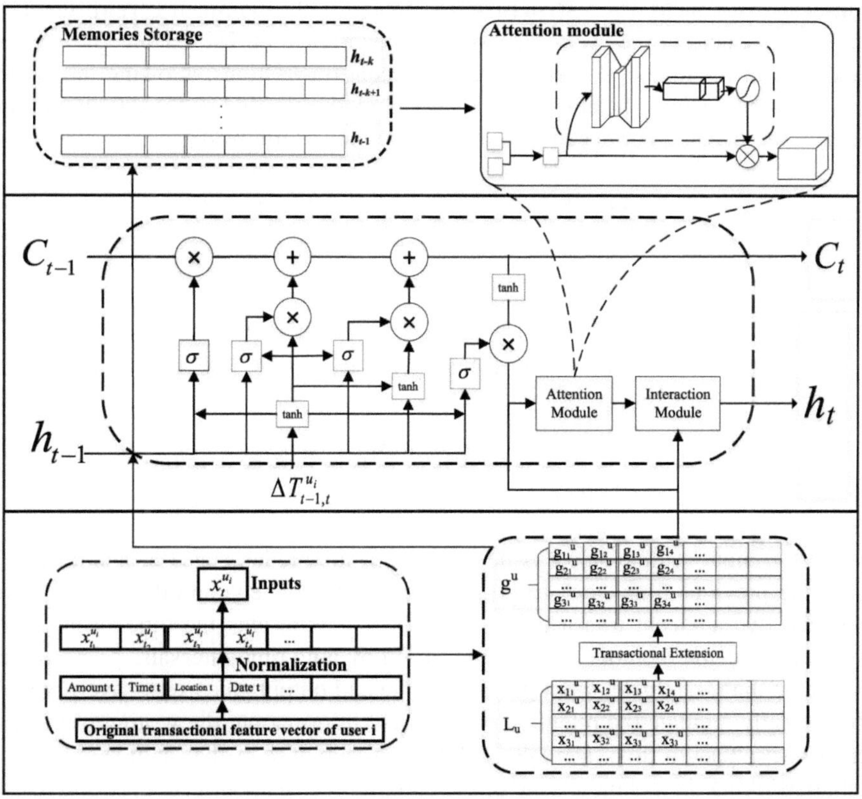

Fig. 8.2 Illustration of the proposed TH-LSTM

Algorithm 1 Training Algorithm of TH-LSTM

Inputs: Transaction dataset: X; Batch generator: B_g; Network parameters: θ; Size of each mini-batch: b_{si}; Number of batches: n_b; Number of epochs: n_e;
Output: Trained model M;
Conduct the transactional expansion: $D \longrightarrow G$;
Initialize the network parameters θ;
for each $j \in \{1, 2, \ldots, n_e\}$ **do**
  for each $k \in \{1, 2, \ldots, n_b\}$ **do**
    $batch = next(B(b_{si}, G))$;
    for each i in $batch$ **do**
      Compute h_i and $\hat{y}_i$ by (13) and (14)
    end for
    Compute the loss by (15)
    Minimize the loss by Adam and update the network parameters θ
  end for
end forreturn M;

Time-Aware LSTM Unit Structure. Compared with traditional LSTM, the TH-LSTM introduces a time-aware gate within its recurrent unit. This enables the explicit modeling of the temporal span between adjacent transactions, allowing the model to dynamically adjust the efficacy of historical memory based on the duration of the behavioral interval. The specific gate unit is defined as follows:

$$s_t = \mathbf{tanh}(W_{sh}h_{t-1} + W_{sx}x_t + W_{st}\Delta\mathbf{T}_{t-1,t} + b_s), \tag{8.1}$$

$$f_t = \sigma\left(W_{fh}h_{t-1} + W_{fx}x_t + W_{fs}s_t + b_f\right), \tag{8.2}$$

$$i_t = \sigma\left(W_{ih}h_{t-1} + W_{ix}x_t + W_{is}s_t + b_i\right) \tag{8.3}$$

$$\mathcal{T}_t = \sigma\left(W_{Th}h_{t-1} + W_{Tx}x_t + W_{Ts}s_t + b_T\right) \tag{8.4}$$

$$\zeta_t = \mathbf{tanh}(W_{uh}h_{t-1} + W_{ux}x_t + W_{us}s_t + b_u) \tag{8.5}$$

$$c_t = f_t * c_{t-1} + i_t * \zeta + \mathcal{I}_t * s_t \tag{8.6}$$

$$o_t = \sigma\left(W_{oh}h_{t-1} + W_{ox}x_t + W_{os}s_t + b_o\right) \tag{8.7}$$

$$\tilde{h}_t = o_t * \tanh(c_t), \tag{8.8}$$

where the input at time step t is denoted as x_t, the hidden state and memory cell from the previous time step are h_{t-1} and c_{t-1}, respectively, and the time interval between two adjacent transactions is $\Delta T_{t-1,t}$. s_t represents the time-aware state, which reflects the memory attenuation caused by long time intervals; f_t, i_t, $\mathcal{T}_t$ and o_t denote the forget gate, input gate, time gate and output gate, respectively, which dynamically regulate the retention of historical information, the writing of current input, the impact of time intervals, and the final output; ζ_t is the candidate memory cell, describing the potential state of the current input without gating; c_t and h_t are the updated memory cell and hidden state, respectively; $\sigma(\cdot)$ and $\tanh(\cdot)$ are the Sigmoid and hyperbolic tangent activation functions; while each W and b represent the weight matrix and bias term learned during the model training process.

Through the above design, TH-LSTM can not only capture the sequential dependencies of the transaction input sequence but also dynamically adjust the forgetting and retention of historical information according to transaction intervals. For example, when the interval between two transactions is too long, the time gate T_t will reduce the influence of previous states, thus avoiding interference from outdated patterns in current modeling; conversely, transactions occurring consecutively in a short period will be assigned higher weights, which helps identify potential centralized fraudulent behaviors.

Model Advantages. A key advantage of the TH-LSTM, in contrast to traditional LSTMs, lies in its ability to explicitly model the time intervals between adjacent transactions. This imbues the recurrent structure with the capacity to respond with fine-grained precision not only to the input sequence itself but also to the rhythm and temporal span of transaction occurrences. Unlike traditional LSTMs, which implicitly rely on sequential information, TH-LSTM overcomes the limitation of being unable to capture the crucial semantic of "how long ago a behavior occurred." By injecting interval information directly into the memory update process through time-aware gates, the model can flexibly adjust the forgetting or retention of historical information based on the duration of the interval.

Specifically, when transactions occur at a high frequency within a short period, the time gates reinforce the influence of recent behaviors on the memory units, making the model more sensitive to potential anomalous patterns. Conversely, when transaction intervals are longer, the model can actively decay outdated memories, reducing interference from irrelevant historical behaviors.

This time-sensitive mechanism not only theoretically enhances the ability to characterize dynamic behaviors but also more closely aligns with the business logic of real-world financial transactions. User payment behaviors often exhibit stable temporal cycles, such as specific consumption periods or fixed transaction rhythms [17]. Fraudulent activities, on the other hand, are typically accompanied by abnormal deviations in this behavioral rhythm. TH-LSTM can effectively capture these time-based behavioral drifts, thereby significantly enhancing model interpretability and business usability while simultaneously improving detection accuracy.

In summary, by deeply integrating temporal factors into the recurrent structure, TH-LSTM establishes a more robust, sensitive, and business-relevant representational foundation for modeling users' dynamic historical behaviors. It also lays a more solid modeling framework for subsequent current-history interaction attention mechanisms.

8.3 Current-Historical Attention Network

In the preceding section, we integrated temporal awareness into the recurrent structure, effectively characterizing the temporal span between adjacent transactions and its influence on memory evolution via the TH-LSTM. However, relying solely on sequential modeling and temporal intervals still presents limitations. Specifically, certain long-term user transaction preferences or stable behavioral patterns may not be directly apparent in the recent transaction sequence. Nevertheless, this information holds significant referential value for discerning the nature of the current transaction. Based on this observation, this section introduces the Current-Historical Attention Network (CH-AN). Building upon the time-sensitive representations derived from TH-LSTM, CH-AN further enhances the interaction between the current transaction state and the global historical memory. This allows for the joint modeling of short-term dynamics and long-term behavioral regularities, enabling the model to more comprehensively capture users' long-range dependencies and structural patterns in their behavior.

As illustrated in Fig. 8.2, the attention module computes an interaction between the sequence of historical hidden states and the current candidate state to derive an attention distribution that reflects historical importance weights. The specific process is as follows:

First, the candidate state $\widehat{h_t}$ and cell state c_t at time step t are concatenated to obtain the current query vector q_t:

$$q_t = Concat(\tilde{h}_t, c_t), \tag{8.9}$$

subsequently, the correlation score $o_{t,i}$ between the query vector and the historical hidden states h_i is calculated as follows:

$$o_{t,i} = tanh(W_{aq}q_t + W_{ah}h_i + b_a), \tag{8.10}$$

and normalized using the softmax function to obtain the attention weights $\alpha_{t,i}$:

$$\alpha_{t,i} = \frac{\exp((o_{t,i}^T v_a)}{\sum_{i=1}^{t-1} \exp(o_{t,i}^T v_a)}. \tag{8.11}$$

All historical states are then weighted and summed according to the attention weights to obtain the final historical context representation e_t:

$$e_t = \sum_{i=t-d_t}^{t-1} \alpha_{t,i} * h_i, \tag{8.12}$$

h_i denotes the hidden state at the i-th historical time step, which stores the transactional behavior features of the user at that time; d represents the length of the transaction memory, which limits the historical range accessible to the current attention mechanism; q_t is the query vector at the current time step, which measures the matching degree between the current transaction and different historical behaviors; $\alpha_{t,i}$ reflects the contribution degree of the historical state to the current prediction, indicating the importance of the i-th historical hidden state in computing the current representation. Through this mechanism, CH-AN can adaptively weight and integrate long-term stable behaviors and short-term dynamic behaviors at the representation layer, thereby preserving short-term sensitivity while compensating for long-term dependency information. It exhibits stronger discriminative power for behavior drift and complex temporal patterns.

CH-AN plays a central role in modeling users' transactional behavior. Its design philosophy centers on dynamically integrating the current transaction state with a user's historical actions to capture long-range dependencies and stable behavioral regularities. Rather than treating all historical behaviors uniformly, CH-AN selectively attends to those prior interactions that are most relevant to the present transactional context. Through this selective mechanism, the model establishes a context-aware and adaptive linkage between current and past behaviors, while simultaneously overcoming the tendency of conventional recurrent architectures to diminish or lose remote dependencies. When the characteristics of an incoming transaction resemble previously observed anomalous patterns, the attention mechanism automatically assigns higher weights to the associated historical states. This weighting amplifies subtle fraud cues and substantially enhances the model's sensitivity and discriminative strength when identifying atypical behavior.

In real-world payment environments, fraudulent users often attempt to obscure abnormal traits by repeatedly imitating legitimate behavioral patterns within short timeframes. Such imitation creates short transaction sequences that appear superficially consistent with normal behavior, making anomalies difficult to detect through short-term patterns alone. CH-AN addresses this challenge by exposing the subtle discrepancies masked beneath these weak similarities. By assigning greater emphasis to historical memories that exhibit strong correlations with potential irregularities in the current transaction, CH-AN improves the model's capacity to distinguish authentic behavior from fraudulent intent. For example, when transaction amounts, frequencies, or counterpart entities diverge from a user's established patterns, the mechanism increases the influence of related historical states during attention computation, enabling sharper recognition of behavioral drift and emerging anomalies.

Together, CH-AN and TH-LSTM form a complementary modeling framework. CH-AN strengthens the selective utilization of long-term behavioral memory, allowing the model to focus dynamically on historical patterns most pertinent to the current transaction. In parallel, TH-LSTM, through its time-aware gating structure, captures the temporal dynamics between adjacent transactions and provides fine-grained modeling of short-term behavioral variations. The integration of these two components not only enhances anomaly detection in complex transactional sequences but also improves interpretability and practical applicability in operational settings. As a result, the combined framework offers a robust, efficient, and theoretically grounded solution for credit card fraud detection.

8.4 Representation Contrast and Visualization

To comprehensively assess the advantages of the proposed TH-LSTM, this study selects a variety of representative sequential modeling methods and feature enhancement frameworks as comparative benchmarks. The selection of comparative methods encompasses traditional recurrent neural networks and their variants, feature aggregation strategies, and deep learning models based on attention mechanisms [1]. This comprehensive approach aims to fully reflect the performance of various methods in capturing dynamic transactional behaviors and modeling long-term dependencies.

(1) LSTM [6]: It is a model that introduces a gating mechanism based on the improved RNN. It is designed to alleviate the problems of gradient vanishing and explosion, and can effectively handle long-sequence inputs. It is widely used in transactional behavior modeling and time-series data processing.
(2) GRU [3]: It is a simplified gated recurrent unit. Similar to LSTM but with fewer parameters, it controls information flow through update gates and reset gates, enabling faster model training while capturing dependencies in sequences.
(3) Bi-RNN [13]: It models transaction sequences in both forward and backward directions, allowing it to capture both past and future dependency information simultaneously. This enhances the ability to understand and predict transactional behavior patterns.
(4) UgRNN [4]: It incorporates an update gate mechanism into traditional RNNs to improve the stability of long-sequence learning. This enables the model to maintain effective state updates when dealing with transaction data spanning long time horizons.
(5) Aggregated LSTM (A-LSTM) [16]: It combines a feature aggregation strategy, taking statistical features such as total transaction amount and transaction frequency as additional inputs to enhance sequence modeling capabilities. This allows the model to more accurately capture the overall trends of user transactional behaviors.
(6) STA-NN [9]: It processes transaction data in the form of 3D tensors through a spatial-temporal attention mechanism, integrating temporal, spatial, and attribute features simultaneously. It enables the model to capture complex behavior patterns, making it particularly suitable for credit card fraud detection and abnormal behavior identification.
(7) Homogeneous Behavior Analysis (HOBA) [12]: It is a feature engineering method based on homogeneous behavior analysis. It generates auxiliary features by mining the similarity of transactional behaviors among users of the same type, strengthening the model's discriminative power for potential abnormal behaviors.
(8) Attention-augmented CNN (A-CNN) [7]: It extracts local patterns from transaction sequences through convolutional operations, converts transaction features into matrix form for input to the CNN, and combines an attention mechanism to achieve enhanced modeling of key behavior features.

(9) HAInt-LSTM [27]: It introduces a self-attention mechanism and additional contextual information into traditional LSTM. This allows the model to highlight key historical behaviors, enhance the ability to capture long-range dependencies, and integrate external information such as user profiles to enrich state representations.
(10) TLSTM [14]: It adds temporal interval modeling to LSTM, dynamically adjusting memory updates based on adjacent transaction intervals through a time gating unit. It enhances the model's sensitivity to irregular time series, making it suitable for financial transaction prediction and anomaly detection.
(11) TAH-RNN [8]: It models transaction sequences at different temporal granularities through a temporally aware hierarchical structure and attention mechanism. It achieves joint capture of long-term and short-term behavioral dependencies, thereby more accurately depicting the evolutionary laws of user behavior.

To intuitively present the transactional behavioral representations learned by each model, this study employs t-SNE for mapping transaction features into a two-dimensional space for visualization, as depicted in Fig. 8.3. Figure 8.3a illustrates the raw transactional representation, i.e., original features without any modeling treatment. In this plot, legitimate samples (blue dots) are highly intermingled with fraudulent ones (red dots), indicating that relying solely on raw features is insufficient for effectively distinguishing normal users from fraudulent behavior, and the underlying structure of users' behavioral patterns is difficult to capture directly.

Figure 8.3b–l showcase the transactional representations generated by different comparative models after learning. It can be observed that these methods, to some extent, are capable of identifying pattern features within transaction sequences, with some fraudulent transactions beginning to exhibit minor clustering trends. However, significant mixing persists overall, and fraudulent behaviors cannot be completely separated from legitimate ones, suggesting that these methods still have certain limitations in OPFD and the characterization of behavioral patterns.

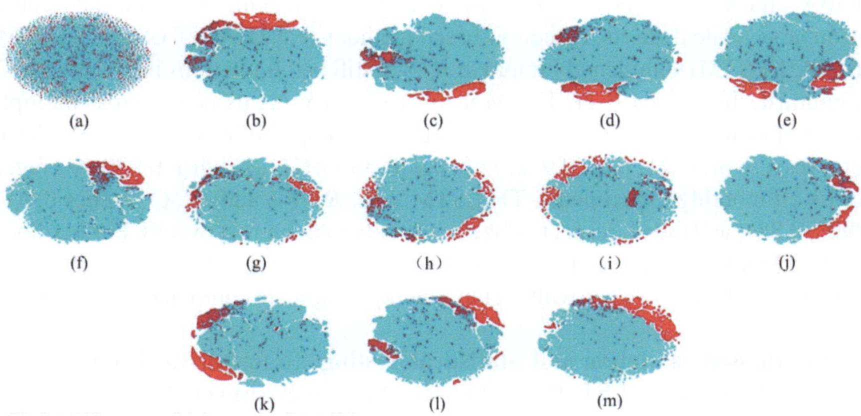

Fig. 8.3 Explorative view of transactional behaviors

In contrast, Fig. 8.3m displays the transactional behavioral representations generated by TH-LSTM. The red dots form distinct clusters, while the blue dots maintain a considerable separation, exhibiting a clear separation state overall. This demonstrates that when modeling transaction sequences, TH-LSTM can effectively capture the long-term dependencies and short-term dynamics of user behavior, thereby strengthening the expression of anomalous patterns and significantly enhancing its ability to recognize fraudulent behavior. This visualization analysis not only intuitively validates the model's advantage in distinguishing legitimate transactions from fraudulent ones but also further reveals the efficacy of the learned transactional representations in terms of feature discriminability and pattern aggregation, providing strong support for model interpretability.

In summary, the comparative analysis of representations and the visualization results collectively validate the robustness and superiority of the proposed TH-LSTM in complex transactional environments. Notably, even when fraudulent and legitimate behaviors exhibit significant overlap, TH-LSTM demonstrates an ability to learn discriminative representations, thereby providing a more robust feature foundation for subsequent classification and detection tasks.

8.5 Experimental Validation and Interpretability Analysis

To comprehensively validate the effectiveness of the proposed TH-LSTM model in the transaction fraud detection task, a multi-faceted experimental framework is employed. This framework encompasses data partitioning strategies, evaluation metrics, comparative experiments, validation on public datasets, and ablation studies, further complemented by an analysis of model interpretability.

As shown in Table 8.1, traditional methods (e.g., LSTM, GRU, and Bi-RNN) demonstrate limited performance in terms of R_e, particularly falling below 0.70 in the March-April migration tests. Feature enhancement methods (e.g., A-LSTM, HOBA, and A-CNN) show some improvements in certain metrics but lacked stability on large-scale datasets. Attention-based methods (e.g., HAINT-LSTM, TLSTM, and TAH-LSTM) significantly improve R_e, yet still had limitations in P_r and AUC. In contrast, the proposed TH-LSTM notably outperforms its peers across multiple metrics. For instance, in the January-February training-testing scenario, TH-LSTM achieves a P_r of 0.921, R_e of 0.972, F_1 of 0.946, and AUC as high as 0.980. Averaged across all monthly experiments, TH-LSTM's P_r, R_e, F_1, and AUC reaches 0.902, 0.908, 0.881, and 0.944, respectively, consistently ranking first overall. Furthermore, TH-LSTM's inference speed (0.027 ms) is comparable to its peers, indicating that it maintains high performance without introducing significant computational overhead.

Public Dataset Validation and Statistical Testing. To further validate the generalization ability of TH-LSTM, this study conducts an experiment by using a public dataset containing 284,807 transaction records from European cardholders in 2013. Due to the lack of specific feature names in this dataset, feature aggregation-based

Table 8.1 OPFD performance of twelve methods

Train	Test	Criteria	STA-NN	A-LSTM	HOBA	A-CNN	LSTM	GRU	Bi-RNN	UgRNN	HAInt-LSTM	TLSTM	TAH-LSTM	TH-LSTM
Jan.	Feb.	P_r	0.761	0.831	0.828	0.835	0.874	0.837	0.864	0.823	0.844	0.847	0.883	**0.921**
		R_e	0.960	0.963	0.956	0.952	0.823	0.911	0.933	**0.989**	0.917	0.925	0.922	0.972
		F_1	0.849	0.892	0.888	0.890	0.848	0.872	0.897	0.898	0.879	0.884	0.902	**0.946**
		AUC	0.874	0.920	0.913	0.916	0.905	0.943	0.956	0.969	0.940	0.926	0.952	**0.980**
Feb.	Mar.	P_r	0.884	0.914	**0.963**	0.949	0.919	0.913	0.879	0.871	0.962	0.917	0.915	0.939
		R_e	**0.729**	0.668	0.642	0.661	0.609	0.692	0.705	0.656	0.539	0.696	0.678	0.711
		F_1	0.784	0.772	0.770	0.779	0.732	0.787	0.782	0.749	0.691	0.791	0.779	**0.810**
		AUC	**0.859**	0.810	0.837	0.839	0.797	0.837	0.840	0.816	0.767	0.840	0.844	0.850
Mar.	Apr.	P_r	0.586	0.564	0.571	0.572	0.552	0.585	0.483	0.594	0.576	0.578	0.568	**0.613**
		R_e	0.990	0.996	0.995	0.994	0.995	0.959	0.958	0.954	0.995	0.995	0.994	**0.996**
		F_1	0.736	0.720	0.726	0.726	0.710	0.727	0.642	0.732	0.730	0.731	0.723	**0.759**
		AUC	0.957	0.960	0.957	0.954	0.954	0.943	0.923	0.941	0.958	0.958	0.956	**0.964**
Apr.	May.	P_r	0.839	0.941	0.954	0.905	0.768	0.831	0.928	0.891	0.971	0.872	0.973	**0.982**
		R_e	**0.945**	0.840	0.818	0.812	0.943	0.893	0.894	0.834	0.829	0.945	0.849	0.887
		F_1	0.889	0.888	0.881	0.856	0.847	0.861	0.910	0.862	0.894	0.907	0.907	**0.932**
		AUC	0.919	0.919	0.907	0.941	0.955	0.938	0.945	0.911	0.913	**0.965**	0.933	0.945
May.	Jun.	P_r	0.970	0.918	0.872	0.893	0.937	0.784	0.916	0.845	**0.971**	0.854	0.824	0.946
		R_e	0.858	0.947	0.945	0.972	0.856	0.941	0.909	0.969	0.930	0.925	0.972	**0.972**
		F_1	0.911	0.932	0.907	0.931	0.895	0.856	0.912	0.903	0.940	0.891	0.872	**0.959**
		AUC	0.928	0.956	0.935	0.946	0.925	0.958	0.950	0.975	0.953	0.956	0.953	**0.983**
Av		P_r	0.808	0.834	0.838	0.831	0.810	0.790	0.814	0.805	0.865	0.814	0.833	**0.880**
		R_e	0.896	0.883	0.871	0.878	0.845	0.879	0.880	0.880	0.838	0.898	0.874	**0.908**
		F_1	0.834	0.841	0.834	0.836	0.806	0.821	0.829	0.829	0.827	0.841	0.837	**0.881**
		AUC	0.907	0.913	0.910	0.919	0.907	0.924	0.923	0.922	0.907	0.929	0.928	**0.944**
Ar		P_r	7.400	7.400	6.200	6.400	7.000	8.600	7.800	8.600	3.600	6.800	6.200	**2.000**
		R_e	5.200	4.600	6.800	6.800	8.200	7.400	7.000	6.800	8.800	4.600	7.400	**2.400**
		F_1	5.800	6.600	7.600	6.800	11.000	8.200	5.600	6.600	5.400	6.200	7.000	**1.000**
		AUC	7.400	6.400	8.800	7.400	8.800	6.400	6.000	7.000	7.200	3.800	5.400	**1.600**
	T_r (ms)		96.86	107.62	102.95	99.67	72.69	113.09	80.09	90.47	95.42	130.26	114.62	100.97
	I_r (ms)		0.027	0.027	0.027	0.027	0.027	0.027	0.027	0.018	0.027	0.027	0.036	0.027

Table 8.2 Performance of different models on a public dataset

Criteria	STA-NN	LSTM	GRU	Bi-RNN	UgRNN	HAInt-LSTM	TLSTM	TAH-LSTM	TH-LSTM
P_r	0.502	0.501	0.501	0.500	0.501	0.501	0.500	0.501	**0.504**
R_e	0.664	0.560	0.608	0.771	0.675	0.682	0.830	0.888	**0.996**
F_1	0.571	0.529	0.550	0.607	0.575	0.578	0.624	0.641	**0.669**
AUC	0.499	0.499	0.500	0.502	0.501	0.500	0.499	0.501	**0.504**

detection methods (e.g., A-LSTM, HOBA, and A-CNN) can not be directly applied and are therefore not included in this experiment. The experimental results, presented in Table 8.2, demonstrate that even under these limitations, TH-LSTM achieves superior performance across key metrics such as P_r, R_e, F_1, and AUC, highlighting the model's robustness and effectiveness in different data environments.

Analysis of the experimental results leads to the following conclusions. First, different time intervals result in distinct changes in users' transactional behavior. Consequently, traditional aggregated features generated based on time windows or intervals, while simple and efficient in feature engineering, fail to fully capture behavioral drift and potential fraudulent activities, thus exhibiting limitations in their detection capabilities. Second, despite the relatively weaker interpretability of RNNs and attention mechanisms, they demonstrate superior performance in fields such as speech recognition, language modeling, machine translation, and image captioning, and are gradually being extended to OPFD. By modeling users' transaction sequences, recurrent networks can more comprehensively capture the dynamic characteristics of transactional behavior, thereby significantly improving detection performance. In summary, although traditional feature aggregation methods are simple and efficient, they remain insufficient in revealing changes in user behavior and fraudulent activities. In contrast, TH-LSTM shows a clear advantage in this task.

Concurrently, to further quantify the performance differences between models, this study performs statistical significance tests, including the Friedman test and the Holm test, with TH-LSTM designated as the control method. Generally, a smaller p-value indicates that an algorithm significantly outperforms others. The significance level is set at 0.1 for the experiments. Table 8.2 presents the A_r of each method, while Table 8.3 shows the p-value results from the Holm test. The results reveal that the differences between TH-LSTM and the compared methods are statistically significant across metrics such as P_r, F_1, and AUC. Furthermore, based on A_v and A_r for each evaluation metric, TH-LSTM demonstrates significantly superior overall performance compared to its peers, further validating its advantage and robustness in OPFD.

Ablation Studies and Feasibility Analysis. To investigate the contribution of each module to the model's performance, ablation studies are conducted on TH-LSTM, and the results are shown in Table 8.4. We sequentially remove the memory unit

Table 8.3 *p*-value of Holm test (significance level = 0.01) between TH-LSTM and its peers

	STA-NN	A-LSTM	HOBA	A-CNN	LSTM	GRU	Bi-RNN	UgRNN	HAInt-LSTM	TLSTM	TAH-LSTM
TH-LSTM (P_r)	0.14305	0.14305	0.21466	0.21466	0.17000	0.04180	0.09878	0.04180	0.48290	0.17648	0.21466
TH-LSTM (R_e)	0.70921	0.70921	0.33917	0.33917	0.09673	0.28486	0.33917	0.33917	0.04802	0.70921	0.28486
TH-LSTM (F_1)	0.10589	0.09841	0.02972	0.06807	0.00013	0.01592	0.10589	0.09841	0.09841	0.10589	0.09841
TH-LSTM (AUC)	0.08705	0.15825	0.01505	0.08781	0.01592	0.15825	0.15825	0.12069	0.08781	0.29258	0.19126

Table 8.4 Ablation study

Train	Test	Criteria	M_0	M_1	M_2	$M_1 + M_2$	$M_1 + M_2 + M_3$
Jan.	Feb.	P_r	0.868	0.857	0.886	0.926	0.925
		R_e	0.825	0.984	0.973	0.955	0.977
		F_1	0.846	0.916	0.928	0.940	0.950
Feb.	Mar.	P_r	0.919	0.941	0.929	0.928	0.925
		R_e	0.602	0.618	0.662	0.694	0.711
		F_1	0.727	0.746	0.773	0.794	0.804
Mar.	Apr.	P_r	0.554	0.575	0.582	0.590	0.608
		R_e	0.994	0.996	0.995	0.995	0.996
		F_1	0.711	0.729	0.734	0.741	0.755
Apr.	May.	P_r	0.796	0.823	0.853	0.886	0.879
		R_e	0.903	0.907	0.914	0.962	0.994
		F_1	0.846	0.863	0.882	0.922	0.933
May.	Jun.	P_r	0.858	0.905	0.949	0.920	0.942
		R_e	0.935	0.924	0.917	0.978	0.980
		F_1	0.895	0.915	0.939	0.948	0.961

(M_1), the historical attention module (M_2), and the interaction module (M_3), and compare the performance under different module combinations. The experimental results show that when only the base model is used, the R_e value is low, which make it difficult to effectively capture hidden fraudulent behaviors. After adding the memory unit M_1, the R_e value improves significantly, indicating that the memory mechanism is critical for modeling users' long-term dependent behaviors. When the historical attention module M_2 and the interaction module M_3 are integrated simultaneously, the model achieves comprehensive improvements in both P_r and R_e, ultimately reaching an F_1 of 0.961 on June. These findings fully validate the complementarity of each module in enhancing the model's discriminative ability.

8.6 Summary

This chapter addresses the challenge of behavioral drift in OPFD by introducing a TH-LSTM that jointly models users' long-term behavioral patterns and current transaction states through a time-aware gating mechanism, a historical attention module, and an explicit historicalâŁ“current interaction unit. By encoding historical trajectories with temporal sensitivity and integrating them with present behavioral signals, TH-LSTM preserves essential long-range characteristics while selectively emphasizing the historical information most relevant to the current transaction, enabling accurate identification of subtle distributional shifts. Compared with conventional sequential models, TH-LSTM strengthens the modeling of interval-dependent memory dynamics, enhances awareness of long-range dependencies, and produces well-separated representations of legitimate and fraudulent behaviors in embedding space. Experimental evaluations on large-scale datasets further confirm that TH-LSTM consistently delivers stronger and more stable performance without incurring additional computational burden. Overall, the model establishes an adaptive and fine-grained behavioral modeling paradigm that improves accuracy, robustness, and interpretability in practical fraud detection systems. Building on this foundation, the next chapter extends the detection paradigm from sequential behavioral analysis to relational inference by introducing graph neural networks, enabling the discovery of collaborative, structure-driven fraud patterns that lie beyond the reach of temporal models.

References

1. Chen, B., Wang, K., Xu, D., Xia, J., Fan, L., Zhou, J.: Global–local attention network and value-informed federated strategy for predicting power battery state of health. Energy **313**, 134088 (2024)
2. Chen, L., Tian, Z., Zhou, S., Gong, Q., Di, H.: Attitude deviation prediction of shield tunneling machine using time-aware LSTM network. Transportation Geotechnics **45**, 101195 (2024)
3. Cho, K., van Merriënboer, B., Gulcehre, C., Bahdanau, D., Bougares, F., Schwenk, H., Bengio, Y.: Learning phrase representations using RNN encoder–decoder for statistical machine translation. ArXiv Preprint ArXiv:1406.1078 (2014)
4. Gao, C., Rios-Navarro, A., Chen, X., Liu, S.C., Delbruck, T.: EdgeDRNN: Recurrent neural network accelerator for edge inference. IEEE Journal on Emerging And Selected Topics in Circuits And Systems **10**(4), 419–432 (2020)
5. Guo, M.H., Xu, T.X., Liu, J.J., Liu, Z.N., Jiang, P.T., Mu, T.J., Zhang, S.H., Martin, R.R., Cheng, M.M., Hu, S.M.: Attention Mechanisms in Computer Vision: A Survey. Computational Visual Media **8**(3), 331–368 (2022)
6. Hochreiter, S., Schmidhuber, J.: Long short-term memory. Neural Computation **9**(8), 1735–1780 (1997)
7. Liu, D., Dong, X., Bian, D., Zhou, W.: Epileptic seizure prediction using attention augmented convolutional network. International Journal of Neural Systems **33**(11), 2350054 (2023)
8. Lu, H., Ge, Z., Song, Y., Jiang, D., Zhou, T., Qin, J.: A temporal-aware LSTM enhanced by loss-switch mechanism for traffic flow forecasting. Neurocomputing **427**, 169–178 (2021)
9. de Medrano, R., Aznarte, J.L.: A spatio-temporal attention-based spot-forecasting framework for urban traffic prediction. Applied Soft Computing **96**, 106615 (2020)
10. Nguinabé, J., Rockefeller, R., Khan, N.M., Rodrigues, P.C.: Bootstrap prediction intervals for the long short term memory (LSTM) recurrent neural network. Expert Systems with Applications p. 127728 (2025)
11. Ntakaris, A., Gabbouj, M., Kanniainen, J.: Optimizing the output of long short-term memory cell for high-frequency forecasting in financial markets. IEEE Trans. on Neural Networks and Learning Systems (2025)
12. Sanchez, T., Zavala-Río, A., Zamora-Gómez, G.I.: on the transient behavior and gain design for a class of second order homogeneous systems. Automatica **149**, 110830 (2023)
13. Schuster, M., Paliwal, K.K.: Bidirectional recurrent neural networks. IEEE Trans. on Signal Processing **45**(11), 2673–2681 (1997)
14. Su, Z., Shen, J., Sun, Y., Hu, R., Zhou, Q., Yong, B.: Deep spatio-temporal fuzzy model for NDVI forecasting. IEEE Trans. on Fuzzy Systems **33**(1), 290–301 (2024)

15. Teng, H., Wang, C., Yang, Q., Chen, X., Li, R.: Leveraging adversarial augmentation on imbalance data for online trading fraud detection. IEEE Trans. on Computational Social Systems **11**(2), 1602–1614 (2024)
16. Wang, C., Shen, D., Li, Y.: Aggregate investor attention and bitcoin return: The long short-term memory networks perspective. Finance Research Letters **49**, 103143 (2022)
17. Wang, F., Yao, H., He, W., Chang, H., Xin, X., Guo, S.: Time-sensitive scheduling mechanism based on end-to-end collaborative latency tolerance for low-earth-orbit satellite networks. IEEE Trans. on Network Science And Engineering **11**(6), 5149–5162 (2023)
18. Xie, Y., Hong, Y., Qiao, S., Yao, J., Liu, G., Pang, S.: A time-aware generative network for enhancing transaction security in consumer electronics. IEEE Trans. on Consumer Electronics **71**(2), 6818–6828 (2025)
19. Xie, Y., Liu, G., Yan, C., Jiang, C., Zhou, M.: Time-aware attention-based gated network for credit card fraud detection by extracting transactional behaviors. IEEE Trans. on Computational Social Systems **10**(3), 1004–1016 (2023)
20. Xie, Y., Liu, G., Yan, C., Jiang, C., Zhou, M., Li, M.: Learning transactional behavioral representations for credit card fraud detection. IEEE Trans. on Neural Networks and Learning Systems **35**(4), 5735–5748 (2024)
21. Xie, Y., Liu, G., Zhou, M., Wei, L., Zhu, H., Zhou, R., Cao, L.: A spatial–temporal gated network for credit card fraud detection by learning transactional representations. IEEE Trans. on Automation Science and Engineering **21**(4), 6978–6991 (2024)
22. Xie, Y., Shan, J., Wei, L., Yao, J., Zhou, M.: GAN-based hybrid sampling method for transaction fraud detection. IEEE Trans. on Knowledge and Data Engineering **37**(10), 5905–5918 (2025)
23. Xie, Y., Zhou, M., Liu, G., Wei, L., Zhu, H., De Meo, P.: A transactional-behavior-based hierarchical gated network for credit card fraud detection. IEEE/CAA Journal of Automatica Sinica **12**(7), 1489–1503 (2025)
24. Xu, Z., Xu, N., Wang, K., Yuan, X., Wang, Y., Yang, C., Gui, W., Cheng, S., Ye, L.: A sampling interval-adaptive transformer for industrial time sequence modeling with heterogeneou s sampling rates in quality prediction. Engineering Applications of Artificial Intelligence **162**, 112374 (2025)
25. Xue, J., Zheng, T., Han, J.: Exploring Attention Mechanisms Based on Summary Information for End-to-end Automatic Speech Recognition. Neurocomputing **465**, 514–524 (2021)
26. Ye, L., Dai, B., Pei, M., Lu, P., Zhao, J., Chen, M., Wang, B.: Combined approach for short-term wind power forecasting based on wave division and seq2seq model using deep learning. IEEE Trans. on Industry Applications **58**(2), 2586–2596 (2022)
27. Zhang, N., Shen, S.L., Zhou, A., Jin, Y.F.: Application of LSTM approach for modelling stress–strain behaviour of soil. Applied Soft Computing **100**, 106959 (2021)
28. Zhang, Z., Wang, Y.X., He, H., Sun, F.: A short-and long-term prognostic associating with remaining useful life estimation for proton exchange membrane fuel cell. Applied Energy **304**, 117841 (2021)

Chapter 9
Graph Neural Network for Online Payment Fraud Detection

This chapter advances the fraud detection paradigm from temporal and behavioral sequence modeling to relational inference by introducing GNNs for structured transaction analysis. While earlier chapters focus on individual user dynamics across time and space, many real-world fraud schemes unfold through coordinated interactions among users, devices, and IP addresses—structures best captured via graph-based representations. A dynamic transaction graph is constructed to model these heterogeneous relationships, and an adaptive neighbor sampling strategy coupled with entropy-based aggregation is proposed to learn robust node embeddings under noise, sparsity, and class imbalance. By exposing latent structural dependencies, this chapter complements earlier deep behavioral models and enables the detection of complex, collaborative fraud patterns—such as collusive rings and synthetic identities—that remain opaque to sequential approaches. It thus marks a pivotal shift toward topology-aware deep learning in online payment fraud detection.

9.1 Background and Problem Statement

Background. In recent years, the rapid growth of online financial transactions has not only provided convenience for users but also created opportunities for malicious actors [23, 27]. Fraudsters continuously evolve their techniques to mimic legitimate user behavior, deliberately blurring the boundary between legitimate and fraudulent activities [28]. This dynamic adversarial relationship between fraudsters and detection models [14] has made the task of fraud detection increasingly challenging. Traditional models often struggle to capture these evolving fraud patterns and to adapt effectively to newly emerging fraudulent behaviors.

Early machine learningâŁ“based approaches to fraud detection relied heavily on handcrafted features and supervised classification models [1, 2, 12]. While such models can perform well on static datasets, they exhibit significant limitations in real-world financial environments. Transaction data inherently contains complex

Y. Xie et al., *Neural Network-Based Deep Learning for Online Payment Fraud Detection*,
https://doi.org/10.1007/978-981-95-8513-7_9

relational and contextual information—including spatial, temporal, and relational dependencies—that cannot be effectively captured through fixed feature engineering [26]. Moreover, fraudsters often disguise their operations by imitating normal transaction behaviors, resulting in overlapping patterns between legitimate and fraudulent transactions [25]. Consequently, traditional feature-based models fail to generalize to new or hidden fraud strategies.

Deep learning methods [6, 24] have shown promise in automatically learning useful representations from raw data, reducing the reliance on manual feature design. However, most deep neural models still treat each transaction independently and overlook the structural relationships among users, devices, and transactions. Such models fail to leverage the rich topological information underlying transaction networks. Furthermore, deep learning—based fraud detection faces two persistent challenges: (1) data imbalance: fraudulent transactions are typically much rarer than legitimate ones [4, 10], and (2) representation dilution: the interaction between fraudulent and legitimate nodes leads to mixed or ambiguous representations, making classification more difficult.

To address these limitations, researchers have turned to GNNs [29], which model entities and their interactions as graphs. GNNs can learn node representations by aggregating information from neighboring nodes, thus capturing complex dependencies that arise from user-to-user, device-to-user, and transaction-to-merchant relationships. Several studies have applied GNNs to fraud detection tasks. For instance, Liu et al. introduced GEM, a heterogeneous GNN that combines activity and device aggregation to enhance representation capability [16]. Wang et al. proposed SemiGNN, which employs attention mechanisms and a multi-objective loss function to improve performance in financial fraud detection [20]. Dou et al. developed CARE-GNN, which incorporates label-aware similarity metrics and reinforcement learning to select reliable neighbors, thereby mitigating the impact of noisy edges [5]. Rao et al. proposed xFraud, which uses self-attention mechanisms to aggregate heterogeneous node information without predefined meta-paths [17].

Despite these advances, existing GNN-based approaches face persistent challenges when applied to transaction fraud detection. Fraudsters often manipulate their network connections—for example, by creating fake device fingerprints, using proxy IPs, or interacting deliberately with legitimate users—to embed themselves within the transaction network. This results in inter-class connections between fraudulent and legitimate nodes. These "cross-type" edges introduce heterophily, meaning that connected nodes often belong to different classes. In such cases, the standard homophily assumption of GNNs—that connected nodes share similar labels or behaviors—no longer holds. When messages from heterophilous neighbors are aggregated, they introduce noisy or misleading information, thereby weakening the model's ability to distinguish between legitimate and fraudulent behaviors.

An additional problem arises from over-smoothing [11, 22]. As GNNs propagate information across multiple layers, representations of nodes from different classes gradually converge toward similar values. In the context of fraud detection, this means that the distinctive features of fraudulent transactions can be diluted by the overwhelming majority of legitimate neighbors. Consequently, the model becomes less discriminative and struggles to accurately identify fraudulent nodes.

To overcome these issues, this chapter introduces the Sampling-and-Gating Graph Neural Network (SaG-GNN). The proposed framework aims to:

1. An adaptive sampling and gating graph neural network method, named SaG-GNN, is proposed for online transaction fraud detection. This method can effectively capture the interactive relationships among transactions and learn discriminative transaction representations, thereby enhancing the model's capability to identify fraudulent transactions.
2. An adaptive neighbor sampling strategy is designed. By dynamically filtering high-quality neighbors through the combination of cosine similarity and edge weights, the strategy can effectively eliminate noise and prioritize nodes with consistent behavioral patterns, thus suppressing the interference from camouflaged nodes. In addition, an oversampling strategy is adopted to strengthen the intra-class connections of fraudulent nodes, alleviating the feature dilution problem caused by class imbalance and the superposition of camouflage behaviors.
3. A metric based on neighbor diversity is introduced, and combined with a gating mechanism to dynamically adjust the intensity of information aggregation, which mitigates the over-smoothing problem induced by the interference of fraudulent nodes.

By integrating these mechanisms, SaG-GNN effectively combats the challenges of fraudsters' disguise strategies, noisy network structures, and imbalanced class distributions. The model enables more robust and discriminative transaction representations, thereby improving fraud detection accuracy in complex, dynamic online environments.

Problem Statement. The rapid evolution of fraudulent transaction patterns poses significant challenges for traditional detection methods, which often struggle to identify newly emerging or subtly disguised fraudulent behaviors. In this context, modeling transactional data as a graph has become an effective approach to capture relational structures and uncover hidden fraud patterns.

The goal of the transaction fraud detection task is to identify fraudulent transactions from large-scale, complex, and highly interconnected financial records. Specifically, each transaction is treated as a node in the graph, while the relationships between transactions—such as shared identifiers, temporal proximity, or behavioral similarity—are used to define edges. Consequently, the task is formulated as a node classification problem, where each node is assigned a label of either legitimate (0) or fraudulent (1).

To achieve this, GNNs are employed to learn discriminative vector representations for nodes by aggregating information from their neighbors. These learned representations are subsequently fed into a classifier to estimate the probability that each node is fraudulent.

9.2 Construction of the Transaction Graph

To support the fraud-node classification task described above, a transaction graph is constructed based on the intrinsic relationships among transaction records. Formally, the transaction graph is denoted as

$$G_t = \{V, S, P, \text{Weight}, E\}, \tag{9.1}$$

where S is the set of transaction records and V is the corresponding node set with $|V| = |S|$. Each node $v \in V$ represents a transaction $s \in S$.

The set Φ consists of m $(m \geq 1)$ logical propositions that describe relational conditions between pairs of transactions. The weight function

$$\text{Weight} : \Phi \rightarrow \mathbb{N}, \tag{9.2}$$

assigns an integer weight to each proposition. Based on these propositions, the edge set E is defined as

$$E = \bigcup_{i=1}^{m} \left\{(a, b)_{w}^{\varphi_i} \mid a \in V \wedge b \in V \wedge a \neq b \wedge \varphi_i(a, b) = \text{True} \wedge w = \text{Weight}(\varphi_i)\right\}. \tag{9.3}$$

For example, one proposition $\varphi_1^{a,b}$ can be defined as

$$\varphi_1^{a,b} = \begin{cases} \text{True}, & a.\text{ip} = b.\text{ip} \wedge |a.\text{time} - b.\text{time}| \leq 1\,\text{h}, \\ \text{False}, & \text{otherwise}. \end{cases} \tag{9.4}$$

After constructing the transaction graph, a Graph Neural Network is applied to learn node representations. In a standard GNN architecture, the update rule for the k-th layer is defined as

$$h_v^k = \sigma\Big(W^k\big(h_v^{k-1} \oplus \mathcal{AGG}_k(\{\, h_{v'}^{k-1} \mid v' \in N_v \,\})\big)\Big), \tag{9.5}$$

where $\mathcal{AGG}_k$ is an aggregation function, such as mean aggregation:

$$\mathcal{AGG}_k = \frac{1}{|N_v|} \sum_{v' \in N_v} h_{v'}^{k-1}. \tag{9.6}$$

After K layers of message passing and aggregation, the final node embeddings are passed to a classifier to determine whether each node is fraudulent.

9.3 Adaptive Neighbor Sampling Strategy

GNNs learn node representations by aggregating information from neighboring nodes. However, traditional methods such as GraphSAGE mainly rely on the homophily assumption—that connected nodes are likely to share similar labels—and use random neighbor sampling during training [8]. This random strategy often ignores the quality of neighbors, which can be problematic in fraud detection scenarios.

In financial transaction networks, some connections are intentionally misleading. Fraudsters may disguise their behavior and create fake links to normal users. When GNNs aggregate information from these noisy neighbors, the target node may receive irrelevant or even harmful signals. This weakens the ability of the model to distinguish between fraudulent and legitimate transactions.

To address this issue, this work introduces an adaptive neighbor sampling strategy based on cosine similarity and edge weights. The idea is to select more informative and reliable neighbors before aggregation, allowing the GNN to learn more discriminative representations.

(1) Cosine Similarity-Based Node Distance.

Given a node $v \in V$ and one of its neighbors $v' \in N_v$, their similarity score is computed using the cosine similarity of their normalized feature vectors r_v and $r_{v'}$. The distance between them is defined as

$$s_{v,v'} = \exp(r_v \cdot r_{v'}). \tag{9.7}$$

The exponential function ensures that all similarity values are non-negative. A higher similarity means that two transaction nodes have more similar behavioral patterns, and therefore the neighbor v' is more informative for v.

(2) Edge Weight Calculation.

In a transaction graph TG, not all transaction relationships are equally informative. Some edges carry stronger fraud-related signals. To capture this, the edge weight between v and v' is defined as

$$w_{v,v'} = \max\{\mu_i \cdot \text{Weight}(\varphi_i)\}, \quad i = 1, 2, \ldots, m, \tag{9.8}$$

where

$$\mu_i = \begin{cases} 1, & \varphi_i(v, v') = \text{True}, \\ 0; & \varphi_i(v, v') = \text{False}. \end{cases} \tag{9.9}$$

Here, $\varphi_i(v, v')$ represents a logical condition satisfied by the edge (v, v'), and $\text{Weight}(\varphi_i)$ is the corresponding edge weight.

(3) Adaptive Sampling Probability.

After computing similarity and normalizing edge weights, the probability of sampling neighbor v' for node v is given by

$$P_{v,v'} = \frac{w_{v,v'} \cdot s_{v,v'}}{\sum\limits_{v'' \in N_v, v'' \neq v} w_{v,v''} \cdot s_{v,v''}}. \tag{9.10}$$

This formulation ensures that neighbors with higher similarity and stronger edge connections are more likely to be selected. Thus, the sampling process focuses on more reliable neighbors while suppressing noise.

In practice, we perform a *Top-$\hat{z}$ neighbor sampling*, i.e., selecting the top $\hat{z}$ neighbors with the highest probabilities:

$$N'_v = \text{Top}_{\hat{z}}\{v' \mid v' \in N_v, P_{v,v'}\}. \tag{9.11}$$

This strategy improves both the stability and quality of neighbor sampling compared to random methods.

(4) Oversampling for Fraudulent Nodes.

Fraudulent transactions are often the minority class and tend to have few direct connections to other fraudulent nodes. As a result, during aggregation, their representations can be dominated by normal neighbors, making it harder for the model to identify them.

To solve this, we design a fraud-node oversampling strategy. For a given fraudulent node v, we expand its neighborhood by introducing additional fraud nodes that show similar behavioral patterns. The extended fraud neighbor set is defined as

$$\bar{N}_v^f = \{v' \in V \mid v' \notin N'_v, y^*_{v'} = 1, s_{v,v'} < d_f\}, \tag{9.12}$$

where $y^*_{v'}$ is the predicted label of node v' (estimated by a multilayer perceptron), and d_f is a similarity threshold ensuring that the introduced nodes are sufficiently similar to v.

Finally, for a fraudulent node v, its complete neighbor set is updated as

$$N_v = N'_v \cup \bar{N}_v^f. \tag{9.13}$$

For normal nodes, only N'_v is used.

In summary, the proposed adaptive neighbor sampling strategy combines cosine similarity and edge weights to filter out noisy neighbors, strengthen meaningful node associations, and reduce the negative impact of fraudulent connections. Moreover, the oversampling mechanism ensures that fraud nodes receive sufficient same-class information during message aggregation, ultimately improving the GNN's ability to distinguish between normal and fraudulent transactions.

9.4 Entropy-based Aggregation Mechanism

After performing the adaptive neighbor sampling described earlier, this section focuses on how to aggregate information from neighbors more effectively. Specifically, we design a time-aware attention mechanism and an entropy-based gating mechanism to improve the quality of message aggregation and alleviate the over-smoothing problem that commonly occurs in GNNs.

(1) Time-Aware Attention Mechanism.

After neighbor sampling, we aggregate information from the neighbors to generate the node representation at the k-th layer. For a given node $v \in V$, its representation at layer k is denoted as h_v^k, where $k = \{1, 2, \cdots, K\}$. The aggregation process can be written as

$$h_{N_v}^k = \sum_{v' \in N_v} \alpha_{v,v'}^k \mathcal{AGG}^k(h_{v'}^{k-1}), \tag{9.14}$$

where $\alpha_{v,v'}^k$ is the attention score indicating how much neighbor v' contributes to node v at layer k, and $\mathcal{AGG}^k$ denotes the aggregation function.

The attention coefficient is computed as

$$\alpha_{v,v'}^k = \frac{\exp(\text{LeakyReLU}(e_{v,v'}))}{\sum_{i \in N_v} \exp(\text{LeakyReLU}(e_{v,i}))}, \tag{9.15}$$

where

$$e_{v,v'} = f(\mathcal{W}^k h_v^{k-1} \,||\, \mathcal{W}^k h_{v'}^{k-1}). \tag{9.16}$$

Here, LeakyReLU is the activation function, $f(\cdot)$ maps high-dimensional features to a scalar, $\mathcal{W}^k$ is the learnable weight matrix, and $||$ denotes concatenation.

In the field of fraud detection, fraudulent users often make many transactions in a short time to gain quick profits. Similarly, legitimate users may also have short-term bursts of activity due to normal spending needs. Since the edges in our transaction graph are built based on shared devices, transactions that occur within short time intervals on the same device are usually more strongly related in behavior and data characteristics.

To model this temporal dependency, we introduce a time decay factor $\widetilde{\delta}_{t_{v,v'}}$ to adjust the attention score:

$$\alpha^k_{v,v'} = \frac{\widetilde{\delta}_{t_{v,v'}} \exp(\text{LeakyReLU}(e_{v,v'}))}{\sum_{i \in N_v} \widetilde{\delta}_{t_{v,i}} \exp(\text{LeakyReLU}(e_{v,i}))}, \tag{9.17}$$

where the time decay factor is calculated as

$$\widetilde{\delta}_{t_{v,v'}} = \frac{t_v - t_{v'}}{\sum_{i \in N_v} (t_v - t_i)}. \tag{9.18}$$

Here, t_v and $t_{v'}$ denote the transaction times of nodes v and v', respectively. This normalization ensures that transactions closer in time have a larger influence, helping the model better capture temporal patterns in user behavior.

(2) Neighbor Diversity and Entropy-Based Gating.

The over-smoothing problem is a common challenge in GNNs. It occurs when nodes from different classes become too similar after multiple layers of message aggregation. Prior studies suggest that noise introduced during aggregation is a major cause of over-smoothing [3, 9].

Ideally, features from same-class neighbors should strengthen class consistency and make the node representations more discriminative. However, in fraud detection, fraudsters often disguise their activities to appear legitimate, creating edges that connect fraudulent and normal nodes. These deceptive connections introduce cross-class information that makes nodes from different classes less distinguishable, worsening over-smoothing.

To mitigate this, we measure the diversity of a node's neighborhood using an *entropy-based metric*. For a target node v, the neighbor diversity $D(v)$ is defined as

$$\Delta(v) = -\sum_{c \in C} P_c(v) \log P_c(v), \tag{9.19}$$

where C is the set of label classes (e.g., normal and fraudulent), and $P_c(v)$ is the proportion of neighbors in class c, calculated as

$$P_c(v) = \frac{|\{v' \in N_v \mid y^*_{v'} = c\}|}{|N_v|}. \tag{9.20}$$

Here, $y^*_{v'}$ denotes the predicted label of node v'.

A larger $D(v)$ means the neighborhood of node v is more diverse, containing nodes from multiple classes, which may lead to more mixed (noisy) feature propagation. To control this, we introduce a gating mechanism that adaptively adjusts how much information node v should aggregate from its neighbors:

$$\gamma_v^k = \sigma(-\text{Norm}(\Delta(v))), \tag{9.21}$$

where Norm$(\cdot)$ is a normalization function applied to all nodes in the graph, and σ is an activation function (e.g., sigmoid). The gate value γ_v^k ranges between (0, 1). When a node is surrounded by many cross-class neighbors, $D(v)$ becomes large, making γ_v^k small and thereby reducing the influence of those neighbors.

Finally, the node update rule at layer k is defined as

$$h_v^k = \sigma\left(\mathcal{W}^k[h_v^{k-1} \,||\, \gamma_v^k h_{N_v}^k]\right). \tag{9.22}$$

Here, σ is the activation function, $\mathcal{W}^k$ is the layer's weight matrix, and $||$ denotes concatenation. This formulation shows that each node representation depends both on its own previous-layer embedding h_v^{k-1} and the aggregated neighbor information $h_{N_v}^k$, weighted by g_v^k.

The gating mechanism helps each node adaptively control the degree of aggregation according to its neighborhood structure. It reduces the influence of dissimilar neighbors and prevents node representations from collapsing into uniform vectors after multiple layers. In this way, the model maintains discriminative representations and alleviates over-smoothing while effectively handling the disguise behavior of fraudsters.

In the task of transaction fraud detection, the goal is to predict whether a given transaction is fraudulent based on the learned node representations. For a target node v, its output representation from the K-th layer, denoted as h_v^K, is passed through a *softmax* function to estimate the probability that the transaction is fraudulent.

The model is trained using the cross-entropy loss function L_{ce}, which serves as the optimization objective. The loss is calculated as follows:

$$L_{ce} = -\sum_{v \in V_{train}} \left(y_v \log \hat{y}_v + (1 - y_v) \log(1 - \hat{y}_v)\right), \tag{9.23}$$

where y_v represents the true label of node v, and $\hat{y}_v$ denotes the predicted probability obtained from the model.

The proposed method follows an inductive learning paradigm, meaning it can generalize to unseen nodes in the graph. Specifically, the model leverages both the intrinsic node features and the learned neighborhood aggregation functions to generate representations for new, unseen nodes, which are then used for prediction tasks such as fraud detection. The framework of SaG-GNN model proposed in this chapter is shown in Fig. 9.1.

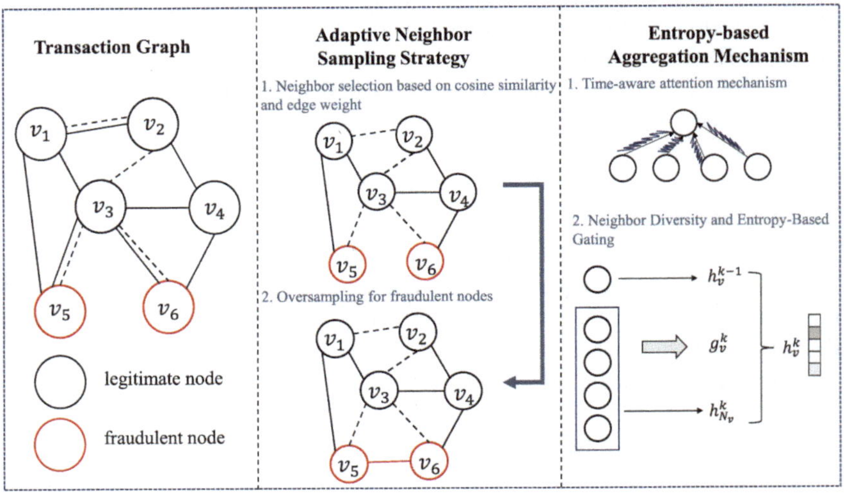

Fig. 9.1 The architecture of SaG-GNN

9.5 Experimental Validation

This section describes the specific experimental design, including the introduction of the dataset, the description of baseline methods, evaluation metrics, as well as the experimental environment and parameter settings. Through a series of extensive experiments, the effectiveness of the proposed SaG-GNN model in the task of online transaction fraud detection is validated.

Experimental Dataset and Construction of the Transaction Graph. The private dataset PR01 contains 5.12 million transactions from a financial company in China. All transactions were labeled by professional investigators, with a label of 1 indicating fraudulent transactions and 0 indicating legitimate ones. For the experiments in this chapter, we selected transaction samples from Nov. 2016 to Jan. 2017, which contained more detailed device information, as the dataset. Table 9.1 presents the total number of samples in the processed PR01 dataset. The dataset was split chronologically, with 70% of the data used for training and the remaining 30% for testing.

Table 9.1 Information of the PR01 dataset

Time	Nov. 2016	Dec. 2016	Jan. 2017
Total transactions	13,607,812	13,397,346	4,749,993
Legitimate transactions	13,597,637	13,363,584	4,711,539
Fraudulent transactions	10,175	33,762	38,454

During data preprocessing, class imbalance was addressed by downsampling the legitimate transactions. Discrete features were encoded using one-hot encoding, while continuous features were normalized using min-max scaling. In addition, PR02 was constructed as a smaller dataset by selecting the latest 10,000 transactions from PR01 for experimental evaluation.

In this chapter, transactions are treated as nodes for constructing the transaction graph G_t. Edges are designed based on logical propositions. Generally, fraudulent behavior exhibits two characteristics: device clustering and temporal clustering. Device clustering indicates that fraudsters, due to financial and regulatory constraints, tend to commit fraud on a limited number of devices, which differs from legitimate cardholders making transactions on multiple devices. Temporal clustering means that fraudsters must complete their activities quickly; otherwise, banks or cardholders may detect their fraudulent behavior.

For the private dataset, the following two logical propositions are used to construct the transaction graph:

$$\varphi_1^{i,j} = \begin{cases} \text{True}, & i.ip = j.ip \\ & \wedge |i.time - j.time| \leq 1\text{h}, \\ \text{False}, & \text{otherwise}. \end{cases} \tag{9.24}$$

$$\varphi_2^{i,j} = \begin{cases} \text{True}, & i.mac = j.mac \\ & \wedge |i.time - j.time| \leq 1\text{h}, \\ \text{False}, & \text{otherwise}. \end{cases} \tag{9.25}$$

Here, ip, time, and mac denote the IP address, timestamp, and MAC address of a transaction. Edges derived from p_1 and p_2 are assigned weights $w_1 = 1$ and $w_2 = 2$, respectively. To illustrate the construction process, a transaction sample in Table 9.2 is used to build the transaction graph shown in Fig. 9.2.

Experimental Setup and Evaluation Metrics. To verify the effectiveness of the proposed SaG-GNN method, this study compares it with seven representative baseline models, including both classical GNN architectures and advanced GNN-based fraud detection models. A brief introduction to each baseline method is given below:

Table 9.2 Transaction sample set

Transaction	Time	Ip	Mac	Amount
a	2016-12-11 07:15	192.168.12.45	A4-5E-60-3B-2F-9C	3,000
b	2016-12-11 07:32	192.168.12.45	A4-5E-60-3B-2F-9C	1,500
c	2016-12-11 08:17	192.168.12.45	3A-19-84-27-50-08	2,500
d	2016-12-11 09:12	192.168.12.45	A4-5E-60-3B-2F-9C	500
e	2016-12-11 09:15	172.16.58.204	3A-19-84-27-50-08	7,000

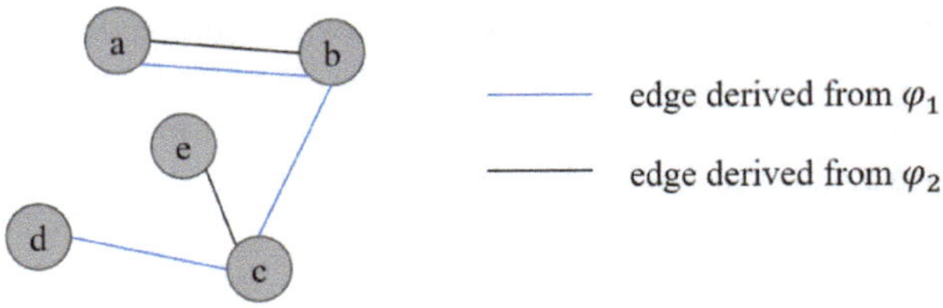

Fig. 9.2 The illustration of transaction graph construction

(1) Graph Convolutional Network (GCN) [13]: It extends traditional convolutional neural networks to graph-structured data, providing an effective deep learning framework for relational modeling. Its core idea is to define graph convolution operations through a first-order approximation of the Laplacian matrix, combining the adjacency matrix and node feature matrix under nonlinear activation to perform representation learning. GCN has been widely applied in node classification and link prediction tasks.
(2) GraphSAGE [8]: It generalizes GCN to an inductive learning framework by introducing random sampling strategies and a set of neighborhood aggregation functions. Unlike transductive methods that rely on the entire graph, GraphSAGE generates node embeddings by sampling and aggregating local neighborhoods, which enables better scalability for large-scale graph data.
(3) Graph Attention Network (GAT) [19]: It introduces the attention mechanism into GNNs. By assigning different importance weights to neighboring nodes through graph attention layers, GAT adaptively aggregates information from neighbors, enhancing the model's representation capability.
(4) CARE-GNN [5]: It is a GNN-based method specifically designed for fraud detection. It proposes a label-aware similarity measure to identify neighbors most similar to the target node and employs a similarity-aware neighbor selector to filter reliable neighbors within each relation. Moreover, it leverages reinforcement learning to adaptively determine the optimal neighbor selection threshold during training.
(5) SSA (Similar-sample + Attention SAGE) [15]: It improves GraphSAGE's random sampling strategy by prioritizing neighbors that exhibit higher behavioral similarity to the target node. By introducing a time-based attention mechanism, it dynamically captures the importance of neighbors with different temporal intervals, leading to improved classification performance for GNN-based fraud detectors.
(6) Relational Graph Convolutional Network (RGCN) [18]: It extends GCN to handle multi-relational data. It aggregates information from local relational neighborhoods, achieving strong performance in link prediction and node classification tasks. To improve efficiency, RGCN applies basis decomposition and block-diagonal decomposition to reduce the number of trainable parameters.

(7) Heterogeneous Graph Attention Network (HAN) [21]: It addresses real-world heterogeneous graphs by generating homogeneous subgraphs through metapaths. It employs a node-level attention mechanism to aggregate information within subgraphs and a semantic-level attention mechanism to combine representations across different subgraphs, capturing both structural and semantic heterogeneity.
(8) Partitioned Message Passing (PMP) [30]: It method mitigates performance degradation caused by heterophilous edges by partitioning message passing according to neighbor label differences.
(9) Graph-based Heterophily Reduction Network (GHRN) [7]: It alleviates the negative impact of heterophilous connections by introducing a label-based high-frequency indicator to detect label variations among neighbors. It then prunes noisy edges, thereby enhancing the quality of node representations.

Performance Comparison. Tables 9.3 and 9.4 report the comparative performance between the proposed SaG-GNN and the baseline models introduced in the previous section, where the highest scores are highlighted in **bold**. The main observations are summarized as follows.

First, classical GNN architectures,including GCN, GraphSAGE, GAT, RGCN, and HAN, are not specifically designed to handle the disguising behaviors of fraudsters. As a result, their performance on the PR01 and PR02 datasets is consistently lower than that of SaG-GNN. During model training, these methods are easily affected by the noisy information produced through interactions between fraudulent and legitimate nodes. Such noise propagates during neighborhood aggregation, distorts the learned representations, and ultimately degrades classification performance. Therefore, when applied to fraud detection scenarios characterized by strong camouflage and complex interaction patterns, conventional GNNs exhibit clear limitations compared with SaG-GNN.

Table 9.3 Experimental results of SaG-GNN and baseline models on the PR01 dataset

Method	R_e	F_1	AUC
GCN	0.655	0.594	0.557
GraphSAGE	0.673	0.598	0.576
GAT	0.863	0.735	0.693
CARE-GNN	–	–	–
SSA	0.867	0.718	0.764
RGCN	0.785	0.871	0.739
HAN	0.862	0.751	0.696
PMP	0.827	0.671	0.875
GHRN	0.809	0.797	0.890
SaG-GNN	**0.884**	**0.904**	**0.922**

Table 9.4 Experimental results of SaG-GNN and baseline models on the PR02 dataset

Method	R_e	F_1	AUC
GCN	0.761	0.811	0.756
GraphSAGE	0.699	0.807	0.818
GAT	0.747	0.815	0.797
CARE-GNN	0.458	0.287	0.790
SSA	0.730	0.804	0.820
RGCN	0.703	0.811	0.824
HAN	0.701	0.802	0.825
PMP	0.715	0.742	0.844
GHRN	0.766	0.800	0.890
SaG-GNN	**0.861**	**0.909**	**0.916**

Second, neighbor-sampling-based methods, such as GraphSAGE, CARE-GNN, and SSA, also perform worse than SaG-GNN. SaG-GNN's superiority mainly stems from its ability to filter out noisy or uninformative neighbors and to provide higher-quality contextual information for minority-class nodes, i.e., fraudulent nodes. Moreover, its explicit modeling of disguising behaviors enhances the robustness of the information aggregation process. Among these baselines, SSA surpasses GraphSAGE due to its improved sampling strategy and attention-based neighbor weighting, which together produce more discriminative embeddings. Although CARE-GNN introduces a label-aware similarity measure based on the L_1 distance to model camouflage, its effectiveness in high-dimensional feature spaces is limited, and its anti-camouflage module only operates during neighbor sampling. In contrast, SaG-GNN performs adaptive information aggregation throughout the message passing process, allowing it to better cope with sophisticated fraudulent disguises.

Finally, PMP and GHRN remain less competitive than SaG-GNN. PMP employs a partitioned message passing mechanism that distinguishes between homophilous and heterophilous neighbors but lacks an effective strategy for filtering low-quality or irrelevant neighbors, making it sensitive to noise. GHRN partially mitigates disguise-induced interference by modifying heterophilous edges; however, it overlooks the scarcity of same-class neighbors for fraudulent nodes, which limits its ability to learn reliable representations. Consequently, both PMP and GHRN exhibit inferior performance to SaG-GNN on these datasets.

Ablation Study. To verify the effectiveness of the key module designs in the proposed SaG-GNN model, this section conducts an ablation study. By removing different modules from SaG-GNN and retraining the model, we evaluate the performance of several SaG-GNN variants with different structural configurations. The designed variants of SaG-GNN are as follows:

1. SaG-GNN1: A variant of SaG-GNN that replaces the proposed adaptive sampling strategy with a random sampling strategy. Specifically, it no longer selects neighborhood nodes based on class relevance and neighbor importance, but instead randomly samples a fixed number of neighbors for information aggregation.
2. SaG-GNN2: A variant that only employs an attention mechanism to measure the importance of different neighbor nodes during information aggregation. It does not adopt the adaptive information aggregation strategy, i.e., it removes the neighbor diversity metric and the gating mechanism used to suppress noise from heterophilous neighbors, which are designed to address fraudsters' camouflage behaviors.
3. SaG-GNN3: A variant that computes node similarity using Euclidean distance.
4. SaG-GNN4: A variant that computes node similarity using L_1 distance.

Table 9.5 present the ablation results on the PR01 dataset. The following observations can be made:

1. Effectiveness of the adaptive sampling strategy: SaG-GNN outperforms SaG-GNN1 in terms of R_e, F_1, and AUC on the PR01 dataset, achieving superior performance across all evaluation metrics. This improvement stems from the proposed adaptive sampling strategy, which effectively filters noisy neighbor information and supplies more same-class neighbors for fraud nodes. By mitigating the negative impact of heterophilous edges and alleviating the scarcity of same-class neighbors during the sampling process, the strategy substantially enhances the overall model performance.
2. Effectiveness of the adaptive aggregation mechanism: SaG-GNN2 performs worse than the full SaG-GNN model on the PR01 dataset. This result indicates that the proposed neighbor diversity metric together with the gating mechanism effectively suppresses information from heterophilous neighbors, thereby enhancing the quality of learned node representations. Without this component, SaG-GNN2 would struggle to mitigate the noise introduced by fraudsters' deceptive behavior. As a consequence, during multi-hop message passing, fraudulent nodes tend to aggregate an excessive amount of information from legitimate nodes, which leads to over-smoothing and ultimately reduces both intra-class compactness and inter-class separability.
3. Effectiveness of the similarity computation method: Both SaG-GNN3 and SaG-GNN4 exhibit inferior performance to the full SaG-GNN model on the PR01 dataset. This performance gap arises because the L_1 distance becomes less

Table 9.5 Ablation results on PR01

Criteria	SaG-GNN1	SaG-GNN2	SaG-GNN3	SaG-GNN4	SaG-GNN
R_e	78.6	84.5	81.0	70.4	**88.4**
F_1	87.2	76.2	86.6	80.7	**90.4**
AUC	88.6	73.8	87.6	83.2	**92.2**

effective in high-dimensional feature spaces and is unable to capture the intricate transactional relationships present in fraud scenarios. Meanwhile, the Euclidean distance disregards the effects of edge weights and the complexity of graph structural patterns, thereby limiting its ability to model node interactions accurately. These results demonstrate that the node similarity computation method proposed in this chapter provides a more expressive and reliable measure, leading to superior detection performance.

In summary, the ablation study confirms that all the designed modules in SaG-GNN are necessary and jointly contribute to its superior overall performance.

9.6 Summary

In this chapter, we propose a novel graph neural network model, SaG-GNN, based on adaptive sampling and aggregation, for identifying fraudulent transactions. SaG-GNN employs an adaptive sampling strategy to filter out noisy nodes and addresses the issue of insufficient neighborhood information for fraud nodes. As a result, it can fully and effectively leverage both attribute and topological information in transaction graphs. Moreover, thanks to the proposed neighbor diversity metric, SaG-GNN is capable of mitigating the effects of heterophilous edges caused by fraudsters' camouflage behavior, alleviating the over-smoothing problem. Extensive experiments on the real-world datasets demonstrate that the proposed SaG-GNN significantly outperforms baseline methods in terms of performance. Additionally, ablation studies further validate the effectiveness of SaG-GNN. Despite its strong performance in modeling local structural patterns through adaptive sampling and aggregation, SaG-GNN is still primarily constrained to neighborhood-level information propagation and lacks an explicit mechanism for capturing fine-grained temporal dynamics and long-range dependencies across the transaction graph. To address these limitations, the next chapter extends the fraud detection framework toward a spatial-temporal-aware graph transformer, which jointly models temporal evolution and global relational interactions to uncover more complex fraud behaviors.

References

1. Bahnsen, A.C., Aouada, D., Stojanovic, A., Ottersten, B.: Feature engineering strategies for credit card fraud detection. Expert Systems with Applications **51**, 134–142 (2016)
2. Cao, R., Wang, J., Mao, M., Liu, G., Jiang, C.: Feature-wise attention based boosting ensemble method for fraud detection. Engineering Applications of Artificial Intelligence **126**, 106975 (2023)
3. Chen, D., Lin, Y., Li, W., Li, P., Zhou, J., Sun, X.: Measuring and relieving the over-smoothing problem for graph neural networks from the topological view. In: Proceedings of the AAAI Conference on Artificial Intelligence. vol. 34, pp. 3438–3445 (2020)

4. Denil, M.: The effects of overlap and imbalance on svm classification. Master's, Dalhousie University (2010)
5. Dou, Y., Liu, Z., Sun, L., Deng, Y., Peng, H., Yu, P.S.: Enhancing graph neural network-based fraud detectors against camouflaged fraudsters. In: Proceedings of the 29th ACM International Conference on Information & Knowledge Management. pp. 315–324 (2020)
6. Fu, K., Cheng, D., Tu, Y., Zhang, L.: Credit card fraud detection using convolutional neural networks. In: International Conference on Neural Information Processing. pp. 483–490. Springer (2016)
7. Gao, Y., Wang, X., He, X., Liu, Z., Feng, H., Zhang, Y.: Addressing heterophily in graph anomaly detection: A perspective of graph spectrum. In: Proceedings of the ACM Web Conference 2023. pp. 1528–1538 (2023)
8. Hamilton, W., Ying, Z., Leskovec, J.: Inductive representation learning on large graphs. Advances in Neural Information Processing Systems **30** (2017)
9. He, D., Guo, R., Wang, X., Jin, D., Huang, Y., Wang, W.: Inflation improves graph neural networks. In: Proceedings of the ACM Web Conference 2022. pp. 1466–1474 (2022)
10. He, H., Garcia, E.A.: Learning from imbalanced data. IEEE Trans. on Knowledge and Data Engineering **21**(9), 1263–1284 (2009)
11. He, K., Fan, H., Wu, Y., Xie, S., Girshick, R.: Momentum contrast for unsupervised visual representation learning. In: Proceedings of the IEEE/CVF Conference on Computer Vision and Pattern Recognition. pp. 9729–9738 (2020)
12. Jiang, C., Song, J., Liu, G., Zheng, L., Luan, W.: Credit card fraud detection: A novel approach using aggregation strategy and feedback mechanism. IEEE Internet of Things Journal **5**(5), 3637–3647 (2018)
13. Kipf, T.: Semi-supervised classification with graph convolutional networks. ArXiv Preprint ArXiv:1609.02907 (2016)
14. Li, Z., Liu, G., Jiang, C.: Deep representation learning with full center loss for credit card fraud detection. IEEE Trans. on Computational Social Systems **7**(2), 569–579 (2020)
15. Liu, G., Tang, J., Tian, Y., Wang, J.: Graph neural network for credit card fraud detection. In: 2021 International Conference on Cyber-Physical Social Intelligence (ICCSI). pp. 1–6. IEEE (2021)
16. Liu, Z., Chen, C., Yang, X., Zhou, J., Li, X., Song, L.: Heterogeneous graph neural networks for malicious account detection. In: Proceedings of the 27th ACM International Conference on Information and Knowledge Management. pp. 2077–2085 (2018)
17. Rao, S.X., Zhang, S., Han, Z., Zhang, Z., Min, W., Chen, Z., Shan, Y., Zhao, Y., Zhang, C.: xFraud: explainable fraud transaction detection. ArXiv Preprint ArXiv:2011.12193 (2020)
18. Schlichtkrull, M., Kipf, T.N., Bloem, P., Van Den Berg, R., Titov, I., Welling, M.: Modeling relational data with graph convolutional networks. In: European Semantic Web Conference. pp. 593–607. Springer (2018)
19. Veličković, P., Cucurull, G., Casanova, A., Romero, A., Lio, P., Bengio, Y.: Graph attention networks. ArXiv Preprint ArXiv:1710.10903 (2017)
20. Wang, D., Lin, J., Cui, P., Jia, Q., Wang, Z., Fang, Y., Yu, Q., Zhou, J., Yang, S., Qi, Y.: A semi-supervised graph attentive network for financial fraud detection. In: 2019 IEEE International Conference on Data Mining (ICDM). pp. 598–607. IEEE (2019)
21. Wang, X., Ji, H., Shi, C., Wang, B., Ye, Y., Cui, P., Yu, P.S.: Heterogeneous graph attention network. In: The World Wide Web Conference. pp. 2022–2032 (2019)
22. Xie, Y., Xu, Z., Zhang, J., Wang, Z., Ji, S.: Self-supervised learning of graph neural networks: A unified review. IEEE Trans. on Pattern Analysis and Machine Intelligence **45**(2), 2412–2429 (2022)
23. Xie, Y., Hong, Y., Qiao, S., Yao, J., Liu, G., Pang, S.: A time-aware generative network for enhancing transaction security in consumer electronics. IEEE Trans. on Consumer Electronics **71**(2), 6818–6828 (2025)
24. Xie, Y., Liu, G., Yan, C., Jiang, C., Zhou, M.: Time-aware attention-based gated network for credit card fraud detection by extracting transactional behaviors. IEEE Trans. on Computational Social Systems **10**(3), 1004–1016 (2023)

25. Xie, Y., Liu, G., Yan, C., Jiang, C., Zhou, M., Li, M.: Learning transactional behavioral representations for credit card fraud detection. IEEE Trans. on Neural Networks and Learning Systems **35**(4), 5735–5748 (2024)
26. Xie, Y., Liu, G., Zhou, M., Wei, L., Zhu, H., Zhou, R., Cao, L.: A spatial–temporal gated network for credit card fraud detection by learning transactional representations. IEEE Trans. on Automation Science and Engineering **21**(4), 6978–6991 (2024)
27. Xie, Y., Shan, J., Wei, L., Yao, J., Zhou, M.: GAN-based hybrid sampling method for transaction fraud detection. IEEE Trans. on Knowledge and Data Engineering **37**(10), 5905–5918 (2025)
28. Xie, Y., Zhou, M., Liu, G., Wei, L., Zhu, H., De Meo, P.: A transactional-behavior-based hierarchical gated network for credit card fraud detection. IEEE/CAA Journal of Automatica Sinica **12**(7), 1489–1503 (2025)
29. Zhang, G., Li, Z., Huang, J., Wu, J., Zhou, C., Yang, J., Gao, J.: efraudcom: An e-commerce fraud detection system via competitive graph neural networks. ACM Trans. on Information Systems (TOIS) **40**(3), 1–29 (2022)
30. Zhuo, W., Liu, Z., Hooi, B., He, B., Tan, G., Fathony, R., Chen, J.: Partitioning message passing for graph fraud detection. ArXiv Preprint ArXiv:2412.00020 (2024)

Chapter 10
Spatial-Temporal-Aware Graph Transformer for Online Payment Fraud Detection

This chapter introduces a spatial-temporal graph transformer that extends graph-based fraud detection with fine-grained temporal modeling and global relational attention. While Chap. 9 focuses on local structural patterns within transaction graphs, many high-impact fraud scenarios—such as bursty micro-payment attacks or coordinated multi-device abuse—unfold over short time spans and limited infrastructures. To capture these transient yet structured behaviors, the proposed model integrates temporal encodings and multi-head self-attention within a graph transformer architecture, enabling the joint learning of localized temporal dependencies and global transaction relationships. This design overcomes the expressiveness bottlenecks of traditional GNNs, which struggle with long-range and heterogeneous interactions. By unifying spatial proximity, temporal intensity, and relational topology, the model excels at identifying concealed, low-signal fraud patterns that evade earlier modeling strategies. Positioned as the conceptual culmination of the book, this chapter synthesizes the deep learning approaches introduced across previous chapters into a holistic framework for dynamic, topology-aware fraud detection in real-world online payment systems.

10.1 Background and Problem Statement

Background. Online financial transactions have become an essential part of modern digital life, enabling seamless payments, mobile banking, and e-commerce interactions. However, with the expansion of these services, fraudulent activities have also evolved in complexity and sophistication. Fraudsters exploit weaknesses in transaction systems and use deceptive strategies—such as impersonating legitimate users, reusing compromised devices, or manipulating time-based transaction patterns—to conceal their identities and maximize illicit gains. The increasing scale and dynamic

Y. Xie et al., *Neural Network-Based Deep Learning for Online Payment Fraud Detection*,
https://doi.org/10.1007/978-981-95-8513-7_10

nature of online transactions pose significant challenges for automated fraud detection systems.

Traditional machine learning-based methods [4, 23] for transaction fraud detection typically rely on supervised or unsupervised models trained on large volumes of historical transaction data. These approaches extract statistical features from structured attributes such as transaction time, amount, and geographical location [1, 20]. While effective in some static scenarios, they often struggle with unstructured information such as device identifiers, Wi-Fi locations, or behavioral logs. Furthermore, these models are limited in their ability to capture the complex interactions between transactions, users, and devices that characterize real-world fraud patterns [18].

Recent advances in GNNs [9] have provided a powerful framework for modeling relational and structural dependencies in complex transaction networks. By representing entities (e.g., users, devices, or transactions) as nodes and their interactions (e.g., shared IPs or device IDs) as edges, GNNs learn latent representations through iterative neighborhood aggregation. This mechanism allows models to capture higher-order relationships that traditional vector-based models cannot. Compared with conventional methods, GNNs offer two major advantages: (1) automatic feature learning: GNNs extract multi-hop relational dependencies directly from graph structures, reducing reliance on manual feature engineering, and (2) relational expressiveness: graphs naturally encode spatial (network) and temporal (sequential) dependencies in transaction data.

Despite these strengths, GNN-based fraud detection still faces critical challenges. Fraudulent behaviors often exhibit spatial-temporal aggregation patterns. Spatial aggregation refers to the reuse of limited resources—such as IP addresses or devices—across multiple fraudulent transactions, since acquiring new devices incurs cost and risk. Temporal aggregation refers to the burst-like occurrence of fraudulent activities within short time spans, as fraudsters tend to act rapidly before being detected by security systems.

Several prior studies have attempted to address these challenges. GEM [12] establishes connections between accounts that appear on the same device within a given time window and then applies filtering. However, its reliance on information restricted to a fixed and local time interval limits its ability to capture broader temporal dynamics. STAGN [11], on the other hand, employs temporal and spatial slices to jointly model spatial and temporal aggregation. Nevertheless, when processing nodes within the same temporal slice, it fails to accurately characterize fine-grained temporal differences among nodes, resulting in a relatively coarse temporal modeling granularity. Moreover, the target node can only aggregate information from its local neighbors within each slice and cannot directly model its interactions with distant nodes in other slices. Therefore, the approach of constructing an independent transaction graph for each temporal slice and performing graph convolution to integrate spatiotemporal information remains insufficient for achieving strong performance in transaction fraud detection.

Another key limitation lies in the locality of standard GNN architectures. Classical GNNs update node representations by aggregating information from neighboring nodes within a few hops [14, 21]. However, distant transactions—which may share subtle but important behavioral correlations—are often overlooked. Although stacking multiple GNN layers theoretically increases the receptive field, this approach introduces information dilution and oversmoothing [8, 13]: as layer depth increases, node representations from different classes become indistinguishable. This phenomenon significantly hampers classification performance, especially when fraudulent samples are sparse or intertwined with legitimate transactions.

To address these challenges, this chapter introduces the Spatial-Temporal-Aware Graph Transformer (STGFormer), a novel heterogeneous graph neural network designed for transaction fraud detection. STGFormer jointly models spatial and temporal dependencies at the node level while incorporating both local and global contextual information. Specifically:

1. It constructs a multi-relational graph where transactions are nodes connected by multiple edge types (e.g., shared IP or MAC addresses), enabling explicit modeling of spatial relations.
2. It integrates a temporal encoding mechanism into the graph learning process, allowing the model to capture fine-grained time-dependent patterns.
3. It employs a Transformer-based global learning module to propagate information across distant nodes, overcoming the locality constraints of conventional GNNs.

By combining these components, STGFormer achieves a balanced representation that preserves local structural dependencies while integrating global contextual knowledge. The model enhances the discriminative power of node representations, improving the ability to identify fraudulent transactions in complex, dynamic environments.

Problem Definition. The task in this chapter aims to detect fraudulent transactions occurring across various platforms, such as banks and financial institutions. We formalize the fraud detection task as a node classification problem on a graph using GNNs. Specifically, a multi-relational graph is defined as

$$G_m = \{V, \{E\}_1^R, X, Y\}, \tag{10.1}$$

where V and E denote the sets of nodes and edges, respectively. An edge $e_{i,j}^r$ represents a connection between nodes i and j under relation $r \in \{1, \ldots, R\}$, where R denotes the number of relation types.

Each node corresponds to a transaction record x, represented as a d-dimensional feature vector $x_i \in \mathbb{R}^d$, and the node feature set is denoted by $X = \{x_1, \ldots, x_n\}$. Y represents the label set for all nodes V. In the transaction graph, each node v represents a transaction whose likelihood of being fraudulent needs to be predicted. The label of node v is $y_v \in [0, 1]$, where 0 and 1 indicate a legitimate transaction and a fraudulent transaction, respectively.

Fraud detection is thus formulated as a binary classification problem. The model is trained using the information from labeled nodes, and subsequently, it predicts the probability of unlabeled nodes being fraudulent.

10.2 Modeling the Spatial-Temporal Dependency

Detecting fraudulent transactions requires an understanding of how suspicious behaviors evolve over both space (i.e., network or device relationships) and time (i.e., transaction sequences). Fraudsters rarely act in isolation; rather, they exploit overlapping infrastructures such as shared IP addresses, reused devices, or repeated merchant channels. Simultaneously, their activities often occur in rapid temporal bursts before detection mechanisms respond. Therefore, a robust fraud detection model must jointly capture where and when fraudulent interactions occur—the essence of spatial-temporal dependency modeling.

Overview of STGFormer Architecture. The *Spatial-Temporal-Aware Graph Transformer* (STGFormer) framework extends conventional graph neural networks by embedding explicit spatial-temporal reasoning into each stage of node representation learning. As shown conceptually in Fig. 10.1, the architecture comprises five major components:

1. Attribute-Driven Embedding Module: It derives initial node embeddings directly from raw transaction attributes without relying on graph connectivity.
2. Temporal Information Learning Module: It applies a learnable time-encoding strategy to represent fine-grained temporal dependencies.
3. Spatial Aggregation Module: It performs intra-relation and inter-relation aggregation to capture spatial relationships between connected transactions.
4. Global Information Learning Module: It utilizes a Transformer-based self-attention mechanism to integrate information across distant nodes.
5. Prediction Module: It classifies transactions as fraudulent or legitimate based on the learned joint representations.

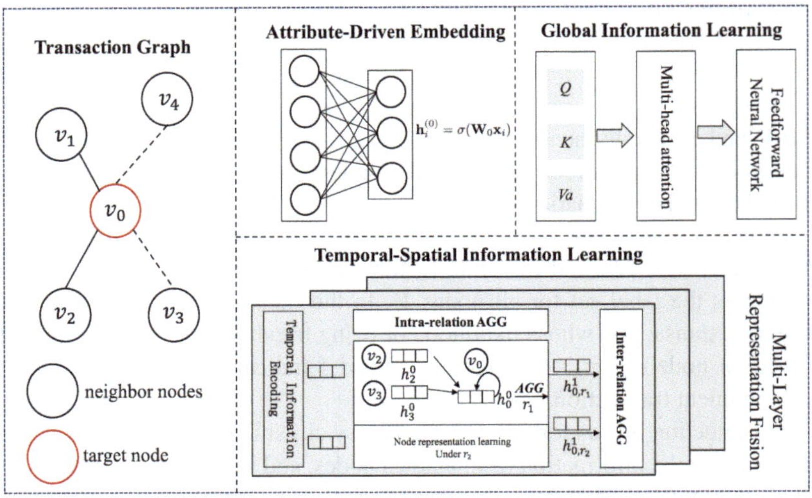

Fig. 10.1 The architecture of STGFormer

Together, these modules enable STGFormer to simultaneously exploit local temporal-spatial signals and global contextual dependencies, ensuring that both short-term bursts and long-range correlations are effectively modeled.

Attribute-Driven Embedding. In many fraud detection settings, fraudulent and legitimate transactions exhibit similar observable features—e.g., transaction amount, location, or merchant category. This similarity arises because fraudsters intentionally imitate normal behavior to avoid detection. Consequently, relying solely on graph connectivity can be misleading, as topological relationships may include noisy or adversarial edges.

To mitigate this issue, STGFormer begins by learning attribute-driven embeddings that provide discriminative initial representations independent of graph structure. For each transaction node v_i, an initial embedding is computed as

$$h_i^{(0)} = \sigma(W_0 x_i), \tag{10.2}$$

where x_i denotes the original feature vector, W_0 is a learnable weight matrix, and $\sigma(\cdot)$ is a nonlinear activation function. This initialization establishes a feature-rich foundation for subsequent temporal and spatial aggregation, enabling the network to separate fraudulent behaviors even before structural information is introduced.

Temporal Information Encoding. Most existing GNNs [2, 22] that incorporate temporal information usually construct separate graphs for each time slice. However, they are unable to distinguish temporal dependencies from different neighboring nodes and, due to structural constraints, cannot allow a target node to interact with nodes from other time periods.

To capture temporal information while fully leveraging structural information, we allow a target node to interact with nodes appearing at any time. Specifically, we adopt a temporal encoding strategy that enables nodes to learn a hidden representation of time. Given a target node v_i occurring at time t_{v_i}, the temporal encoding is defined as

$$p_{v_i}[2i] = \sin\left(\frac{t_{v_i}}{10000^{2i/d_t}}\right), \tag{10.3}$$

$$p_{v_i}[2i+1] = \cos\left(\frac{t_{v_i}}{10000^{(2i+1)/d_t}}\right), \tag{10.4}$$

$$e_{v_i} = \text{T-Linear}(p_{v_i}). \tag{10.5}$$

Here, T-Linear is a learnable linear projection and d_t is the dimensionality of the temporal encoding. This formulation also allows modeling of the relative temporal difference between nodes v_i and v_j.

By adding the temporal encoding, the hidden representation of node v_i is updated as

$$h_{v_i}^{(t_{v_i})} = h_{v_i}^{0} + e_{v_i}. \tag{10.6}$$

In this way, the model captures both the temporal properties of the target node and the relative temporal relationships between the target node and its neighbors. Subsequently, message passing via a graph neural network further integrates structural and temporal information, effectively capturing local spatio-temporal dependencies in the graph.

Spatial Information Learning. The spatial dimension of a transaction graph encodes the connections between transactions through various shared attributes, such as IP address, MAC address, or device identifier. These connections reveal critical behavioral patterns; for instance, multiple fraudulent transactions may originate from the same IP within a short time window.

To capture spatial dependencies, we employ a **multi-relation aggregation** strategy. Each relation type r (e.g., "transaction-IP-transaction," "transaction-MAC-transaction") defines a separate adjacency set $\mathcal{N}_r(v_i)$. For a target node v_i at layer l, we first aggregate the neighborhood information while also modeling differences between the node and its neighbors:

$$h^1_{\mathcal{AGG}} = \mathcal{AGG}\Big(h_j^{l-1,t'} \mid v_j \in \mathcal{N}_r(v_i)\Big), \tag{10.7}$$

$$h^2_{\mathcal{AGG}} = \mathcal{AGG}\Big(h_i^{l-1,t} - h_j^{l-1,t'} \mid v_j \in \mathcal{N}_r(v_i)\Big), \tag{10.8}$$

$$h^{l,t}_{v_i,r} = \text{COMBINE}\big(h^1_{\mathcal{AGG}}, h^2_{\mathcal{AGG}}\big). \tag{10.9}$$

Here, $h_j^{l-1,t'}$ denotes the $l-1$th layer embedding of neighbor v_j under relation r with timestamp t', $h_i^{l-1,t}$ is the embedding of node v_i with timestamp t, $l \in \{1, 2, \ldots, L\}$, $r \in \{1, 2, \ldots, R\}$, and $\mathcal{AGG}(\cdot)$ represents a neighborhood aggregation function. The COMBINE$(\cdot)$ operation can be realized via concatenation, weighted summation, or a gated mechanism.

Since different relation types contribute differently to fraud detection, we introduce a relation-level attention mechanism to quantify their importance. The final representation of node v_i at layer l is

$$h_i^{(l,t)} = \sum_{r=1}^{R} \alpha_r^l\, h_{v_i,r}^{(l,t)}, \tag{10.10}$$

where α_r^l denotes the normalized importance of relation r at layer l, computed as

$$w_r^l = \frac{1}{|V|} \sum_{i \in V} q^\top \tanh\left(W_2 h_{v_i,r}^{(l,t)} + b\right), \tag{10.11}$$

$$\alpha_r^l = \frac{\exp(w_r^l)}{\sum_{i=1}^{R} \exp(w_i^l)}. \tag{10.12}$$

Here, q, W_2, and b are trainable parameters representing the relation-level query vector, weight matrix, and bias vector, respectively. This mechanism dynamically emphasizes relations that are most informative for each node, enabling the model to capture subtle yet meaningful spatial structures.

Multi-Layer Representation Fusion. Representations learned at different GNN layers capture information at varying receptive-field scales. Lower layers encode local, fine-grained interactions, while deeper layers provide broader contextual understanding. To leverage these complementary features, STGFormer fuses multi-level embeddings through concatenation or gated summation:

$$h_i^{(\text{fused})} = \text{Fuse}\big(h_i^{(1)}, h_i^{(2)}, \ldots, h_i^{(L)}\big). \tag{10.13}$$

This fusion enhances the expressiveness of the learned node representations by combining short-range and medium-range spatial-temporal patterns, thereby forming a rich local embedding that serves as input to the subsequent global information learning stage.

In summary, the spatial-temporal modeling process in STGFormer allows each transaction node to encode its intrinsic attributes, temporal behavior, and structural relationships simultaneously. Through joint aggregation and adaptive weighting across relations and time, the model captures both *who interacted with whom* and *when those interactions occurred*—critical cues for uncovering coordinated fraud activities.

10.3 Learning Global Information

While the spatial-temporal modeling process in STGFormer effectively captures local dependencies among transactions, real-world fraud detection often requires a broader perspective. Fraudulent behaviors may occur across distant nodes that share no direct connections but exhibit correlated activity patterns. For example, coordinated fraud rings may distribute transactions across multiple accounts or devices to evade detection. Conventional graph neural networks struggle to model such long-range dependencies because their message-passing operations are inherently local. To overcome this limitation, STGFormer introduces a Transformer-based global information learning module that enables full-graph interaction through self-attention.

Motivation for Global Context Learning. Standard GNNs update node representations by aggregating information from a limited neighborhood, typically within k hops [14, 21]. Although stacking more layers increases the receptive field, this often leads to over-smoothing [8, 13], where the representations of different nodes become indistinguishable. In contrast, the Transformer architecture [16] allows each node to directly attend to all others, enabling the capture of both local and global dependencies without relying on explicit neighborhood constraints.

In the context of transaction networks, this capability is crucial. Fraudulent nodes that are far apart in the graph may share latent similarities in their behavioral signatures, such as transaction frequency, device reuse, or temporal bursts. The Transformer-based module in STGFormer therefore complements the local GNN aggregation by introducing an all-to-all communication mechanism that integrates these global relationships.

Inspired by the attention mechanism [16], this chapter applies a dedicated Transformer layer to each node. This module enables nodes in the graph to directly interact with one another, allowing information aggregation from distant nodes across the entire graph. Specifically, we apply a multi-head attention mechanism to the obtained embedding matrix (denoted as $H^{(v_i)} \in \mathbb{R}^{n \times d_1}$). These embeddings contain both the attribute information of each node and its spatiotemporal relationships with its neighbors.

We first introduce the single-head attention method and then extend it to the multi-head mechanism. For single-head attention, we perform linear projections on the embeddings to obtain the Query, Key, and Value matrices, as follows:

$$Q^{(v_i)} = H^{(v_i)} W^{Q}, \tag{10.14}$$

$$K^{(v_i)} = H^{(v_i)} W^{K}, \tag{10.15}$$

$$V^{(v_i)} = H^{(v_i)} W^{Va}, \tag{10.16}$$

where W^{Q}, W^{K}, and W^{Va} are learnable projection matrices.

Thus, the single-head attention function is defined as

$$\begin{aligned} \text{Attention}(H^{(v_i)}) &= \text{softmax}\left(\frac{Q^{(v_i)} K^{(v_i)\top}}{\sqrt{d_k}}\right) Va^{(v_i)} \\ &= \text{softmax}\left(\frac{(H^{(v_i)} W^{Q})(H^{(v_i)} W^{K})^{\top}}{\sqrt{d_k}}\right) H^{(v_i)} W^{Va}. \end{aligned} \tag{10.17}$$

Multi-Head Attention and Representation Fusion. To enhance model stability and capture diverse relational patterns, STGFormer employs multi-head attention, which executes multiple self-attention operations in parallel:

$$\text{Multihead}(H^{(v_i)}) = \left(\|_{m=1}^{M} head_m\right) W^{O}, \tag{10.18}$$

$$\begin{aligned} head_m &= \text{attention}_m(H^{(v_i)}) \\ &= \text{softmax}\left(\frac{(H^{(v_i)} W_m^{Q})(H^{(v_i)} W_m^{K})^{\top}}{\sqrt{d_k}}\right) H^{(v_i)} W_m^{Va}. \end{aligned} \tag{10.19}$$

Multi-head attention enables the model to learn different perspectives of inter-node relationships, improving representational richness. Following the self-attention operation, STGFormer adopts the standard Transformer sequence of residual connections and layer normalization to preserve gradient stability.

Advantages of the Transformer-based Global Module. The incorporation of the Transformer subnetwork provides several key benefits:

1. Long-range dependency modeling: Nodes that are several hops apart can directly exchange information without layer stacking.
2. Over-smoothing mitigation: By integrating a non-local communication mechanism, the Transformer module alleviates the tendency of deep GNNs to produce homogeneous representations.

Overall, the Transformer-based global information learning module enhances STGFormer's capacity. By combining this module with the spatial-temporal graph layers, STGFormer achieves a unified framework capable of encoding both fine-grained local details and holistic global dependencies within transaction networks.

10.4 Experimental Validation

This section presents the experimental setup and results that validate the effectiveness of the proposed Spatial-Temporal-Aware Graph Transformer (STGFormer) model for online transaction fraud detection. We describe the dataset, baseline methods, evaluation metrics, and implementation details, followed by a comprehensive analysis of experimental results and ablation studies.

Dataset and Graph Construction. Experiments were conducted on a large-scale private financial dataset. Each transaction was modeled as a node, and edges represented relationships such as shared IP or MAC addresses. The private dataset was provided by a major financial institution in China. It contains approximately 5.12 million real transaction records, including about 140,000 confirmed fraudulent transactions. To ensure rich contextual information, data from Nov. 2016 to Jan. 2017 were selected for experimentation. Transactions from the first month were used for training, while the remaining data were divided chronologically into five test sets, denoted PR1 through PR5. The model was trained under strict temporal constraints to prevent data leakage from future transactions.

In this dataset, each transaction node is connected to others through two types of relations:

1. Transaction-IP-Transaction: connects transactions that occur on the same IP address.
2. Transaction-MAC-Transaction: connects transactions sharing the same MAC address.

Baseline Methods. To evaluate the proposed model, STGFormer was compared with a range of classical and state-of-the-art baselines, including both homogeneous and heterogeneous graph neural network methods, as well as specialized graph-based fraud detection models.

(1) GCN [7]: It aggregates neighbor features to learn local spatial structures.
(2) GraphSAGE [6]: It employs sampling-based aggregation for efficient representation learning in large-scale graphs.
(3) GAT [17]: It integrates attention mechanisms to weight the importance of neighboring nodes during aggregation.
(4) RGCN [15]: It extends GCN to heterogeneous graphs by distinguishing multiple edge types.
(5) HAN [19]: It aggregates semantic information across meta-paths using a two-level attention mechanism.
(6) CARE-GNN [3]: It introduces label-aware similarity and reinforcement learning to select trustworthy neighbors for fraud detection.
(7) SSA [10]: It improves GraphSAGE by sampling neighbors based on similarity and incorporating temporal attention mechanisms.
(8) PMP [25]: It employs class-aware aggregation to balance homophilous and heterophilous neighbors, mitigating class imbalance.
(9) FRAUDRE [24]: It integrates fraud-aware operations and imbalance-sensitive loss functions to improve robustness.
(10) GHRN [5]: It uses label-driven high-frequency indicators to prune heterophilous edges and enhance robustness.

Implementation Details. Model training was performed using the `PyTorch` framework on an Ubuntu 20.04.5 LTS system. The Adam optimizer was used with a learning rate of 0.01. The number of Transformer attention heads was set to 2, and one graph convolution layer was employed. The hidden dimension was set to 64, and the batch size was 512.

All experiments were executed on an RTX 2080Ti GPU (13.4 TFlops single precision) with an Intel i9-10900X CPU (20 cores, 3.7 GHz) and 64 GB of memory.

Results and Discussion. As shown in Tables 10.1, 10.2, 10.3, 10.4 and 10.5, STGFormer consistently outperforms all baseline methods across all evaluation metrics on the PR1-PR5 datasets, demonstrating stable and robust performance. These results indicate that STGFormer exhibits strong generalization capability in fraud transaction detection. The overall performance gains can be primarily attributed to the joint modeling of spatio-temporal dependencies, as well as the effective integration of local structural information and global contextual information, which enables more expressive and discriminative node representations.

When compared with several representative fraud detection approaches, STGFormer maintains clear performance advantages. GHRN mainly focuses on local structural information and employs a label-based high-frequency indicator to identify and prune heterophilous edges, which helps alleviate performance degradation under structurally mixed and highly camouflaged scenarios. However, this method primarily emphasizes structural pruning and does not explicitly model temporal dependencies or global information, thereby limiting further performance improvements. PMP introduces a class-aware mechanism during feature aggregation to mitigate class imbalance and demonstrates certain effectiveness in distinguishing information from homophilous and heterophilous neighbors. Nevertheless, as its modeling strategy is

Table 10.1 Experimental results of different models on the PR1 test dataset

Method	R_e	F_1	AUC
GCN	0.620	0.681	0.876
GraphSAGE	0.605	0.678	0.877
GAT	0.692	0.686	0.865
CARE-GNN	0.799	0.690	0.911
SSA	0.636	0.610	0.826
RGCN	0.666	0.788	0.830
HAN	0.576	0.626	0.752
PMP	0.719	0.705	0.823
FRAUDRE	0.826	0.758	0.908
GHRN	0.813	0.793	0.891
STGFormer	**0.855**	**0.821**	**0.922**

Table 10.2 Experimental results of different models on the PR2 test dataset

Method	R_e	F_1	AUC
GCN	0.593	0.714	0.852
GraphSAGE	0.684	0.779	0.879
GAT	0.750	0.776	0.865
CARE-GNN	0.862	0.839	0.941
SSA	0.679	0.540	0.874
RGCN	0.621	0.771	0.794
HAN	0.518	0.647	0.740
PMP	0.766	0.734	0.844
FRAUDRE	0.821	0.744	0.920
GHRN	0.839	0.810	0.905
STGFormer	**0.881**	**0.865**	**0.956**

largely confined to local neighborhood structures, its performance becomes less stable when handling fraud scenarios with complex temporal behaviors. FRAUDRE incorporates a fraud-aware module together with an imbalance-oriented loss function to address graph inconsistency and class imbalance issues, achieving competitive results, but its overall performance still falls short of STGFormer.

In addition, comparisons with classical graph neural network models constructed on single-relation graphs, such as GCN, GraphSAGE, and GAT, as well as multi-relation models including RGCN and HAN, reveal that generic GNN architectures do not exhibit clear advantages in fraud transaction detection tasks. Although multi-relation graphs can capture more complex interaction patterns, directly applying general-purpose GNN models may introduce redundant or noisy information if the heterogeneity among node interactions is not carefully modeled. In contrast, by

Table 10.3 Experimental results of different models on the PR3 test dataset

Method	R_e	F_1	AUC
GCN	0.817	0.896	0.869
GraphSAGE	0.702	0.640	0.832
GAT	0.821	0.898	0.871
CARE-GNN	0.853	0.877	0.982
SSA	0.732	0.834	0.798
RGCN	0.618	0.758	0.792
HAN	0.639	0.778	0.815
PMP	0.734	0.790	0.884
FRAUDRE	0.898	0.913	0.982
GHRN	0.868	0.812	0.917
STGFormer	**0.902**	**0.916**	**0.983**

Table 10.4 Experimental results of different models on the PR4 test dataset

Method	R_e	F_1	AUC
GCN	0.821	0.899	0.856
GraphSAGE	0.723	0.793	0.882
GAT	0.846	0.913	0.875
CARE-GNN	0.808	0.707	0.915
SSA	0.672	0.799	0.737
RGCN	0.642	0.772	0.818
HAN	0.873	0.930	0.926
PMP	0.880	0.416	0.797
FRAUDRE	0.874	0.903	0.979
GHRN	0.900	0.814	0.930
STGFormer	**0.935**	**0.940**	**0.980**

explicitly incorporating temporal dependencies and global information, STGFormer is better aligned with the dynamic nature of fraud behaviors, leading to superior detection performance.

Ablation Study. To further examine the contributions of different components, we performed ablation experiments with two model variants:

1. STGFormer w/o TIE: removes the temporal information encoding module, preventing the model from learning time-dependent behaviors.
2. STGFormer w/o GIL: omits the global information learning module, limiting the model to local spatial-temporal interactions.

To evaluate the specific impact of the temporal encoding module on model performance, this section conducts a series of ablation experiments comparing the original STGFormer with its variant, STGFormer w/o TIE. The experimental results are

Table 10.5 Experimental results of different models on the PR5 test dataset

Method	R_e	F_1	AUC
GCN	0.829	0.897	0.864
GraphSAGE	0.775	0.549	0.728
GAT	0.861	0.897	0.859
CARE-GNN	0.821	0.759	0.904
SSA	0.524	0.682	0.648
RGCN	0.661	0.784	0.827
HAN	0.856	0.904	0.879
PMP	0.651	0.756	0.897
FRAUDRE	0.834	0.819	0.909
GHRN	0.830	0.808	0.900
STGFormer	**0.893**	**0.912**	**0.982**

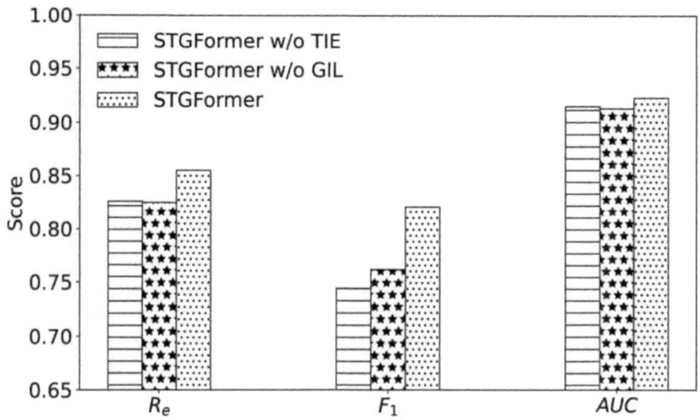

Fig. 10.2 Ablation study results on the PR1 dataset

illustrated in Figs. 10.2, 10.3, 10.4, 10.5 and 10.6. It can be observed that when temporal dependencies are not considered, STGFormer achieves superior performance compared to STGFormer w/o TIE, which excludes temporal information. This performance gap arises because STGFormer w/o TIE aggregates only spatial information while ignoring the differences between nodes associated with distinct timestamps. Consequently, STGFormer consistently outperforms its time-agnostic variant, demonstrating the effectiveness and superiority of the proposed temporal encoding strategy.

To investigate the effectiveness of the Transformer-based global information learning module, we conduct corresponding ablation experiments to compare the performance of the complete STGFormer model with its variant, STGFormer w/o GIL. The experimental results are presented in Figs. 10.2, 10.3, 10.4, 10.5 and 10.6. Compared with STGFormer w/o GIL, the full STGFormer consistently achieves superior performance in terms of R_e, F_1, and AUC, indicating that incorporating

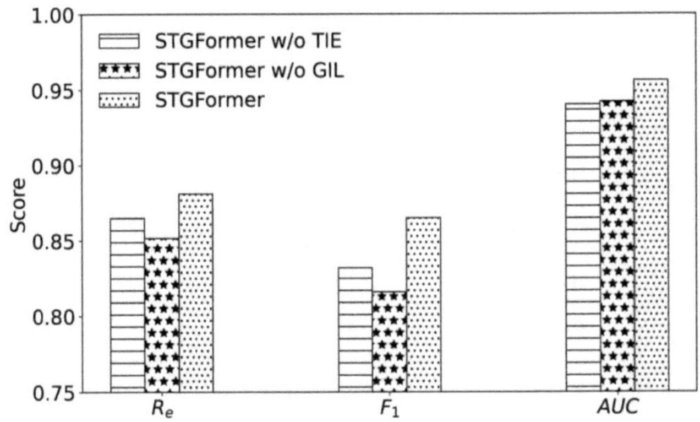

Fig. 10.3 Ablation study results on the PR2 dataset

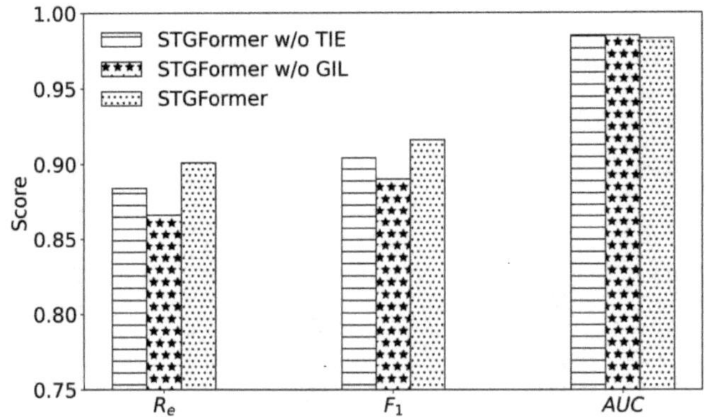

Fig. 10.4 Ablation study results on the PR3 dataset

global information significantly enhances the discriminative capability of node representations. Although introducing global information for node representation learning incurs additional computational and time costs, it leads to substantial performance improvements. For instance, on the PR5 dataset, the F_1 is improved by at least 10%, which clearly demonstrates the effectiveness of the introduced Transformer layers.

10.5 Summary

In this chapter, a heterogeneous graph neural network model named STGFormer is proposed for online transaction fraud detection. By integrating a time-encoding strategy with heterogeneous graph convolution operations, the model effectively learns node-level spatial-temporal representations, capturing local dynamic patterns of transaction behavior. On top of the stacked GNN layers, a Transformer-based

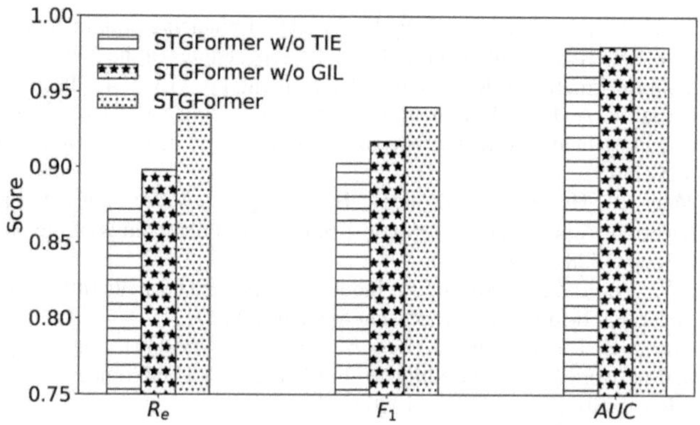

Fig. 10.5 Ablation study results on the PR4 dataset

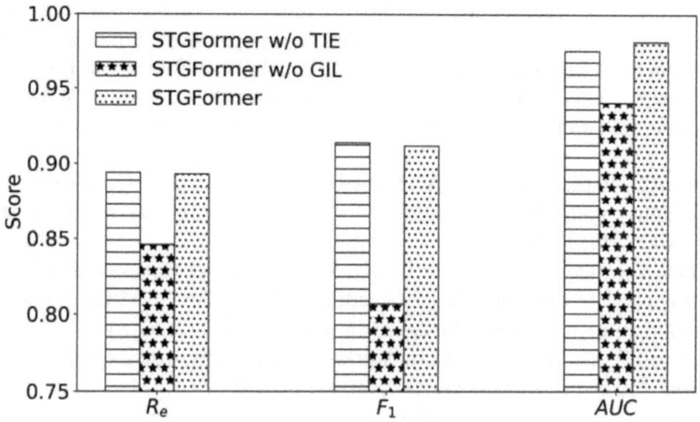

Fig. 10.6 Ablation study results on the PR5 dataset

global information learning module is constructed to leverage information from distant but semantically related transactions, thereby enhancing intra-class compactness and inter-class separability. Finally, a MLP classifier is employed to identify fraudulent transactions. Experimental results on two financial datasets demonstrate the superior performance of STGFormer in the transaction fraud detection task.

References

1. Bahnsen, A.C., Aouada, D., Stojanovic, A., Ottersten, B.: Detecting credit card fraud using periodic features. In: 2015 IEEE 14th International Conference on Machine Learning and Applications (ICMLA). pp. 208–213. IEEE (2015)
2. Chen, Z., Zhang, W., Yan, J., Wang, G., Wang, J.: Learning dual dynamic representations on time-sliced user-item interaction graphs for sequential recommendation. In: Proceedings of the 30th ACM International Conference on Information & Knowledge Management. pp. 231–240 (2021)

3. Dou, Y., Liu, Z., Sun, L., Deng, Y., Peng, H., Yu, P.S.: Enhancing graph neural network-based fraud detectors against camouflaged fraudsters. In: Proceedings of the 29th ACM International Conference on Information & Knowledge Management. pp. 315–324 (2020)
4. Fiore, U., De Santis, A., Perla, F., Zanetti, P., Palmieri, F.: Using generative adversarial networks for improving classification effectiveness in credit card fraud detection. Information Sciences **479**, 448–455 (2019)
5. Gao, Y., Wang, X., He, X., Liu, Z., Feng, H., Zhang, Y.: Addressing heterophily in graph anomaly detection: A perspective of graph spectrum. In: Proceedings of the ACM Web Conference 2023. pp. 1528–1538 (2023)
6. Hamilton, W., Ying, Z., Leskovec, J.: Inductive representation learning on large graphs. Advances in Neural Information Processing Systems **30** (2017)
7. Jiang, B., Zhang, Z., Lin, D., Tang, J., Luo, B.: Semi-supervised learning with graph learning-convolutional networks. In: Proceedings of the IEEE/CVF Conference on Computer Vision and Pattern Recognition. pp. 11313–11320 (2019)
8. Li, Q., Han, Z., Wu, X.M.: Deeper insights into graph convolutional networks for semi-supervised learning. In: Proceedings of the AAAI Conference on Artificial Intelligence. vol. 32 (2018)
9. Li, Y., Xie, S., Liu, X., Ying, Q.F., Lau, W.C., Chiu, D.M., Chen, S.Z., et al.: Temporal graph representation learning for detecting anomalies in e-payment systems. In: 2021 International Conference on Data Mining Workshops (ICDMW). pp. 983–990. IEEE (2021)
10. Liu, G., Tang, J., Tian, Y., Wang, J.: Graph neural network for credit card fraud detection. In: 2021 International Conference on Cyber-Physical Social Intelligence (ICCSI). pp. 1–6. IEEE (2021)
11. Liu, Z., Chen, C., Li, L., Zhou, J., Li, X., Song, L., Qi, Y.: Geniepath: Graph neural networks with adaptive receptive paths. In: Proceedings of the AAAI Conference on Artificial Intelligence. vol. 33, pp. 4424–4431 (2019)
12. Liu, Z., Chen, C., Yang, X., Zhou, J., Li, X., Song, L.: Heterogeneous graph neural networks for malicious account detection. In: Proceedings of the 27th ACM International Conference on Information and Knowledge Management. pp. 2077–2085 (2018)
13. Oono, K., Suzuki, T.: Graph neural networks exponentially lose expressive power for node classification. ArXiv Preprint ArXiv:1905.10947 (2019)
14. Papp, P.A., Martinkus, K., Faber, L., Wattenhofer, R.: DropGNN: Random dropouts increase the expressiveness of graph neural networks. Advances in Neural Information Processing Systems **34**, 21997–22009 (2021)
15. Schlichtkrull, M., Kipf, T.N., Bloem, P., Van Den Berg, R., Titov, I., Welling, M.: Modeling relational data with graph convolutional networks. In: European Semantic Web Conference. pp. 593–607. Springer (2018)
16. Vaswani, A., Shazeer, N., Parmar, N., Uszkoreit, J., Jones, L., Gomez, A.N., Kaiser, Ł., Polosukhin, I.: Attention is all you need. Advances in Neural Information Processing Systems **30** (2017)
17. Veličković, P., Cucurull, G., Casanova, A., Romero, A., Lio, P., Bengio, Y.: Graph attention networks. ArXiv Preprint ArXiv:1710.10903 (2017)
18. Wang, D., Lin, J., Cui, P., Jia, Q., Wang, Z., Fang, Y., Yu, Q., Zhou, J., Yang, S., Qi, Y.: A semi-supervised graph attentive network for financial fraud detection. In: 2019 IEEE International Conference on Data Mining (ICDM). pp. 598–607. IEEE (2019)
19. Wang, X., Ji, H., Shi, C., Wang, B., Ye, Y., Cui, P., Yu, P.S.: Heterogeneous graph attention network. In: The World Wide Web Conference. pp. 2022–2032 (2019)
20. Whitrow, C., Hand, D.J., Juszczak, P., Weston, D., Adams, N.M.: Transaction aggregation as a strategy for credit card fraud detection. Data Mining and Knowledge Discovery **18**(1), 30–55 (2009)
21. Wu, S., Sun, F., Zhang, W., Xie, X., Cui, B.: Graph neural networks in recommender systems: a survey. ACM Computing Surveys **55**(5), 1–37 (2022)
22. Yang, M., Zhou, M., Kalander, M., Huang, Z., King, I.: Discrete-time temporal network embedding via implicit hierarchical learning in hyperbolic space. In: Proceedings of the 27th ACM SIGKDD Conference on Knowledge Discovery & Data Mining. pp. 1975–1985 (2021)

23. Yee, O.S., Sagadevan, S., Malim, N.H.A.H.: Credit card fraud detection using machine learning as data mining technique. Journal of Telecommunication, Electronic and Computer Engineering (JTEC) **10**(1-4), 23–27 (2018)
24. Zhang, G., Wu, J., Yang, J., Beheshti, A., Xue, S., Zhou, C., Sheng, Q.Z.: Fraudre: Fraud detection dual-resistant to graph inconsistency and imbalance. In: 2021 IEEE International Conference on Data Mining (ICDM). pp. 867–876. IEEE (2021)
25. Zhuo, W., Liu, Z., Hooi, B., He, B., Tan, G., Fathony, R., Chen, J.: Partitioning message passing for graph fraud detection. ArXiv Preprint ArXiv:2412.00020 (2024)

MIX
Papier aus verantwortungsvollen Quellen
Paper from responsible sources
FSC® C105338

If you have any concerns about our products,
you can contact us on
ProductSafety@springernature.com

In case Publisher is established outside the EU,
the EU authorized representative is:
Springer Nature Customer Service Center GmbH
Europaplatz 3, 69115 Heidelberg, Germany

Printed by Libri Plureos GmbH
in Hamburg, Germany